Crash Course in PERSONAL DEVELOPMENT

WITHDRAWN FROM STOCK

Crash Course in PERSONAL DEVELOPMENT

NATIONAL COLLEGE
OF IRELAND
LIBRARY

BRIAN CLEGG

WITHDRAWN FROM STOCK

Barcode No:..39006010015883
Dewey No:..650.1
Date Input...01/11/02
Price.....€ 24.57

First published in 2002

Apart from any fair dealing for the purposes of research or private study, or criticism or review, as permitted under the Copyright, Designs and Patents Act 1988, this publication may only be reproduced, stored or transmitted, in any form or by any means, with the prior permission in writing of the publishers, or in the case of reprographic reproduction in accordance with the terms and licences issued by the CLA. Enquiries concerning reproduction outside these terms should be sent to the publishers at the undermentioned addresses:

Kogan Page Limited
120 Pentonville Road
London N1 9JN
UK

Stylus Publishing Inc.
22883 Quicksilver Drive
Sterling VA 20166-2012
USA

© Brian Clegg, 2002

The right of Brian Clegg to be identified as the author of this work has been asserted by him in accordance with the Copyright, Designs and Patents Act 1988.

British Library Cataloguing in Publication Data

A CIP record for this book is available from the British Library.

ISBN 0 7494 3832 0

Typeset by Saxon Graphics Ltd, Derby
Printed and bound in Great Britain by Clays Ltd, St Ives plc

Contents

WITHDRAWN FROM STOCK

Introduction

Personal development is a broad topic – this book might just as easily (though more clumsily) have been titled 'Making the best of your life' or 'Getting things the way you want them to be'. In writing three books for the Kogan Page *Instants* series, *Instant Time Management*, *Instant Stress Management* and *Instant Negotiation*, I was surprised to discover just how tightly interwoven these topics were.

In each case, the important thing was to be clear just what it was what you wanted to achieve (in life, in a negotiation), then take steps to maximize the extent to which you were in control. There's no magic formula that will guarantee that you will succeed in every endeavour, but by taking charge, by developing the skills and techniques that will enable you to have better control of your time, manage stress and negotiate better with others, you will ensure that your chances are the best they can be.

The tried and trusted techniques from the *Instants* books have been combined to form a unified course that will enable you to develop yourself without taking up too much of your valuable time.

This book comprises two main sections. In Chapter 1 – Getting the basics – we lay the foundation of understanding on which the exercises and techniques are built. It is very important to have this understanding before engaging in activity like personal development – without understanding why you are undertaking the exercises you will not feel totally in control. This chapter is short and can be read in a couple of hours.

The second section contains a programme of exercises and techniques – exercises to develop your personal skills and techniques you can bring to play when working with others. The programme is split into units, designed to be manageable in your spare time in a week, though if you want to take the crash course to its extreme, each unit can be fitted in to a day. Each unit also introduces one or two recommended books. Wider reading is an essential when working on personal development, and though it is not necessary to read all (or even any) of these specific books, they have been selected to enhance the impact of the course.

At the back of the book you will find a review section to pull together what you have learned, including a collected reading list (in case you decide not to go with the books at the time of working through the programme) and tables that support the techniques or can be used to pick and choose individual techniques for a specific requirement. You will also find Web links for further reading and to help with the exercises.

Be prepared to learn, but also be prepared to have fun – personal development is for *your* benefit and should never be a chore.

1 Getting the basics

WHAT'S IT FOR?

Making the most of your life

The whole point of this course is to help you to make the most of your life. We have a natural tendency to ignore the big questions and deal with the lesser issues. In the classic book *Parkinson's Law*, C. Northcote Parkinson (1961) imagines a meeting with two key items on the agenda – whether or not to rebuild a nuclear power station and whether or not to erect a new bike shed. Those present spend very little time on the power station and lots on the bike shed. This is because everyone understands bike sheds, and the amount of money needed to put one up – whereas hardly anyone can understand a nuclear power station, or visualize the immense sums of money required to build one.

In part, then, we tend to skip over the big questions because we find it difficult to get our minds around them. It's also because they can be frightening. And because we feel they are so big there's nothing we can do about them, so we might as well concentrate on the trivia.

As an individual, one of the biggest questions you face is 'How can I make the most of my life?' and the natural tendency for all the above reasons is to ignore it, and get on. Yet without taking that step back, without looking at what you really want out of life and what steps you can take to make a move towards it, you aren't ever going to come close.

There are those who would say, 'Don't try'. After all, sometimes what we want out of life is genuinely unachievable. It doesn't matter how much I want it, I'm never going to play football for England. As it happens I don't want it all, which is just as well. But without recognizing what your underlying wants and desires are, and at least making some effort to getting part of the way if not all the way, you are going to remain frustrated and unfulfilled. At the heart of this issue is a matter of control.

Taking control

Many of the exercises and techniques in this course are about taking control. Taking control of your time. Taking control of your stressors. Taking control of your dealings with other people. Having a degree of control doesn't mean that you will always get what you want. There are always limits, always restrictions. Yet almost all of us could be much more in control than we typically are, and this is a vital aspect of feeling that you are on the way to achieving what you want out of life.

It's interesting that when the stress levels of different jobs are compared, it isn't the complexity of the job, or the pressure the individual is under, that determines whether or not he or she becomes stressed. It is the degree of control that it's possible to exercise. This is why a cleaner can be more stressed than a managing director. A ballet dancer can be more stressed than an air traffic controller. Of course, that air traffic controller could be hugely stressed if his or her systems are overloaded, so control begins to evaporate, but with appropriate support what at first seems one of the most stressful jobs in the world doesn't have to be. Taking control is at the heart of personal development.

THE KEY ELEMENTS

In this course we are going to concentrate on three key factors that influence your ability to take control and make the most of your life: being able to handle time, stress and other people. Traditionally these factors have been classified separately as time management, stress management and negotiation skills. There is still some benefit in considering each separately when exploring the external requirements, but once it is realized how closely related these areas are, it becomes clear that a unified course of personal development is the best way to deal with all of them.

Time management

Time management is a discipline that everyone acknowledges is worthwhile while simultaneously ignoring it. There seems to be something in the human spirit that rebels against time management, despite realizing the benefits. It's like eating the right food – we might acknowledge the benefits of eating lots of fruit and vegetables, we can even enjoy eating fruit and vegetables – but still pig out on junk food.

This ability to ignore time management is very sad. There are plenty of variations on the theme of 'so much to do, so little time to do it in'. Few of us have time to get everything completed. Few of us manage to effectively balance work and home life, business and pleasure, stress and stress relief. Good time management is more than a nit-picking discipline that will appeal to those who like everything in its place, it is a vehicle for getting more done and having a better life. If only it can be made practical.

Time management is mostly common sense. So why is it such a problem? It's as if there's something inside us that rebels against it. In fact, there's a whole bunch of reasons that conspire to make our time management fail. One is a leftover from our teens. Most teenagers spend a fair amount of time being told what they should do when, and they don't like it. Because time management can be seen as an imposed control on our time, it kicks in the urge to fight back, to refuse stubbornly what is obviously good for you just for the sake of it.

Another problem is laziness. Like it or not, most of us are lazy. We can't be bothered with the whole thing. We aren't very enthusiastic about change. And anyway, it's just an admin matter, isn't it? It's not exciting, important stuff, like creating or selling or whatever we like doing best – it's routine. Yawn.

Then there is the swamps and alligators problem. The old saying goes something like 'when you are up to your armpits (substitute part of the anatomy of your choice) in alligators, it's hard to think about draining the swamp'. Of course I'll get my time management sorted out, but wait until this crisis is out of the way. When I've got some time, I'll do something about it. Only thanks to a lack of time management, we never get the time, because there's always some new crisis, some new pressure.

Finally, there's the misconception that is fostered by some well-meaning approaches to time management. The fallacy that time management is closely related to having a neat, tidy desk and a well-ordered filing system. The fact is, the way we work most effectively is a very personal thing. You can't take a 'one size fits all' approach to working. For some, having a clear desk and everything labelled and in its place is an essential – but it would be a mistake to say that this is the solution for everyone.

Stress management

Stress is a recognized killer and a major contributor to workplace illness. Companies are worried about stress because of reduced effectiveness; individuals can find that the impact of stress blights their health and happiness. Yet stress is a complex phenomenon. It can't be painted in black and white. We all need a degree of stress to drive us on to achieve. Neither total lack of stress nor stress to excess is good for you.

At the physical level we have a pretty good understanding of what stress is about. When the brain senses a demand for exertion it signals the release of various hormones from glands around the body. These active agents, like adrenaline, noradrenaline and cortisol prepare the body for action. Muscles tense up, the heart beats faster, the blood supply is concentrated where it is needed, moving away from 'low need' areas like the digestion and the skin. All this is designed to provide a wave of energy to enable you to react appropriately to the trigger: to fight or to run away. To survive.

Sometimes that survival urge is real – escaping a burning building or an attack. More often it is a driver to get the extra mile. You might be an athlete or an actor, a manager giving a business presentation or a fire fighter. In any role, stress can make all the difference. Everyone who has ever gone on stage knows too well that feeling in the pit of the stomach that says 'Why the hell am I here?' – but without that stress there wouldn't be the huge return that makes it all worthwhile.

If things were that simple, stress management would be about getting more stress, but the reality is quite different. Our bodies were designed for stress as a special case, where all too often it's the norm. Also, when we get the surge of adrenaline and other hormones, we don't usually do anything to make use of those changes to our body. We can't fight or run away – we just have to sit and take it. This happens with stresses as widely separated as the rigours of driving and bringing up children.

One-off examples of such stresses aren't as much of a problem, it's the combination of stress without a physical response and frequent, almost constant exposure that does the real damage. Someone who is constantly on the edge of stress can be easily tipped into over-reaction – road rage is a classic example – by trivial incidents. And the body simply isn't built for long-term, stress-heightened activity. Without an outlet, the outcome can be an increased risk of heart disease and other medical conditions.

This course can't provide all the answers to dealing with stress. In some circumstances it will be necessary to get professional help, or to look to others to help deal with your stress. But in the personal development course you will find a toolkit of anti-stress techniques to help in most circumstances.

Negotiation

It's hard to imagine life without negotiation. Practically every business interaction, from the largest corporate merger to a meeting to decide the site of a new desk, depends on negotiation. So does arranging ground rules with your children. In fact there are few human transactions where there isn't room for discussion and modification of terms.

The good negotiator calls on a whole raft of skills. He or she needs to be an effective communicator, combining the abilities to sell and to listen. The negotiator must be able to balance tactical and strategic considerations. Good business negotiators know their company inside out – and know just as much about the other side too. As if this isn't enough, good negotiators also need flexibility – the ability to explore what is possible, changing goal from a hypothetical summit to a more reachable hill.

There is good news and bad news here. Many of the skills of negotiation cannot be learned without practice. But this doesn't mean that you have to plunge into a corporate merger as a virgin negotiator. Every day you are negotiating – at home, on the way to work, in the office. Negotiation is a natural part of life.

But why negotiate at all? From either side of a negotiation, there is a practical need. If you are selling (in the widest sense of the word), you want to get the best price with the best terms. If you are buying you also want the best price and terms, but strangely this now means something quite different. Some negotiations are more about finding an agreed version of reality, but even here points of view will drive parties to pull the result in a particular direction.

Negotiations can be distinguished from other forms of social interaction by the fact there is a specific, pre-identified, desired outcome. It might be a purchase or a pay deal, it might be where to go for dinner or how late a child can stay out at night. The desired outcome is to reach agreement on the subject – but each party in the negotiation has his or her own slant on what would be the best flavour of outcome. Each is trying to move the result into his or her own preferred solution space.

It should never be forgotten, though, when dealing with negotiations that this remains a social interaction between human beings. Mechanical 'negotiations' can be disastrous. The unbending application of a series of rules can make a negotiation run out of control, never getting to a conclusion. Negotiation is not a pure science – it is a blend of logic and emotion, of gut feel and calculation. Neither the human nor the calculated side is enough on its own. There is a need for both.

Expanding the topics

Before launching into the course, let's spend a little more time on each of these three topics.

TIME MANAGEMENT

It doesn't exist

Having established the value of time management in personal development, it's rather unfortunate that there is no such thing as managing time. Remember Lewis Carroll's masterly summary of the problems of dealing with time:

> Alice sighed wearily. 'I think you might do something better with the time,' she said, 'than wasting it in asking riddles that have no answers.'
> 'If you knew time as well as I do,' said the Hatter, 'you wouldn't talk about wasting it. It's him.'
> 'I don't know what you mean,' said Alice.
> 'Of course you don't!' the Hatter said, tossing his head contemptuously. 'I dare say you never even spoke to Time!'
> 'Perhaps not,' Alice cautiously replied; 'but I know I have to beat time when I learn music.'
> 'Ah! That accounts for it,' said the Hatter. 'He won't stand beating. Now, if you only kept on good terms with him, he'd do almost anything you liked with the clock. For instance, suppose it were nine o'clock in the morning, just time to begin lessons: you'd only have to whisper a hint to Time, and round goes the clock in a twinkling! Half-past one, time for dinner!' *Alice in Wonderland*

Time is not amenable to management, nor to argument, it continues to tick away at an irritatingly constant sixty minutes per hour.

If that were all there were to it, this would be an extremely short part of the course, but there's more. We can influence the demands on our time – both in quantity and execution – and the effectiveness with which we use the time we've got. Time management might be impossible, but resource management certainly isn't. You'll find throughout the course that the term time management is used for convenience – but bear in mind that it's a useful fiction.

You can't waste it...

There hardly seems to be a day that goes by without another report from a group of pompous management consultants announcing how much time office workers waste on something or other. Flavour of the month is surfing the Internet and text messaging, but once they go away, something else will emerge. This is a shame, because with the possible exception of spending it on writing reports like those, you can't waste time any more than you can manage it.

What you can do is give relative weightings to the different activities you could have undertaken in a particular chunk of time. This is not a trivial activity, which is why such reports are so misleading. The weighting you give to an activity is dependent on many things. For instance, it is time dependent. Say you were approaching the deadline for completing a major piece of work. The courier is standing waiting for you to finish. The board is about to meet to discuss your recommendations. It is not a good move to put everything to one side and start looking for your passport, which you will need for your holiday three months later. However, come the morning of the holiday, looking for that passport will be higher up your priorities. It's obvious, isn't it? Yet few of us make such prioritization well.

The attitude you have to an activity depends strongly on its outcomes, which are not always obvious. A classic advertisement for the *Guardian* showed a thug pushing over a poor, defenceless person. It was the sort of thing that made you want to bring back corporal punishment. Then it showed the same scene from a different angle. Now you saw the danger that was facing the poor defenceless person, and how the apparent thug's push saved him or her from harm. So-called time wasting is sometimes like this. That Internet browsing could be recreational, but equally it could generate information that is valuable to the business or improve the individual's creativity.

A final consideration is the balance between business and social activity. A more accurate interpretation of what is often labelled time wasting is 'time spent on social activity that could be spent on business'. This is not a justification for undertaking social activities in office hours, just a more useful description of what is happening.

...but you can manage demands and usage

If time can't be managed or wasted, what's the point? Time management is about taking control of the demands that are made on your available time. About ensuring that the use you make of your time has the best fit with your personal goals and requirements. It is about saying 'No' where it's appropriate. It is about getting the right balance. For this reason, the first requirement in setting about time management is not to get your diary sorted or your desk tidy, it is to establish just what your personal goals are – without being clear about these you have no frame of reference in which to allocate time.

When achieving a balance, remember the importance of both business and social demands. Often we assume that business must always have the priority. A British Airways director once commented that it was a shame he hadn't had the chance to see his children growing up, but the pressures of work didn't allow him much contact with them. If he had taken a wider view of time management, he would have realized that he could legitimately allocate more time to his family. So many people miss out on a social life, yet will say that they are working 'for the family' – the balance simply isn't right. This is not to say that the social life must always come first, or that it is somehow wrong to have your career as a central driving force of your life – just that time management has to take in a bigger picture.

As you use the exercises and techniques you will find many different ways to improve time management, but there is one approach that is so fundamental that it is worth bringing up straight away. Time management is often about dealing with big tasks – activities that can take over, given the chance. The magic wand that the good time manager can wave to overcome these rampant tasks is chunking. Breaking up a task into manageable chunks is an absolute essential for time management. After all, the whole business of balancing your time is rather like juggling. These big tasks are equivalent to trying to juggle with cars – it's impossible. However, by breaking them up, you are reduced to juggling with wing mirrors or steering wheels, a much more practical possibility. Dealing with a single large task without breaking it down is difficult enough – dealing with many large tasks, both business and social, is an impossibility.

This need to break up major tasks into chunks may seem obvious, but when you are faced with a big job it is all too easy to plunge in. Time is short; you need to get started. Taking the (brief) time required to break down the task into chunks will pay back handsomely, but it is a very human failing not to do so.

The influences

Time management would be extremely easy if it weren't for all the factors that conspire to stop you from being organized.

The first, and perhaps biggest, factor is you yourself. You might have a very clear picture of what you want to achieve today, and how you are going to do it. Unfortunately, soon after starting you get a craving for a Mars bar which sends you down to the shop. Then you get distracted, thinking about something you should have done last weekend, or the holiday you are planning. Then you decide you had better check the post. Somehow most of the day has slipped away without getting started.

If this weren't bad enough, there are the other people too. Just popping in for a chat, or asking for some information right away, even though it is going to take you three hours to collect it, and you are already working on another urgent project. There are the phone calls and e-mails, the cries for help and the demands for attention. People are out to capture your time whenever they can. Other people aren't always negative contributors, of course. Delegation is a highly effective time management tool, as long as you resist the urge to constantly monitor the activity. People can free up time for you, if you can go about it the right way.

Even without other people, the rest of the world can eat away at your time. Just the smell of fresh coffee or hot rolls can be enough to distract. Technology can be a great time consumer. PCs are wonderful business tools, but they also provide a temptation to tinker. I'll get that important memo written when I've just got my desktop arranged the way I want it. Oh, and while I'm at it, I'll just delete a few files. And install that new program off the magazine cover disk. Don't forget technology's ability to be positive, though. Sending off a quick e-mail when an idea occurs to you is the fastest way to free up your mental resources for other requirements.

Many of the exercises and techniques in this course are about modifying or controlling these influences. That is, bringing them into line to help make your use of time more effective and satisfying.

Facing reality

There is one real problem, even if you manage to do everything this course suggests. That's the difference between perception and reality. You might know very well that you work best from mid-afternoon to mid-evening at a desk covered in pizza boxes, wearing torn jeans and listening to rock music. However, if your boss has the perception that to be a good worker you have to conform to standards of dress and time-keeping, it doesn't honestly matter how good your time management is, you are still going to suffer. This isn't fair, but it is very real.

Like it or not, having the appearance of being effective is just as important as actually getting the job done. Ideally, you ought to be able to do things your own way, but bear in mind that redundancies often come the way of those who are considered non-conformist, however good they are at their job. The changing face of work is mitigating this problem to some extent. As more and more people spend time working at home, for instance, they have a much better opportunity to work the way they want to, rather than the way their boss wants them to. Even so, it is essential to be politically and socially aware to survive.

You will find, therefore, that some of the recommendations for time management, like overcoming the myth of the tidy desk, do need modifying to suit your particular environment.

Being comfortable

An essential start down the road of managing your own contribution to time management is being comfortable. This isn't a matter of getting a comfy chair with arm rests at the right height and all the rest (though it's not a bad idea), it's about being comfortable with the time management environment. If having a clear desk helps you feel comfortable in your work, that's fine. If piles of clutter make you comfortable, that's fine too. Probably.

Probably, because there are two types of clutter. Mess becomes a problem for time management when it gets in the way. When you can't work properly because of the clutter. Most importantly when you can't find something because it's somewhere in one of ten huge piles. If, however, like many clutter lovers you can genuinely say 'It might be a mess, but I know where everything is', stick with it. Your clutter is your filing system. Clearing it up will just result in things going missing.

If you are a naturally tidy person, that's great, but don't feel too smug. The chances are that those who can say 'It might be a mess, but I know where everything is' have a more natural system – the brain, after all, doesn't store things in neat compartments. A loose, flowing system can cope better with a complex mix of information than a rigid matrix. You might be able to put your hands on any document in under a minute, but your colleague with a cluttered desk could probably produce the ten most important documents of the moment in a couple of seconds.

Not letting go

A particular danger for some personality types is over-monitoring. You have to keep checking and tinkering all the time. If you delegate a task, it's fine to set milestones and expect updates. But it's a disaster if you are constantly on top of those doing the work, getting in the way of anything being done. It is the classic problem for the small-time entrepreneur whose business is growing. He or she has taken on staff, but won't trust them to get on with the job. It is seen equally often when a junior manager starts to have reports.

If you are to make sensible use of your time, you have to be prepared to let go. Not entirely – you still have an interest. But you need to find ways to get the essential information as quickly as possible, at appropriate intervals, without interfering with the running of the business, and without distracting you from what you really should be doing.

Sometimes, managers don't delegate a task because it's not important enough. This seems crazy when stated so bluntly, but that's what happens. Your staff are all experts, with plenty to do. Here's a simple enough task, so you might as well do it and let them get on with their real work. There's an element of reality in this. If you are a manager of highly professional staff, it ought to be part of your role to deflect the garbage from them. Ideally, though, you should be deflecting it to someone else (or even better, making sure it never gets done at all).

Clutching at straws

When we finally realize just how much we (and others) are doing to mess up our own time, it is not uncommon to clutch at straws. To search for some sort of miracle cure that will make everything better. It might be a set of rules to obey, or an off-the-shelf time management system. None of these approaches is necessarily bad. But there are pitfalls attached. The biggest danger with a system is that it becomes a time-waster in its own right. Rules are more insidious, but carry their own dangers.

The rules

It's an attractive proposition that there should be a set of rules for ideal time management. Just follow these seven (or ten, or twelve... or whatever) prescriptions and you will change your life. It's easy (at least to specify), you can stick them on a card and laminate them, and you can have a nice, easy checklist. Done that, done that... okay, now my time is managed.

Unfortunately there are two problems with rules in this sort of circumstance. Rules are ideal for a simple, confined world. It's fine to have rules when you are playing Monopoly, because you know that the players will always have the same starting positions, and that no one is going to come along and totally rearrange the board into three dimensions overnight. Life very definitely ain't like that. As already discussed with the matter of the tidy desk syndrome, everyone is not the same and will not respond the same way to a standard rule. What's more, the world is constantly changing, thrashing about, riding a roller coaster of influences. A rule that was valuable today may be worthless tomorrow.

This being the case, is it possible to put together a course like this which includes a set of time management exercises? Luckily, yes. Partly because the approach is driven by principles rather than rules. Not 'Have six action areas' and 'Never spend more than 20 minutes on phone calls each day', but 'Establish your priorities in work and private time' or 'Restrict phone calls to appropriate slots in the day'. Even so, some of the exercises here will not be particularly valuable for you as an individual. Don't worry – by breaking the requirement down into a lot of small components it is possible to mix and match your ideal set of techniques.

Shiny systems

Time management is awash with shiny systems. Attractive personal organizers with all sorts of sexy stationery. Special software that allows you to allocate time to the nearest minute, then track your performance. You'll find some references to these systems in the course. Feel free to try some of them out. If they work for you, great. But just like the approach to clutter on the desk, don't feel that you are a failure if time management systems leave you cold. You can manage just as well with a diary and a notebook.

The most important consideration is not to be lured into unnecessary use of systems. Remember that the vendors of paper-based systems are in business to sell paper. It's in their interests to introduce as many new and different forms as they think they can get away with selling. Now they may well have very good time management principles at heart, but think twice before buying every new piece of stationery. Similarly, the computer-based systems have a pitfall. Because computers are so good at adding and checking and monitoring, they always provide the option of inputting much more information than you really need. It's quite possible to find that your time management system is taking up too much of your time. Make sure that you are only filling in the information that is necessary.

The basic requirements

Whether or not you go for an all-singing, all-dancing system, you will need some tools to help with your time management. These might be electronic or something as simple as a notebook. There are four key requirements. A diary, both to schedule meetings and (probably more important) your own activities. A contact list – names, address, phone numbers and e-mail addresses as a bare minimum. A task list – things to do. And a general notebook. Somewhere, for example, to keep track of your progress on some of the exercises you will be undertaking.

STRESS MANAGEMENT

Where stress comes from

When we're managing stress it helps to know where it's coming from. For any individual there are liable to be a range of causes, some very personal, some general to all of us. If you think through a typical day, you can see a set of classical stress inducers.

- A blaring noise from your alarm clock wakes you up.
- You are tired because you stayed up too late last night.
- You are worried about your promotion interview this afternoon.
- Your children demand your attention, when you are in a hurry to get ready for work…
- …because you are late.
- Heavy traffic makes you later still.
- Bad drivers cut you up and slow you down.
- The computer isn't working properly again.
- When you ring support you get stuck in a voice-handling queue.
- …and so on.

Stressors are attacking you from all sides – and from inside. The exercises in this course will provide you with tools to handle stress in yourself and others, and will be looking at some of the more common causes of stress. In general the exercises emphasize the small, frequent causes of stress, as these are often the ones that we ignore at our peril. Everyone is aware of the stressful impact of a death in the family, or of moving house. In this book I intentionally flag up some of the lesser stressors that continuously nibble away at our sanity.

Internal stressors

It would be nice to blame 'them' for all our stress, just as it's tempting to say that time management would be easy without 'them'. If only they left me alone to get on with things, everything would be fine. Sadly, it's just not true. A sizeable chunk of bad stress comes from within. This can operate at a simple practical level. Your ability to take control of your time can have a significant impact on stress. Here's where we see the benefit of taking overall control of your personal development, rather than slotting time management, stress management and negotiation into separate compartments.

Equally important is the whole mix of emotional confusion that can erupt in any of us. Because our emotional sides are beyond conscious control, they can be a prime cause of stress. Your feelings can stress you long after you are out of reach of the original causes of stress. You might start with a small amount of external stress – your son is being very difficult, so you get angry and smack him. But the stress you then generate for yourself from guilt and frustration at your own lack of control can far outweigh the original trigger.

In our materialistic world, it might seem strange that a practical book should dwell on the spiritual, but spiritual influences cannot be ignored when it comes to internal stresses. Almost everyone feels the need for something more, something beyond the everyday; the lack of spiritual content in our lives can be a prime source of stress. This underlying need is reflected in the questions addressed by the major religions – 'What's the point?' 'Is there anything more to life?' 'You live and then you die and that's it?' Uncertainty about where life is taking us and the ever-present reality of death produce internal stress, while many find that spiritual sources provide a relief and defence against a whole range of stressors, not just the physical.

External stressors

Though the internal is important, we can't ignore external stressors. They are there all the time. Some are immense one-off shocks to the system. Bereavement, moving house, divorce, going on holiday (yes, it causes stress). Others are small but constantly nagging – driving on congested roads or constant hassles at work. We have already seen that because, whatever the stress, our bodies react as is if we are in physical danger, we end up with a potentially damaging hormonal reaction. This means that often there is more danger from the small but constantly present stresses than a big, one-off event. However, you do also need to be aware of the dangers when several big, stressing events occur in one year.

Why me?

Stress doesn't affect everyone in the same way. A number of reasons, mental and physiological, will determine how an individual responds to stress. Some of us are more quick-tempered or more naturally calm. Some of us have more self-esteem and feel more in control, hence are better able to let stress wash over us. Even our state of heath will change our ability to cope with stress.

Crash Course in PERSONAL DEVELOPMENT

WITHDRAWN FROM STOCK

Crash Course in PERSONAL DEVELOPMENT

NATIONAL COLLEGE
OF IRELAND
LIBRARY

BRIAN CLEGG

WITHDRAWN FROM STOCK

KOGAN
PAGE

This doesn't mean that there's nothing to be done about it. We may not be able to (or even want to) change our personalities, but there is plenty that can be done to help even if you are naturally inclined to respond to stress in the wrong way, or to bring stress on yourself. That's the point of the stress components of this course – to help with managing stress so that you can improve your natural level of stress control.

Medical stuff

Care has to be taken when attempting stress management. Some apparent stress symptoms have a medical cause. If you are suffering from symptoms like dizziness, chest pains, palpitations and faintness it's not enough to think that you are stressed and attempt to manage it – you could equally be suffering from a heart condition. If you have physical symptoms, make sure that you check with your GP rather than assuming that they are down to stress.

Similarly, an inability to sleep or headaches or stomach conditions, all potentially stress-induced, can have physical causes that need treatment – don't make assumptions, check with the doctor. Finally, don't assume that depression is necessarily stress-induced. There are two clear forms of depression – exogenous, caused by external influences, and endogenous, coming from internal causes. An endogenous depression is totally unconnected to any stressors you may have, and will not respond to stress management. Such a depression does not imply that you are mentally ill – it is a recognized physiological condition. Again, if you are suffering from depression or its consequences (sadness and misery, tiredness and sleep difficulties, eating disorders, difficulty concentrating or making decisions), check with your GP, don't make assumptions.

Control and relief

So far the picture of stress has been fairly unpleasant. While we need an element of stress in our lives to add flavour and keep things moving, the level of stress we all are under far exceeds these requirements, and generally is of a destructive rather than constructive nature. We need mechanisms to bring stress under control and to relieve the damage it can cause. Broadly, we can divide ways of controlling our response to stress into three types – physical, emotional and spiritual. We can also build defences against stress, preventing the stress getting through in the first place.

Physical control

Stress is a physiological consequence of the stressor, and as such responds to physical control. At the extreme this can involve the use of drugs, but more frequently it can be a matter of giving the body the natural defences to be able to handle stress, and enabling a physical outlet when stress manifests itself.

Human beings have never before had such a sedentary life. Much work is now chair-bound, whether you are sitting in front of a computer screen or driving a car. The TV ensures that our entertainment is often low energy too. We don't walk as much as we used to. Recent reports have shown that women, who traditionally had less of a problem with diseases caused by insufficient exercise, have now caught up with men. A major factor in being able to deal with stress is to be able to improve your physical condition. Often this involves basics like better sleep, better eating and more exercise. This isn't a health book, but we will be looking at ways to achieve this with a particular view to stress management – for instance, finding ways to exercise that don't bore you to death.

There are also physical controls that go beyond basic health improvements. Many find massage particularly effective. Aromatherapy may not be entirely proven, but there are enough people who do feel a benefit from it (and bearing in mind the nature of stress, the perception of benefit is enough) to make it worthwhile trying. Although we tend to think of stress as very much an internal thing, we shouldn't ignore these physical aids.

Emotional control

A large degree of our response to stress is dependent on our emotional state and self-image. If we are depressed and unhappy, stress will have a disproportionately large impact. We've all been in the position of snapping at someone for a very minor offence when we are already feeling miserable. Help with your emotional state can make all the difference to how you cope with stress.

Similarly, as we have already seen, self-confidence and feeling in control of your life are immensely valuable when it comes to fending off negative stress. Something as apparently flimsy as attitude and self-esteem has a very big impact. One of the strands you will find in the techniques is looking at building your self-esteem.

It's because of the importance of being in control that the apparent level of stress in a job isn't always a good indicator of the impact it will have on the individual. People with apparently stressful careers – company directors, successful self-employed people, surgeons, air traffic controllers – are much less likely to succumb to stress-related illness than those with apparently low-stress jobs. It's because production line workers or cleaners have so little control and, hence, much less self-esteem that they are more susceptible to stress. Appropriate emotional control can be a lifesaver.

Spiritual control

There's a dichotomy in our world. We have never been more rational, scientific and analytical. Yet everyone will at some time feel a yearning for something more, something beyond the everyday. This need for something more has led to a huge interest in everything spiritual. A reviewer of my book on stress management suggested that it was good stuff, as long as you missed out the 'New Age' bits. That's way off beam. This isn't about getting in touch with your navel, it's simply recognizing that most human beings have a spiritual element (even if they don't recognize it as such). It might be going to church. It might be in their feelings about their football team. But this isn't cultist claptrap – it's just being honest about the factors that influence our stress levels.

The specific approach taken isn't really of concern here, though there are several different suggestions in the techniques. The important consideration is the power of having a spiritual dimension to your life in helping control stress. Many religions stress prayer or meditation as a means of building spiritual calm, which has the practical effect of reducing the impact of stress. In fact, properly used, such spiritual tools can be the most effective stress relievers, as they can be used in any circumstances and have a very powerful effect. Accepting a spiritual dimension to your life can also help overcome difficulties with 'the big issues' that are rarely thought about or discussed in ordinary life, so remain a nagging worry on the threshold of consciousness.

Stress defences

Sometimes the best way to control stress is to avoid it ever reaching you. There are lots of good ways to reduce the impact of sitting in a traffic jam as you queue with the other commuters on the way to work, but it would be even better if you could avoid the queue in the first place. In this particular instance, defences might be anything from taking a different route to not commuting at all.

The natural temptation is to think that most of our stressors are inevitable. I mentioned earlier (see page 10) the BA director who bemoaned the fact that his work had made it impossible for him to see his children growing up. He thought that he had no choice. In fact, he had made a decision that his career, and the level of personal wealth that went with it, was more important than his family life. It's not for me to say whether or not he made the right decision, but it was a decision, not an inevitable fact. Because the decision was never made consciously, we treat it as if it doesn't exist. That's a mistake. The same goes for stress factors. Often we assume that we can't avoid the stressors and so need controls to cope. Before reaching that stage it's worth making the decisions that force the stressors on you visible rather than leaving them implicit.

Keeping the balance

While building your personal resources against stress, bear in mind that your aim is not to totally eliminate stress from your life but to achieve a better balance. This is important to remember both so you don't feel frustrated that you haven't achieved perfection and to avoid the inclination to remove positive stressors which drive you on to achieve success without endangering your health and happiness.

NEGOTIATION

What sort of relationship?

Your approach to negotiation is going to differ depending on the type of relationship you have with the other party. Is it a one-off interaction, or will it be a long-term relationship? What you are attempting to achieve is likely to be quite different in each case.

The one-off

In an isolated negotiation your goal has to be what you get out of the session – because there won't be another chance. Of course not all one-off negotiations involve a single negotiating session. You can have a single goal with multiple meetings (for instance, when selling a house), but with less significant deals a single session might be your only chance for success.

This one-off nature gives a special freedom to be a little more dramatic than usual. You may feel that it is appropriate to go for broke – to push for a win–lose. The easiest examples are those involving simple sales, but the lessons apply whatever the negotiation. For instance, buying a house you could offer not just 10 per cent under half the asking price. Sometimes it will be accepted. Often it won't, but at least you can guarantee plenty of leeway in your negotiating position.

Remember, though, that one-off deals cut both ways. If you are too hard in your bargaining it is quite possible that the other parties will pull out – and then you may regret your daring. It is also quite likely that the one-off nature was an illusion, accidentally or intentionally. It could be that because of changes of circumstances you need to deal with the same person again. I know of, for instance, someone who was really unpleasant to the boss who had made him redundant. He made his negotiations on redundancy as difficult as possible for the boss. A while later he got a job for another firm, only to find out that in the meanwhile his previous boss had also moved to that firm. He had the doubtful pleasure of being made redundant twice in two years by the same man. How much the second event was influenced by previous negotiations, is hard to say, but it would be very naïve to suggest there was no possible connection.

It may also be the case that, despite all the signs, you are being tried out for a longer relationship. A company might negotiate a one-off deal with no suggestion that there is anything more to it. If the contacts are treated well, they may later (knowingly) come back to establish a long-term contract. Go into that one-off deal with the intention of taking them for everything they've got and that long-term contract could well be in jeopardy.

So feel free to be hard on someone whose house you are buying, or whose assets you are buying up when his or her company leaves the country – but make sure you have done your homework and minimized the chances of this backfiring.

The long term

Handling a negotiation that is part of a long-term relationship is a very different affair. Here lifetime value becomes a crucial component of the consideration. The other stakeholders may continue to influence your life and business for a long time to come. In reaching a negotiation you have to consider not only what you can get today, but how that outcome will influence future negotiations and relationships.

If you have the total upper hand – let's say you are a political dictator with enormous powers – you may feel that this is irrelevant because you are always going to be in charge. History has some important lessons that you shouldn't ignore, though. Most dictators find that their power cannot be sustained forever, and then the results of earlier negotiations may come home to roost. You may not actually be running a country, but even someone in a position of power in a company or simply with 'Yes' or 'No' authority in a negotiation should consider that this degree of control may not stay with them for life – at some point, the boot may be on the other foot.

In most negotiations, though, we are not in a position of absolute power and the long-term view means that win–win becomes a golden opportunity. If you can reach an outcome that all parties consider to be positive, then each will go away from the negotiation in a better state for future relationships to flourish.

Because of the uncertainty of the future, the long-term view should be the default stance when looking at negotiating. Unless you can be reasonably sure that there will be no future comeback, your aim should be to establish win–win (though, of course, win–win that particularly benefits you).

Knowing it all

A major weapon in handling negotiations is to be well prepared beforehand. The nature of negotiation is to have movement. If no movement occurs in a negotiation, in effect you haven't negotiated, you have just talked at each other. To be able to deal with such movement, to be able to continue to put your case given the changing circumstances, you will need to know not only your starting point, but the territory surrounding it.

The catalogue of information the good negotiator needs will obviously vary hugely from negotiation to negotiation, but the essence of the requirement is to minimize the risk of needing a piece of information on the spot and being unable to access it. Some fundamentals are to know just what is being negotiated, what your goals are as a stakeholder in the negotiation and what your variables are – the aspects of the negotiation that can be changed to produce an acceptable output.

There will be other categories of information that will be specific to your company and business. The negotiator, or his or her support staff, needs to really know the company and the requirement inside out. Why do you need so much? You can't tell in which direction the discussions will move. If, for instance, you were trying to sell staples to a company and they said 'You already sell us pencils – can we do some kind of bundled deal?', you would not be in a very good position if you didn't know about existing deals, and your company's other product lines (even if personally you only ever dealt in staples). Flexibility is an essential for good negotiation, and flexibility means knowing which way it's safe to move, and which way it isn't.

Knowing your opponent

That's not the end of it, either. You might know your side of the negotiation perfectly, but you also need to know as much as you can about the other stakeholders. That is very obvious in the industrial dispute example above, but less so in the buying and selling examples. Here the seller needs to know as much as possible of the set of information the buyer needs to know. About other vendors they deal with, about other requirements they might have, and so on. Similarly, the good negotiator on the buying side needs to know the vendor inside out – and the vendor's competitors.

Arguably, this knowledge of the other stakeholders is more important than all but the most basic information about your own side. You will usually be able to pull together most internal information quickly if required. Information about the other parties may take longer to obtain.

A key requirement here is to keep your eyes open. Observing the other stakeholders, how they behave and any documentation you are shown will help. Sometimes you may see something accidentally. I recently went into a gift shop. While I was waiting to be served, I noticed a paper on the counter. As a habitual reader, my eyes flicked along the text as I waited. This document told me the mark-up on each of a number of products the shop sold. Such information, innocently obtained, might have been very valuable if I happened to be in negotiation with that shop.

Knowing your deal

Movement means you have to have a wide knowledge of your company and your products and your competitors and the other stakeholders. But movement also has another impact on the knowledge required. You need to know the deal itself. Because if your picture is of the state of negotiations yesterday and things have moved on since then, you may end up arguing from the wrong position and giving way unnecessarily. I have seen a buyer reinstate a starting price after his colleagues had knocked it down to two thirds, simply by not being on top of the deal. It lost the company a hefty sum of money.

This is not usually a problem in a small, quick negotiation, where the posi tion and any variables can easily be held in the heads of any stakeholders, but where the whole deal is complex, with many variables and perhaps many stakeholders, simply keeping a clear picture of the state of the deal is an essential for effective negotiation.

Setting targets

On the ground, dealing with the tactics of negotiation, there isn't time to assess every possibility and decide whether or not a particular suggestion from another stakeholder is acceptable. To make this tactical operation more practical, another strategic essential is to set targets. These should be clear, simple and quantifiable.

Targets need to specify what your ideal goals are in undertaking the negotiation. They should also define your room for manoeuvre. Where appropriate it may be helpful to have this in the form of a table or chart, making it easy to combine a number of variables and see how you are doing against target. For instance, if your variables on a sale included quantities, price, delivery cost, timing and bundled consumables, you might want to know what cut in price you would be happy with if the customer took twice as much product over a longer timescale. This shouldn't need to be a tactical consideration – good strategic target setting would mean that you could read off a ballpark response to a set of figures.

Are the others involved telling the truth?

Some aspects of negotiation are purely tactical though – never more so than the assessment of just what it is that the other stakeholders are telling you. It might be very foolish for them to tell you absolutely everything up front, but this is quite different from telling you lies. Once you suspect a stakeholder of lying, it is difficult to continue the negotiation as if nothing had happened. Yet initially this is probably the best policy, as an apparent lie does not have to be what it seems.

Even if the stakeholder is telling an intentional untruth, there is a whole spectrum you need to be aware of. It could be an out-and-out lie to get business – 'We can deliver all of that three weeks ahead of the competition', but actually the company has neither the ability nor the will to do so. Car salesmen are notorious for the out-and-out lie. If you have a strong suspicion, the lie can often be made to crumble by applying conditions to it ('If you're so sure, presumably you won't mind a hefty penalty clause') or, at the extreme, walking away.

Other lies are more excusable because the lie applies to the present while the promise is for the future. This sounds more complicated than it is. You are buying a coffee maker for each office in your company. You say to the supplier 'With an order this big, do you supply a pack of coffee with each machine?' He replies with a straight face 'Of course.' Technically it's a lie, because he never has before – but he certainly will in your case, so the lie is not disadvantaging you in the negotiation.

All this presumes that you can accurately detect a lie, but given that the justice system has never managed to find a way to do this, with all the technology and weight of the law at its disposal, it is highly unlikely that you can always get it right in a negotiation. It could be that the person across the table is simply nervous. The body language of nervousness is close enough to that of lying to make it easy to confuse the two. It could be that each of you is interpreting a statement in a totally different way. Neither of you is lying, but each would find the other's version untrue. In the end, negotiation often comes down to the old Russian saying picked up by the Reagan administration – trust, but verify.

Sensitive to the moment

However hard you plan, all planning, all strategic consideration is, in the end, guesswork. This is something we don't generally like to hear. A lot of effort frequently goes into planning, and that's fine as long as you accept you are dealing with probabilistic contingencies, rather than what is really going to happen. There is something very irrational about the human brain – once it has a clear picture of how things are going to be, it's a disappointment when things turn out differently. This can happen quite painfully in negotiation.

You reach a point in the discussions where you decided (for instance) that it was appropriate to take a break. But no one wants to. They are really enjoying themselves (it can happen). But it's in the plan, so you insist on a break. The whole impetus is lost and the negotiations collapse. It is crucially important to be aware of your plans, but sensitive to the moment, picking up on the cues that say things are going differently to the way you might have expected.

Often the most obvious difference between an experienced negotiator and a newcomer is this ability to 'fly by the seat of the pants'. The more your plans are a straightjacket, the less you can make the best out of the negotiation. Plans are there to support you – I'm not suggesting you ignore them – but there are times when you need to ignore the constraints and go with the flow of the discussion. Being sensitive to the moment does not mean abandoning your plans. It means being constantly aware of them, but when an opportunity arises, as it will, that wasn't catered for, it should be given full consideration.

Getting this one right will require plenty of mistakes along the way. Like most interpersonal skills, negotiation can rarely be learned without failure. If you are an inexperienced negotiator, watch how a seasoned professional acts – when he or she sticks to the script, when they go with the moment.

Widening the picture

It may be that the negotiation starts off with the intention of being a one-off transaction, but the variables that are used to manage the negotiation widen the picture, whether they involve taking in different products or services, or going from a single deal to a more strategic agreement.

This often happens in pay negotiations. The employees want more money than the employer intends to put on the table. So the employer widens the picture, moving in the strategic direction. 'I can't give you five per cent now, but we could phase it over the next three years.' Or 'The only way I can afford to give you five per cent is to fix pay at that level for the next four years. It will be tight this year, but I can plan on the basis of no further increases.'

Similarly, a purchasing negotiation might be for a single batch of a consumable product. The buyer says 'I can't afford that, could you drop by 10 per cent?' The seller says 'Not on a one-off sale, my overheads won't take it. But you need widgets every month. If we can agree to a contract for the next three years, I can keep prices down to the level you want. What's more, I can hold them down for the whole period.' A nice example of win–win. The buyer gets a lower price. The vendor gets a cash flow lasting for three years, instead of a one-off sale followed by the need to start all over again.

Don't be afraid to widen the picture. Sometimes this can be in a direction that is relatively painless to the stakeholder, but it still may result in big rewards. Publishers usually present authors with contracts specifying a (very small) percentage royalty on each sale. Often authors negotiate for a rising percentage. So after selling (say) 5,000 books, the percentage goes up. The author feels better, as there's the possibility of doing better than expected, while the publisher isn't too worried, as he or she won't have to pay more unless the book is making a decent profit. A similar approach occurs in any negotiation that results in getting a percentage of the profits of an enterprise as well as a straight fee. It's widening the picture, but in a fail-safe direction.

Getting time right

Time is always a factor in negotiation. Time to plan and prepare in advance of the sessions. Managing time in the sessions. The timing of your moves and tactics. How time is employed can often make a big difference. The aggressive negotiator will often use time as a bludgeon, coming up with negotiating stances like 'I can offer you this, very special deal, but you have to make up your mind and agree today. It won't be on the table any longer.'

It is fine to be the one applying time pressure, but being on the receiving end is generally a signal to put the brakes on. If a stakeholder is trying to get you to accept quickly, chances are they have something to hide – they are trying to get you to agree before you can consider all the implications or look more carefully at the alternatives. It is often sensible to say 'I'm sorry, but I really don't understand why this has to be done in such a hurry. If you can't be bothered to wait until we've got everything straight, you obviously don't want to do business.' Effectively calling their bluff, perhaps to the extent of walking away from the table and seeing what happens.

However, a time constraint can sometimes be a legitimate variable to accept. A good example is the process of placing a potential best-selling book with a publisher. Usually, publishing is a buyer's market. The publisher can pick and choose between offerings with little concern if they get it wrong. Occasionally, though, there will be a book comes along that is an obvious best-seller. Suddenly it's a seller's market, and the publishers are trying to outdo each other to get the book.

In such circumstances, a publisher will sometimes make a pre-emptive bid, saying to the author 'We will give you £X,' where X is perhaps two or three times the amount so far discussed, 'but only if you sign up today.' As always the negotiator, in this case the author, is taking a risk. He or she may get more elsewhere. There's no knowing how far the bids will go. But equally, they may never get up to this figure, and there's the reassurance that a contract will actually be in place the same day, and the publisher isn't suddenly going to get distracted by another project. It's not an easy call, but the time factor is less of a disaster here.

Slowing things down not only gives time to consider all possibilities and look for potential snares, but can also be beneficial to the emotional side of negotiation. It is all too easy to get carried away with the excitement of negotiation, to lose a temper or get over-enthusiastic about a doubtful proposition. Time gives the chance to take the edge off the emotional response and mix in the logical. As we will see in the next chapter, good negotiation requires both intuition and logic, but under time pressure logic is often squeezed out of the equation, resulting in erratic and dangerous decisions.

The matter of price

You can't talk about selling for long before price comes up. It would be very strange if this wasn't the case. Yet the first consideration when dealing with price is to make sure that it isn't over-valued. It shouldn't always dominate a negotiation. Instead, price should be seen alongside a whole host of other variables (see the next section). It's only in context that it is meaningful. Take a simple example. You are buying computer printers for your company. One supplier offers a unit price of £200, the other £120. Which do you go with?

The answer should be, 'I don't know, there's insufficient information.' For instance you may be waiting for me to tell you that the annual consumables cost of the first printer is £100 and the second is £200. And so on. Yes, price is important, but it is usually so visible (and we are often so fixed on the short-term view) that it sometimes is given excessive importance.

If you are selling there always comes that uncomfortable moment when you've got to set a price. From the strategy section, you will already have an idea of what you want and need to get. Setting that initial price on paper is a good idea – a price list gives a false air of officialdom to a price. The level needs to be pitched so that it is not outrageously high in market terms, but not so low you haven't room to still be comfortable after manoeuvre.

I have seen it suggested that you should avoid round number prices (like £10, £100 or £1,400), because this suggests a starting price for negotiation. Apart from the fact that this is what your price is likely to be, I'm not totally convinced about this argument. There's some justification for using the standing retail trick of £399.95 instead of £400, but I'm not sure if £403 is really somehow better than £400 too.

When you have to lower a price as a seller, make sure it's in decreasing increments, making it harder and harder to get too far down, emphasizing that you are running out of space to move. One piece of advice I would certainly follow is never give anything away (on price or any other variable), wait for the buyers to ask (and don't be too quick to accept). In fact silence is often an underrated negotiating skill. You can often get people to negotiate themselves down, given enough silence.

There's always another lever

As we've already seen, price is but one of a huge host of variables. Here's a representative sample in no particular order:

- maintenance cost;
- consumable cost;
- delivery charges;
- delivery time;
- expenses;
- materials;
- finance;

- guarantees and warranties;
- product quality;
- packaging;
- bulk discount;
- delayed payment;
- ...and so on.

If you are in trouble in a negotiation and don't have the leeway to move on a particular variable, remember just how many other options there are. If the other stakeholder points out that you are 10 per cent more expensive than your rival, you can argue, 'yes, but we can deliver in a week to their month, and you don't have to pay a penny with us until the summer', or whatever.

Your USP

In sales and marketing there is one acronym that is engraved on everyone's heart – USP. The Unique Selling Proposition is something almost every company could make more of than it does at the moment. It's what's special about your product, your services, your business, your people that makes them different from the rest. A good USP is simple, readily understood by the employees and readily understood by the customers. An old, but well known one is the John Lewis Partnership's 'never knowingly undersold'.

Unfortunately USPs do get out of date and devalued. 'Never knowingly undersold' is something many companies could say nowadays, and it's arguable that John Lewis would be better working on quality and service lines. However, the point is still that a USP makes a lot of difference when selling.

When you are negotiating, your USP should be to the fore. If, for example, you were in a business where support generally operated in office hours and you had 24-hour support, it should be something that was worked into your negotiations as strongly as possible, in many different ways. Your USP should be a prime tool in selling your side of the negotiation, provided it is strong enough. Just make sure it truly is unique.

Using emotion

Emotion inevitably enters into negotiations. Any interaction between people will be flavoured by emotion, and the intuition and gut-feel that is a vital part of negotiation is impossible without it. The negotiator's aim has to be to use emotion effectively without being controlled by it. As soon as you lose your temper, you have given away control of the negotiation. However, you can use the whole gamut of emotion – from anger to joy – to put across your message and reinforce your position.

Exactly how emotion is employed in negotiations depends very much on the people involved. There are individual variations, but also cultural inclinations. Some cultures consider a vivid display of emotion such a normal part of everyday life that they would think that a negotiator who didn't show emotion regularly had something to hide. Other cultures consider shows of emotion in business a sign of weakness. If you are to use emotion effectively, part of your preparation needs to be finding out as much as you can about the other stakeholders in the negotiation, establishing their personal and cultural attitudes.

The emotions that are most frequently and safely employed in most Western negotiations are anger and friendliness. Anger has to be used sparingly, and almost artificially. It's fine to appear angry and even to feel some anger, as long as you haven't lost control to the anger. Anger is best employed to counter an outrageous suggestion from the other side, and even will be most effective if it very quickly turns into sorrow that they can think they can treat you this way.

Usually, though, there is most leverage from warmth and friendship. The more you can put this across, the harder it will be for the other stakeholders to comprehensively rip you off. To get the value out of warmth and friendship you will need to maximize the human contact between the parties. This is why it is always best that at least part of the negotiation takes place face-to-face. You can do plenty over the phone or by e-mail, but these remote communications lack the emotional linkage. It's much easier to stop thinking of someone as a person if you haven't had a face-to-face meeting with them lately, and it's a great disadvantage to someone if you don't think of them as a person.

But, like the anger, can't you fake it? Not so easily. A short burst of anger is relatively easy to generate, but faked warmth is usually easily detected – and dangerously off-putting. By far the easiest way to fake warmth is to actually feel it, to think of the other stakeholders as real people and to like them for their humanity. For all but the most consummate actors, finding something to like about almost anyone else is easier than generating a convincing fake.

Dealing with people

I can't reiterate enough that negotiations are human relations, with all the flaws and difficulties (and fun) that accompany all human relations. I was speaking recently to the director of a major financial institution. He had been involved with merger negotiations with another large institution, a Swiss organization. By mid-afternoon on the first day, things were going well, but were tense. The Swiss negotiators wanted a coffee break. The other stakeholders wanted to continue. For a period the negotiation nearly fell through. The Swiss negotiators were prepared to drop a whole multi-billion dollar deal over a cup of coffee. That's people for you.

It's all very well to say that negotiation requires you to balance logic and gut-feel, but sometimes human nature introduces a third factor that is neither of these – sheer bloody-mindedness. Everyone has moments when they operate irrationally, over-reacting to a stimulus or being ridiculously intransigent. In such circumstances, an understanding of human nature and a willingness to work around it are essential.

The natural reaction when someone else goes into extreme irrationality is to follow them. When they insult your family, you insult theirs. When they threaten to walk out, so do you. But the good negotiator is enough in control to be able to handle over-reaction and irrationality calmly, bringing the negotiation back on track. You have to be prepared to apologize, overcoming pride when you know you have done nothing wrong. Often, the over-reaction will have been triggered by misunderstanding. Calmly, slowly, point out what was really intended. Verbally sympathize with their viewpoint, even if you don't inside. Until the stakeholders can be brought back out of irrationality, no progress can be made.

Often such over-reaction is simple human nature, but occasionally it will be cynically used as a bargaining counter, with the intention that you give way on some issue in order to stop the irrationality. It's a classic child's technique, that all too often works for children so that the adults can get a bit of peace. While it is important to soothe the other stakeholders, it is equally important to totally ignore any conditions they are putting on their return to normal. Keep assuring them there was no bad intention and apologizing for any misunderstanding, without ever moving an inch on any concessions. There is a limit to how long any over-reaction can be sustained in the face of sympathy (though it can totally finish negotiations if you over-react back). Before long, with no concessions required, the other stakeholders will pull back to normality.

Culture shock

Time and again, cultural differences have caused problems in negotiations. Anything from how the other stakeholders are addressed to how much price haggling is allowed and expected will have cultural variants. Cultural upsets are sometimes used as a cynical bargaining chip, but often arouse genuine upset in the parties to a negotiation, disrupting the whole process.

Cultural differences will bring in different expectations, difficulties in communication, and differences in attitude to timing. It might be, for instance, that representatives of two cultures are meeting for the first time for a social event on the evening before a formal negotiation. One culture might expect to have early discussions on the subject of the negotiation. The other might expect to stick to social niceties. This second group would find the first pushy, while the first would find their opponents evasive. Neither is doing anything wrong, apart from not anticipating the other's cultural reaction.

It's a good thing before a negotiation with a different culture to immerse yourself as much as possible in their tradition. Talk to other people who have already dealt with them. Read up on the culture. Talk to a friendly person from the same culture. Try to get a picture of how they are likely to react to something and why.

Sometimes taking such care can result in amusing circumstances. After all, you aren't necessarily the only one who has done their homework. A famous example was the first meeting of IBM and Apple to discuss a new business venture. These two companies might have been from the same country, but their cultures were poles apart. IBM was all East Coast, button-down formality; Apple was West Coast, beard-and-sandals openness. Each did their homework. At the first meeting the Apple folk turned up wearing suits and white shirts. The IBM team were in jeans and T-shirts. Each had made an effort to match the other's culture – and the result was positive. Each was impressed by the other's attempts. The humour of the situation helped break down barriers. Negotiations went a great deal better thanks to this.

Like many human issues, once you have established a basic level of trust between stakeholders, it makes a great deal of sense to get the issue out into the open. If there are aspects of the behaviour of the other team that you don't understand, ask them about it. Not in a derogatory way, but with a genuine interest. If, for instance, you found that a Spanish negotiator never turned up until mid-afternoon for the lunchtime session, you might be irritated at his recurrent lateness. Berate him about this, and the whole negotiation would probably collapse. But ask him about it in a positive way and he will be happy to let you know that he can only work in the afternoon after a siesta – and you, no doubt, will cease to be irritated and be happy to accommodate him.

Building trust

Trust is an essential for effective negotiation. In negotiations without trust, the stakeholders are like fighters, circling each other looking for advantage, never daring to turn their back in case they are attacked when they aren't looking. The fundamental requirement to be able to establish a win–win outcome is a degree of trust.

You can help your chances of successful negotiation by making it easier for the other stakeholders to trust you. It's a peculiarity of trust that it is much more dependent on what you do than on what you say. It doesn't matter how wonderful you are when speaking, if you act differently there can be no trust. 'Do what I say, not what I do' is not an acceptable motto for a negotiator.

Why are actions so important? Because as soon as you say one thing and do another, the other stakeholders are going to think 'It doesn't matter what he says, he's going to do something different.' And the whole basis of negotiation is talking in order to establish what will be done in the future. If, on the other hand, the other stakeholders think 'I can always rely on her to do what she says she's going to do,' they will feel more open to discuss things with you. They will accept your word on the way things are. And the negotiations can proceed.

A little endorsement

If you need to build trust relatively quickly, the normal approach is to use endorsement. It's a term that has become sadly devalued thanks to the advertisers' use of endorsements by famous people as a way of selling products. Cynically, we know that the famous athlete who is raving about the sports drink probably can't stand the stuff, but is being paid enough to say anything. This isn't endorsement, it's prostitution. But true endorsement still has a value.

If you are negotiating to sell your services, it can be very helpful in building trust if you have satisfied customers who will tell your potential buyer just how great you have been. Too often we are embarrassed at the thought of seeking out endorsement – we don't like asking other people to praise us. Yet this is a hugely valuable tool in building trust in the artificial confines of the negotiation. Whatever your negotiation look for the opportunity to make honest use of endorsement.

Listening

I had initially intended 'listening' to come after the next section, 'talking' – but that would be getting things back to front. Good communication, good negotiating, starts with listening. The fact is that most of us are pretty good at talking, but hopeless at listening. We tend to spend the time when others are talking getting ready for our next bit of speech. This makes for bad communication, because it's usually quite clear that we aren't giving full attention. If, when you are listening, something occurs to you, make a quick note, don't keep worrying at it in your mind. If necessary, get the speaker to reiterate to make sure you don't lose track. But when you are listening, do just that. Listen.

Just by listening, *really* listening, you will have put yourself ahead of the majority of negotiators. You will have won more trust from the other stakeholders – because you were obviously really interested in what they were saying – and you will have a grasp of exactly what they are saying, not a vague synopsis.

Talking

Talking is equally at the heart of negotiation. It might seem that talking is something that can be left to nature, that it's something everyone can do, but the way that you handle your input can be crucial. The aim should be to be relaxed, to be positive and to be fluent. There is nothing that will beat practice in this field. Especially bearing in mind the need to listen to the other parties, you have to be able to spring into speech with very little thinking time.

Don't take this as an excuse for waffling. Give yourself a second or two to collect your thoughts. A useful approach if you feel you aren't sure where to start is to try to pull together what has already been said. Echo back what you have heard from the other parties – make sure there is clear understanding. And make appropriate use of notes to ensure that you have a range of openings available to you. Most of all a negotiator needs to be able to engage his or her brain before speaking, sadly a rare ability. Before undertaking negotiation for real, get some practice in. Undertake some mock negotiations with your colleagues. It doesn't matter how much you learn valuable techniques, your communication skills will benefit most from being used.

Assertive or aggressive?

Aggression invokes the ancient fight or flight response. The other stakeholders will respond as they are programmed. They will either run away or fight back. Running away could mean literally leaving the negotiating table or finding ways to avoid discussion. Fighting back could be anything from getting aggressive in their turn to physical violence. None of these responses will help conclude the negotiation.

But curbing aggression does not mean that you have to give in to whatever the other stakeholders want. The appropriate position is to be assertive. It's unfortunate that assertiveness has been taken up as a clarion cry of fringe groups – it somehow seems to fit with self-defence and holistic medicine. This misses the point. Being assertive is simply a matter of ensuring that your viewpoint is heard and that you get an appropriate chance to get your way without being aggressive.

The first, and most important aid to being assertive rather than aggressive is to be calm. Nothing can be more unnerving than appropriately applied calm. By staying calm, you appear to be in the right (whether or not you are). By staying calm you can help defuse the situation. And by staying calm you will not say things that you might regret (and that will damage your negotiation). With calm as a foundation you can build up assertiveness. The essential is to get your point across, whatever the opposition, in a calm and positive way.

If you want your point to be heard, it's best not to disagree. If you launch in with 'I see what you are saying, but…' the people in opposition have already switched off. You are contradicting them and they won't like it. Much better to build on what they are saying. Starting with something like 'That's right, and we could…' is much more likely to succeed because you are being inclusive ('*we* could') and you have used *and* instead of *but*, making your statement seem a constructive addition rather than an argument. It might seem such picky concentration on words is unnecessary but such words set the tone of the negotiation. The more you can seem positive and agreeable, even if your remarks are in total contradiction, the harder it will be to dismiss you.

A final thought on being assertive – have plenty of supporting material. It is easier to stay assertive if you can cite examples and endorsements for your point of view. That way you aren't just saying 'This is the way things should be because I say so' which can slip easily from being assertive to just being bossy. Exuding calm, staying positive, reiterating your point and using plenty of supporting material – being assertive – won't guarantee a result, but it will maximize your chances of success.

Plotting out the journey

As you undertake a negotiation, change is always occurring. Unless there is movement, as we have already seen, there is no successful negotiation. However, in a complex deal it is very easy to lose track of the different variables and the state of play. It can be useful to have some sort of record of the situation, making it clear just where you have got to, particularly in an exploratory negotiation (in a selling negotiation you may not want the other parties to remember too much).

In such circumstances, consider having a large whiteboard or similar vehicle, showing the state of play. Apart from anything else, this frees up mental resources in the negotiators that would otherwise be taken up with remembering what has happened so far. Whether you are exploring or selling, you want the negotiation to come to a conclusion; without an end, it will have been a total waste of time. Plotting out the journey you have taken will make it easier to reach a conclusion.

GETTING STARTED

With these three components of time management, stress management and negotiation fixed firmly in mind, let's move on to the course itself, a series of 30 units that can be undertaken on a weekly or daily basis – or however best suits you. The next chapter gives a brief introduction to the layout, and provides a checklist to record progress.

2 Work plan

INTRODUCING THE COURSE

Each of the 30 units consists of a number of elements. There are five exercises or techniques. Exercises are designed to be performed immediately to help develop your creative skills. They will normally take between five and twenty minutes to undertake. Techniques are additions to your toolkit that can be brought into play as and when you have a need to take control, to move your life closer to the way you want it to be. It is sensible to read through the techniques, and note when you might next find the technique useful, but it will not usually be practical to undertake the technique straight away. Some items are marked exercise/technique – these form general techniques, but should also be undertaken immediately as an exercise.

How you organize the course is up to you. You could take a day over each unit, or a week – or however long you like. It's up to you how long you want the 30 units to take.

Each unit also contains one or more unit books. The unit books are intended to help expand your horizons and give more opportunities for development of your people management skills. You aren't expected to read every book we recommend, but the more you can get in, the more effective the course will be. Most of our recommendations are available from public libraries, or you can build your own management library by buying them – there are links to online bookshops stocking them at our support Web site www.cul.co.uk/crashcourse.

The support Web site, www.cul.co.uk/crashcourse, is packed with Web links to broaden your reading, and is designed to extend your knowledge base into the Web.

The next short section provides a checklist to monitor your progress. You may also find it useful to make some notes on the exercise and technique pages to help record your progress.

When you have completed all the units, there is a final section that provides an opportunity to recap and to revisit the unit books.

CHECKLIST

Unit 1: A taster

1.1 Where did it go? ☐
1.2 The top ten list ☐
1.3 A personal project ☐
1.4 Little successes ☐
1.5 Another lever ☐
Unit book ☐
Web links ☐

Unit 2: Fundamentals – understanding your motives

2.1 Talent spotting ☐
2.2 If I were rich ☐
2.3 Dream day ☐
2.4 Obstacle map ☐
2.5 What's it worth? ☐
Unit books ☐

Unit 3: Finding the switches – understanding your stressors

3.1 Control freaks ☐
3.2 The big stuff ☐
3.3 How do you react? ☐
3.4 Physical checks ☐

3.5 Emotional and spiritual checks ☐
Unit books ☐
Web links ☐

Unit 4: What comes first? – prioritization

4.1 Principles ☐
4.2 Focus ☐
4.3 Priorities ☐
4.4 Pareto ☐
4.5 Drawn and quartered ☐
Unit book ☐

Unit 5: There's nowhere like home – work/life balance

5.1 Scrap the briefcase ☐
5.2 How long? ☐
5.3 Reading up ☐
5.4 Banning homework ☐
5.5 Because I'm worth it ☐
Unit book ☐
Web links ☐

Unit 6: I can't concentrate – handling distractions

6.1 The red hat ☐
6.2 Deflecting distraction ☐
6.3 Jump-start ☐
6.4 Waiting room ☐
6.5 Caught in the Web ☐
Unit books ☐

Unit 7: Chunking it up – breaking down your goals into manageable items

7.1 Chunking ☐
7.2 Tasks, tasks ☐

- 7.3 Task list stragglers ☐
- 7.4 We don't deliver ☐
- 7.5 Against the buffers ☐
- Unit book ☐
- Web links ☐

Unit 8: Stopping – saying 'No' and throwing things out

- 8.1 Why not 'No'? ☐
- 8.2 No, I can ☐
- 8.3 Meet yourself half way ☐
- 8.4 No action, no report ☐
- 8.5 No news is good news ☐
- Unit book ☐

Unit 9: Managing meetings – don't let them rule your life

- 9.1 Agenda bender ☐
- 9.2 Garbage in, garbage out ☐
- 9.3 Crowd control ☐
- 9.4 Go casual ☐
- 9.5 Coherent discussion ☐
- Unit books ☐
- Web links ☐

Unit 10: A pat on the back – self reward

- 10.1 Cherry-picking ☐
- 10.2 Little treats ☐
- 10.3 Doggie chocs ☐
- 10.4 Pat on the back ☐
- 10.5 I did that ☐
- Unit books ☐
- Web links ☐

Unit 11: Look around you – dealing with the environment

11.1 Quiet corners ☐
11.2 How wide is your door? ☐
11.3 Home, sweet home ☐
11.4 Environmental stuff ☐
11.5 Coping with change ☐
Unit books ☐
Web links ☐

Unit 12: Giving it away – sharing your burdens

12.1 Letting go ☐
12.2 Be prepared ☐
12.3 Delegation difficulties ☐
12.4 It's mine ☐
12.5 Mentor mine ☐
Unit book ☐
Web links ☐

Unit 13: Making communications work for you – rather than for them

13.1 The e-mail of the species ☐
13.2 E-mail it away ☐
13.3 Calling by numbers ☐
13.4 Fluffy phones ☐
13.5 Paper mountains ☐
Unit book ☐

Unit 14: Filling the gaps – using your spare time

14.1 TV turn-off ☐
14.2 You are what you eat ☐
14.3 Play! ☐
14.4 The spiritual path ☐
14.5 Different values ☐
Unit books ☐
Web links ☐

Unit 15: Devils and angels – anger and laughter

15.1 Handling confrontation ☐
15.2 Laugh! ☐
15.3 Rage ☐
15.4 Don't do that ☐
15.5 When you lose your temper ☐
Unit book ☐
Web links ☐

Unit 16: Easing off – relaxation

16.1 Touchy-smelly ☐
16.2 Ritual relaxation ☐
16.3 Breathing is good for you ☐
16.4 Pushing waves ☐
16.5 Medicinal reading ☐
Unit books ☐
Web links ☐

Unit 17: Dealing with a troublemaker – de-stressing the interaction

17.1 Sulkers ☐
17.2 Nemesis ☐
17.3 Bully off ☐
17.4 Cut the aggro ☐
17.5 Slowing the pace ☐
Unit book ☐
Web links ☐

Unit 18: Getting what you want – assertive behaviour

18.1 Are you assertive? ☐
18.2 Broken record ☐
18.3 Broken CD ☐
18.4 Setbacks ☐
18.5 Personality types ☐
Unit book ☐
Web links ☐

Unit 19: Make the break – getting away from it all

19.1 Don't bury yourself ☐
19.2 Café life ☐
19.3 Get away ☐
19.4 Walkies! ☐
19.5 Going solo ☐
Unit book ☐
Web links ☐

Unit 20: Bumf bashing – dealing with bureaucracy and paperwork

20.1 Penalizing pen-pushing ☐
20.2 A file in a cake ☐
20.3 Scheduling admin ☐
20.4 Bureaucratic bounce-back ☐
20.5 Sharing chores ☐
Unit books ☐

Unit 21: The inner you – dealing with physical issues

21.1 Hot spots ☐
21.2 Stress workout ☐
21.3 Sleep! ☐
21.4 Stimulants stink ☐
21.5 Integral exercise ☐
Unit book ☐
Web links ☐

Unit 22: Development through knowledge – using information to your advantage

22.1 Capture ideas ☐
22.2 Lifetime value ☐
22.3 Web research ☐
22.4 Knowing the opposition ☐
22.5 Knowing your products and services ☐
Unit book ☐
Web links ☐

Unit 23: Seeing through the fog – understanding what they're really saying

23.1 Listen well ☐
23.2 Are they telling the truth? ☐
23.3 Play that back ☐
23.4 Remote negotiation ☐
23.5 Appearing naïve ☐
Unit books ☐
Web links ☐

Unit 24: Finding the levers – making negotiation work for you

24.1 It's yours right now ☐
24.2 Starting prices ☐
24.3 Throwing in the condiment ☐
24.4 There's always an 'if' ☐
24.5 Doing a special ☐
Unit book ☐
Web links ☐

Unit 25: Selling yourself – don't shoot yourself in the foot

25.1 Talking yourself down ☐
25.2 Getting endorsements ☐
25.3 Delightful deals ☐
25.4 Selling your wider strengths ☐
25.5 Being you ☐
Unit book ☐

Unit 26: Making the choice – supporting your decisions

26.1 Taking notes ☐
26.2 The timescales game ☐
26.3 Basic option evaluation ☐
26.4 Sophisticated option evaluation ☐
26.5 Options with guts ☐
Unit book ☐
Web links ☐

Unit 27: Going beyond the obvious – dealing with others differently

27.1 I agree… ish ☐
27.2 Exploring trust ☐
27.3 Beautiful barter ☐
27.4 You won't win them all ☐
27.5 Aim high to get more ☐
Unit books ☐
Web links ☐

Unit 28: Be prepared – planning for success

28.1 Stage fright ☐
28.2 Your USP ☐
28.3 Setting targets ☐
28.4 Future visions ☐
28.5 Don't leave the next step in others' hands ☐
Unit book ☐
Web links ☐

Unit 29: Putting it across – communicating your message

29.1 Using emotion ☐
29.2 I'll be honest… ☐
29.3 Yes… eventually ☐
29.4 Using silence ☐
29.5 Body language ☐
Unit book ☐

Unit 30: A sense of calm – further relaxation

30.1 Relaxing by numbers ☐
30.2 Music soothes the savage breast ☐
30.3 Cornered rats ☐
30.4 Meditation ☐
30.5 Low power dressing ☐
Unit book ☐
Web links ☐

3 The course

Each unit comprises a mix of exercises – activities to undertake now as you read the book – and techniques that can be used later, whether working alone or with others. Sections marked as exercise/techniques can be used straight away as an exercise, but also provide a technique to use later on.

Unit 1:
A taster

In this first unit we get a taste of things to come with an exercise to discover just where your time goes, a technique that can be used to ensure that you get more of what you want to do done, a look at working on a personal project, a technique to enhance your self-esteem and a fundamental technique for negotiation.

Do try out the exercises as you go. Put them off until later and you probably won't ever do them. Read through the techniques. Make notes about how and when you can use them. And make sure you give them a try in the next appropriate forum.

Unit book

There's no obligation to read all, or any, of the unit books, but you will find that they provide excellent support to the course and strengthen your self development.

Personal development is strongly dependent on understanding your motivation and needs. Charles Handy's excellent *The Hungry Spirit* explores the gap between the drivers of corporate culture and what we really need as human beings. Although usually labelled a business book – and Handy has impeccable business credentials – this is much more about thinking through the way you live your life.

You can find more information on our unit books, or buy them, from our support site: www.cul.co.uk/crashcourse.

Web links

Links to Web sites on general self development can be found at www.cul.co.uk/crashcourse.

1.1 Exercise: Where did it go?

Preparation None.
Running time Five minutes.
Resources Diary, paper.
Frequency Once.

It is often difficult to appreciate just where your time has gone. Look back over the last typical week you had. Your diary will probably help. Starting with the 168 hours you have in the week, allocate each to one of a number of headings. Try: Sleep, Paid work, Social, Maintenance (both self and belongings), Unpaid work and Study. You should be able to fit all your activities into these headings without too much trouble.

Now have a look at how that time balances out – a bar chart is a good way of getting an overview of the implications. How do you feel about the relative times you spend on your different activities? We aren't going to do anything actively with this data right now, but it will be an important input to the decisions you will be making. In the exercise *How long?* in Unit 5 we will look at achieving a better balance between work and social, but the purpose of this exercise is to understand your position.

Feedback Balance is fundamental to self development. Remember there isn't any wasted time, just time that is used more or less effectively for your purposes.

Outcome Without a reasonable feeling for where your time is going now, you are unlikely to have a good idea of the balance and the need for change. Although this exercise doesn't result in immediate action, it will give you an essential picture of your starting point.

Variations The best way to put together a summary like this is to keep a log for a week, noting as you do it which category your activity fits into. Not many people do this as it seems too much hassle. It's a pity, because without a log it is very difficult to be realistic about the way you spend your time, and keeping one for a week is very little burden. Give it a try.

Time management	✪✪✪✪
Stress management	✪✪
Negotiation skills	✪
General development	✪✪✪
Fun	✪✪

1.2 *Exercise/Technique: The top ten list*

Preparation None.
Running time Five minutes.
Resources None.
Frequency Weekly.

Note your top ten concerns for the coming week. Put the list somewhere very visible. If you have staff, e-mail them a copy.

Whenever you start a task, glance at the top ten list. Does the task influence your top ten? If it doesn't, you may still do it, but bear in mind its relative unimportance. If you are asked to do something which doesn't fit with your list and you are short of time, say 'No'. (Find it difficult? There will be plenty of help in Unit 8.) Next week, when you draw up your list, make sure there are changes. There may be ongoing priorities, but if everything stays the same from week to week you are stagnating.

Feedback This is a good exercise to start early because it can stand alone.

Outcome The top ten list cuts through your potential activities to the essentials. It's great both for work and at home. I was introduced to the idea of sharing the list with staff by Nick Spooner, MD of Internet commerce company Entranet. Nick used his top ten list to communicate priorities to his staff. Before long they all had their own lists in public view. This has significantly improved the company's effectiveness. A side effect of the top ten list is to reduce irrelevant interruptions. A meaningful look at the list as someone comes close can cause them to reassess their priorities.

Variations It may be necessary to have several lists. For example, top ten customers and top ten milestones. The actual subjects need to be matched to your line of business, but don't be tempted to have more than two or three – you need to be able to take in the lists at a glance.

Time management	✪✪✪✪
Stress management	✪✪✪
Negotiation skills	✪✪
General development	✪✪
Fun	✪✪

1.3 Technique: A personal project

Preparation None.
Running time 10 minutes.
Resources Output from personal goal sessions, notebook.
Frequency Annual.

Personal development is as much about your home life as it is about work, but many people put work first. This exercise encourages you to widen your view. The aim is to establish a new personal project – an activity towards a goal outside work that isn't currently under way. However busy you are, this is worthwhile.

Take a couple of minutes to consider anything you have on goals and skills, values and obstacles (if you don't have anything, try one or two of the first five exercises in the chapter). Identify an activity in your personal life that isn't happening or isn't being handled very well. Ideally it should be an activity that can be brought to a conclusion in a reasonable frequency – no more than six months. Now feed this activity into your plans. Ensure that you do something on it every week, perhaps only a few minutes, but keep it alive. Now at least one personal project has made it into your priorities.

Feedback Resist the temptation to push this activity aside when time gets tight. You needn't spend long on it, but make sure you spend some time on it weekly.

Outcome By forcing a goal outside work into your focal activities you are helping even out the balance most of us have got drastically wrong.

Variations It's just possible that your balance is so far the other way that you have to use this exercise to get another work topic into your focal activities, but that is rare. Don't add several activities at once. Get one up and running and then consider more. Don't drop anything to add this first one. As you change the balance further you will need to, but for one new activity there should not be a need to drop anything.

Time management	✪✪✪✪
Stress management	✪✪✪
Negotiation skills	✪
General development	✪✪✪✪
Fun	✪✪✪✪

1.4 Exercise/Technique: Little successes

Preparation None.
Running time Two minutes.
Resources None.
Frequency Several times.

Self-esteem is an important contributory factor to managing stress – and without a handle on your stress levels you are going to find self development almost impossible. If your self-esteem is low, you are much more likely to succumb to stress-related illness. One of the undermining factors that keep self-esteem low is the diminishing spiral that says 'I never achieve anything', so you feel bad about not achieving, so you get stressed and achieve even less.

This is a very quick exercise that can have a surprisingly powerful effect on self-esteem. Spend a couple of minutes jotting down a handful of small achievements you have made in the day. However bad a day you've had, you should be able to find something positive to say – force yourself to generate at least three; don't take no for an answer. Repeat this exercise each day for a week or two.

Feedback Stick to small achievements for this exercise. We will look at stress relief out of bigger achievements in a different topic (*I did that* in Unit 10). No one is going to have a big achievement every day, but we all have a series of small achievements that will prove the fictional nature of the destructive view that everything about your life is terrible and you never succeed at anything.

Outcome It might seem that such a small success – it might just be 'I got to work on time' or 'I told my children a bedtime story' – is small beer compared to your problems. It doesn't matter; much of the stress from lack of self-esteem derives from an imagined bleak picture that 'everything' goes wrong for you. Realistically this can't be true – and proving it to yourself can really help.

Variations You could do this on a day-by-day basis, or (perhaps better) accumulate a list of all the little plusses across the period of time you are running the exercise.

Time management	✪
Stress management	✪✪✪✪
Negotiation skills	✪
General development	✪✪
Fun	✪✪✪

1.5 Technique: Another lever

Preparation None.
Running time 10 minutes.
Resources None.
Frequency Once.

There is always another lever to pull. You will see this coming out in various techniques throughout this book, but it is worth emphasizing as a general concept because it is so important. Your ability to negotiate depends on making movements in the various variables under your control. In a sales negotiation, for instance, such variables will generally include price, quantities, delivery costs, timing and so forth.

When undertaking a negotiation, you should always be using these variables to get concessions out of the other stakeholders. The good news is that however many variables you think there are, there can always be more.

Before any negotiation take ten minutes to think about the variables. Set yourself the task of adding two more (though it may be that you can find many). Get them lined up, considering their potential impact on the stakeholders and their impact on you. Don't let the other negotiators win the lever war.

Feedback Just as a good card player keeps his or her cards well hidden, you don't want all your levers exposed up front. Keep a few winners back to pull out in case the other stakeholders come up with something difficult to handle. Remember to think outside the individual product to anything your company and the stakeholder companies are (or could be) involved in.

Outcome The ability to add in another variable can both counter a surprise step from the other stakeholders and improve your own position in the negotiation.

Variations None.

Time management	✪
Stress management	✪✪
Negotiation skills	✪✪✪✪
General development	✪✪
Fun	✪✪

Unit 2: Fundamentals – understanding your motives

It's easy when trying to sort out your time management and handle your stress to plunge in and try to untangle the minutiae. The trouble is, such an approach misses out on a fundamental point –what's it all for? Why do you want the time in the first place? Why do you want to develop yourself? This unit is inward looking, but not in a vague philosophical way – it uses simple and enjoyable exercises to help you clarify what you really want in life.

Do try out the exercises as you go. Put them off until later and you probably won't ever do them. Read through the techniques. Make notes about how and when you can use them. And make sure you give them a try in the next appropriate forum.

Unit books

Anthony Jay and Jonathan Lynn's superb books *The Complete Yes Minister* and *The Complete Yes Prime Minister*, based on the classic TV series, combine wonderful humour with startling accuracy. Most importantly for this unit, we see how the motives and actions of those involved diverge, buried under a pile of hidden agenda.

You can find more information on our unit books, or buy them, from our support site: www.cul.co.uk/crashcourse.

2.1 Exercise: Talent spotting

Preparation None.
Running time Five minutes.
Resources None.
Frequency Annual.

Time for some self-assessment. Run through the activities you undertake, both at work and in your social life. Trying not to be modest, what do you do well? What have you had positive feedback about? Put together a list of one-liners on your talents. Don't separate work and social: they are all talents.

Now extend out along the timeline. What did you do years ago that you were good at, but haven't done since? Also, think yourself into the future. Is there anything that you've never actually done, but think you would be good at? This is not a matter of impossible dreams, but talents you feel you may well have, given the chance.

It might be necessary to do a second cut at your list, combining similar items that have arisen from different sources.

Feedback The point of the time management aspect of self-development is to ensure that more time is available for the things you really want to do. One of the useful starting points is the talents you can bring to play. It may be that some of your talents appear useless, there may be things you are good at but hate – it doesn't matter, it's still worth establishing what they are.

Outcome Out of this exercise you should get a one page talent list. We will use this as input to various other exercises – keep it somewhere easily accessed, whether it's in an appropriate folder on your PC, in your personal organizer, or in a particular file (or pile) in your system.

Variations There isn't much variation here. It's probably best to revisit your talents annually, or after a burst of training, but they usually change quite slowly, so it isn't the end of the world if you don't polish them too often. Like anything that is only updated irregularly, your talent list is easy to forget. Why not put an entry in your schedule to revisit it?

Time management	✪✪✪✪
Stress management	✪✪✪
Negotiation skills	✪
General development	✪✪✪✪
Fun	✪✪✪

2.2 Exercise: If I were rich

Preparation None.
Running time Five minutes.
Resources None.
Frequency Annual.

The first step to time management isn't getting a diary or scheduling tasks, it's finding out what you want to do with your time. This exercise helps establish your desires. Imagine you have come into a huge sum of money. You will never have to work again. Take a minute to enjoy the thought and its immediate implications.

Now jot down the main activities you undertake – between 10 and 20. Don't differentiate between work and social activities – list everything significant. Then draw up three columns: Yes, No and New. Assign all your activities to one of the first two columns. What would you do anyway? What would you instantly dismiss?

With the first two columns filled in, consider the third. It would be helpful to have completed the *Talent spotting* exercise before doing this. Given the freedom provided by your riches, what else would you do? Try to be realistic, considering your talents, but be happy to stretch yourself.

Feedback Don't skip this and other early exercises because they seem 'wishy-washy'. They are essential. Without this step, the reasoning behind choosing your focal activities and allocating your time is missing.

Outcome The outcome of the exercises in this unit is a clearer understanding of what you want to do with your time.

Variations Personal goals change, though often slowly. What you wanted to do while at school will often be very different to your feelings after a few years in a job. Having a family, changing careers, redundancy – plenty of outside forces alter your needs, as do internal pressures like the mid-life crisis. You should refresh this list when you hit such a milestone. You may want to revisit it annually – at New Year or on a birthday is a good point. To make sure it happens, put it in your diary.

Time management	✪✪✪✪
Stress management	✪✪✪
Negotiation skills	✪
General development	✪✪✪
Fun	✪✪✪✪

2.3 Exercise: Dream day

Preparation None.
Running time Five minutes.
Resources None.
Frequency Once.

Along with the other activities at the start of the chapter, *Dream day* helps clarify what you want to do with your time. Without this knowledge, there is little point in developing skills at using time better, because there is no yardstick by which to measure 'better'.

Make sure you are relaxed. Find an armchair in a quiet setting. Get a cup of coffee. Play some music that helps you unwind. Now put together a schedule for a dream of a day. In detail (including, for instance, what you do between waking up and getting dressed), map out exactly what you would do if you had a whole 24 hours with total control over your time.

Now pick out the activities that you want to carry forward. You may have to modify an unreachable dream to become practical (if stretching) – still, make sure that the key aspects of your dream day are reflected in your output.

Feedback Resist the urge to censor. After extracting the useful cues, you can bin the output. So if your dream day involves a jacuzzi with a film star or shooting next door's cat, don't worry – get it down, then think about the practical goals you can deduce.

Outcome This exercise is useful in combination with *If I were rich* to round out your dream goals.

Variations There are other ways to tease out desires. If your mind works well with categories, break down what you would like to do into categories, and sub-categories and so on (a mind map works well). Think what you would do if you were stranded on a desert island with plenty of physical resources and lots of time. Or locked in a shopping mall for a weekend with all the contents of the mall available to you. Try using different slants to widen your picture of your personal goals.

Time management	✪✪✪✪
Stress management	✪✪✪
Negotiation skills	✪
General development	✪✪✪
Fun	✪✪✪

2.4 Exercise: Obstacle map

Preparation Personal goals.
Running time Five minutes.
Resources Notebook.
Frequency Annual.

Before performing this exercise, try some of the earlier ones to establish your personal goals. This exercise will help where you have a goal, but no clear way of achieving it. If you don't have problems like this, you don't need this exercise – but you are unusual. Take a goal from the early exercises – a way you want to change your life, or just something you want to do. If it isn't obvious how to achieve your goal, try this exercise. First note what the goal is. Jot down a few short phrases identifying not just what you want, but what it implies, what surrounds the goal.

Now make a few one-line notes summarizing your starting point. What is different from your goal? What would have to change? Finally, fill in the obstacles that are preventing you from moving immediately to your goal state. What is lacking? What is getting in the way? Sometimes the obstacles will be the starting point itself – don't worry, still list them.

Feedback If there weren't obstacles, your goals would have already been achieved. Explicitly identifying the obstacles is very valuable because often you are so focused on where you are now, or where you want to go, that you don't consider what's in the way.

Outcome The result of this exercise is to generate a new set of goals, overcoming the obstacles you have identified. For example, if a goal was 'To run my own courier business', one obstacle might be 'No employees' – so a new goal might be 'Recruit appropriate employees'.

Variations You might find this technique easier if you use a large sheet of paper, turned sideways. Draw three boxes, from left to right: Starting Point, Obstacles and Goal. Using this structure may help you visualize what is going on. Resist any inclination to jump straight to the obstacles: the sequence of goal, then starting point, then obstacles is essential.

Time management	✪✪✪✪
Stress management	✪✪
Negotiation skills	✪
General development	✪✪✪
Fun	✪✪

2.5 Exercise: What's it worth?

Preparation Some of the early exercises.
Running time Five minutes.
Resources Notebook.
Frequency Once.

This is an exercise to undertake when you have a reasonably clear picture of your personal goals. The first exercises in this unit develop these – if you haven't done them yet, please do them before this one. Start with a list of these goals on a piece of paper – don't try to keep the goals in your head.

Put four columns alongside your goals: Cash, Thrill, Leverage and Availability. Give each goal a rating in the first three columns. Cash should indicate direct earnings. Thrill should show how much of a buzz you will get out of achieving the goal. Leverage indicates how much achieving this goal can support other goals. Rate them as accurately as you can. For example, try to put figures in the cash column rather than 'low' or 'high'.

Finally fill in the Availability column, indicating whether the chances of achieving the goal are low or high, and whether this is likely to be a one-off source, or continuing.

Feedback Without knowing how you value your goals, it is hard to allocate time to them. For example, writing a book usually scores low on Cash. In fact, for many authors, it's on a par with working in a hamburger restaurant. Yet the activity often scores high on Thrill, and has considerable potential to support other goals like consultancy. Too often we only consider the cash dimension – having a value list helps ensure that we don't fall into that trap.

Outcome This exercise explores the relative values of the activities and goals that you aspire to. It isn't possible to simply prioritize these goals, but these values should give you a better idea of the balance you need to achieve.

Variations You may wish to reassess your values when reassessing your personal goals. See the Variations section of *If I were rich*.

Time management	✪✪✪✪
Stress management	✪✪✪
Negotiation skills	✪✪
General development	✪✪✪
Fun	✪✪✪

Unit 3:
Finding the switches – understanding your stressors

Just as it is important to understand your personal drivers that make you want to use your time more effectively and develop, it's also important to have a grasp of what stresses you, both internally and externally, if managing that stress is to be part of your development. This unit focuses on understanding what causes you stress.

Do try out the exercises as you go. Put them off until later and you probably won't ever do them. Read through the techniques. Make notes about how and when you can use them. And make sure you give them a try in the next appropriate forum.

Unit books

There's nothing like humour to ease away stress. Practically anything by P. G. Wodehouse is worth a try – *Summer Lightning* for instance – for top, stress-relieving qualities. Alternatively, try his modern equivalent, the humorous fantasy writer Terry Pratchett – take for example the superb *Wyrd Sisters*. In either case, practically anything from the author's prodigious output would do.

You can find more information on our unit books, or buy them, from our support site: www.cul.co.uk/crashcourse.

Web links

Links to stress management and Terry Pratchett Web sites can be found at www.cul.co.uk/crashcourse.

3.1 Exercise: Control freaks

Preparation None.
Running time 15 minutes.
Resources Notepad.
Frequency Once.

The degree to which you are in control of your life, both in and out of work can have a major impact on your stress levels. Take a sheet of paper and divide it into three columns: work, evenings and weekends (if you work shifts, change the headings accordingly). Spend a few minutes listing the major activities that you do in each column. Remember to include 'crossover' activities like commuting – it doesn't matter where.

Now, think yourself into each activity. How much do you feel in control? (Your perception is the most important thing here.) How much can you decide what to do when? Does your input matter, or are you following a pattern set by someone else? Are you following rules or interpreting principles? Note that time is a major factor in control. A deadline that is prepared for doesn't take control away from you. A deadline that is dropped on you at a moment's notice, or which you don't prepare for, can be debilitating. Label each activity H (high), M (medium) or L (low) for the level of control you have.

Feedback Note the low control areas for positive action. Think about each of them. Are there any where it is possible to take more control? Can you deal with the stress arising using any of the principle categories you'll find in the next section: physical control (exercise, drugs etc), mental control (thinking in a different way etc), spiritual control (achieving calm through spiritual means etc) or defence (taking action to avoid the stressor reaching you)?

Outcome As with all the exercises in this unit, the outcome is not a final result but a direction to consider when using the techniques we will later add to your armoury. Keep your list of low control areas as a stimulus for use in future exercises.

Variations None.

Time management	✪✪
Stress management	✪✪✪✪
Negotiation skills	✪✪
General development	✪✪✪
Fun	✪✪

3.2 Exercise: The big stuff

Preparation None.
Running time 10 minutes.
Resources Notepad.
Frequency Once.

Big events in your life, whether positive or negative, are stressful. This exercise looks at what you have been through in the last year or so, and are likely to go through this year. Spend a few minutes noting events that fit into each of these categories.

- Very high stress: death of close person, divorce or separation, jail or major injury.
- High stress: marriage, job loss, retirement, serious illness, pregnancy, birth, adoption, sexual problems, major change in financial status, death of friend, lots of arguments.
- Medium stress: large loan, debt, change in responsibilities at work, child leaving home, family disputes, change in home conditions.
- Low stress: other big events and stressors including holidays, parking tickets etc.

Feedback This scale is a simplification of the life crisis table developed by Holmes and Rahe. They give each potential stress item a detailed score. All we are trying to do here is get a feel for the amount of pressure from major events. Note that isolated events of this kind do not pose a great threat to your overall stress levels. It is sustained stress that causes the damage – and this could come either from chronic minor stressors or from a series of major events (or both).

Outcome The major events will provide particular stress points and contribute to your overall levels of stress. Having a feel for whether you are in a period with a high level of major stressors will help you decide whether you need to concentrate initially on defence – which really only works against minor stressors – or control.

Variations None.

Time management	✪
Stress management	✪✪✪✪
Negotiation skills	✪
General development	✪✪✪
Fun	✪

3.3 Exercise: How do you react?

Preparation None.
Running time Five minutes.
Resources Notepad.
Frequency Once.

We all have different ways of reacting to pressure, but broadly all these approaches fit into two categories, which were given the labels Type A and Type B by the US doctor Meyer Friedman in the 1960s. Spend a few minutes thinking which of these behaviours best fits your typical reaction to a situation. Try to be honest.

Type A		**Type B**	
Find other people get in the way	☐	Like working with other people	☐
Feel on edge a lot	☐	Usually feel laid back	☐
Have angry outbursts	☐	Take things calmly	☐
Think failure is a major problem	☐	Forgive failure easily	☐
Hold in emotions	☐	Let emotions go	☐
Always trying to achieve more	☐	Comfortable with the way things are	☐
Find life a constant struggle	☐	Find life generally easy	☐
Like to work to deadlines	☐	Like to work without deadlines	☐

Feedback While Type A behaviour is more likely to lead to stress-related illness, it is also associated with getting things done. Often those who get to the top in their jobs will have some Type A characteristics. The problem, as always with stress, is not a simple one. It's also true that there is nothing harder to do than to change a reaction that is based on your personality. This is possible – and stress management techniques can help – but if you are naturally more inclined to Type A, you will find it difficult to move towards a balance with Type B.

Outcome By being aware of your position you can decide how (and if) you need to try to move the balance between Type A and Type B. Remember that this is not a black-and-white decision – you aren't trying to convert from Type A to Type B, but to achieve a healthy balance.

Variations None.

Time management	✪✪
Stress management	✪✪✪✪
Negotiation skills	✪
General development	✪✪✪
Fun	✪✪

3.4 Exercise: Physical checks

Preparation None.
Running time Five minutes.
Resources Notepad.
Frequency Once.

Just how stressed are you right now? This is the first of two activities checking out the sorts of reactions that stress typically induces. Are you subject to several of these physical symptoms?

Regular indigestion ☐
Inability to sleep well ☐
Aches and pains that respond to massage ☐
Eczema, spots and other skin complaints ☐
Frequent headaches ☐
Frequent minor infections ☐
Difficulty catching your breath ☐
Feeling dizzy or shaky ☐
Breaking out in a cold sweat ☐
Tingling in your palms ☐

Feedback Note that not all physical symptoms of these kinds are caused by stress. If you have symptoms that continue, check with your doctor.

Outcome This exercise and the next are simply to help you establish how much you are already in a state of chronic stress. They provide helpful background to stress management.

Variations None.

Time management	✪
Stress management	✪✪✪✪
Negotiation skills	✪
General development	✪✪✪
Fun	✪

3.5 Exercise: Emotional and spiritual checks

Preparation None.
Running time Five minutes.
Resources Notepad.
Frequency Once.

Stress reactions aren't limited to the physical – after all, stress is irritatingly holistic. This second activity looking at typical stress symptoms considers the effects on your emotion, mind and spirit. How many, if any, of these sound familiar?

- You forget things a lot ☐
- You find decision making difficult ☐
- Your driving has deteriorated ☐
- You feel restless ☐
- You get frustrated with others ☐
- You are unusually impatient ☐
- You experience mood swings ☐
- You lack concentration ☐
- Everything seems pointless ☐
- You can`t keep on top of things ☐
- You feel defensive ☐

Feedback As with physical symptoms, bear in mind that many of these reactions can be due to illness as well as pure stress. Don`t hesitate to get medical advice if it is appropriate.

Outcome These checks are simply to help you establish how much you are already in a state of chronic stress. They provide helpful background to stress management.

Variations None.

Time management	✪
Stress management	✪✪✪✪
Negotiation skills	✪
General development	✪✪✪
Fun	✪

Unit 4: What comes first? – prioritization

Most of us spend too much of our time chasing around in circles. We've all got too much to do and too little time to do it in. If we are to make more effective use of our time we need to take a step back and look at what we are trying to achieve. Based on the values and goals established in Unit 2, it should be possible to prioritize your excessive activities and get them into some form of order.

Sometimes prioritization means being able to say 'No'. This is something many of us find difficult, and is a big enough problem to require its own unit.

Do try out the exercises as you go. Put them off until later and you probably won't ever do them. Read through the techniques. Make notes about how and when you can use them. And make sure you give them a try in the next appropriate forum.

Unit book

Occasionally we will be recommending unit books that combine a number of functions – that's the case with this unit's recommendation, *Fermat's Last Theorem* by Simon Singh (not to be confused with the book of the same name by Amir Aczel). Like all good popular science books it contributes to personal development by broadening your outlook, but this particular book also provides a marvellous example of handling priorities from the way that the mathematician Andrew Wiles put the solution of Fermat's last theorem at the top of his personal list.

You can find more information on our unit books, or buy them, from our support site: www.cul.co.uk/crashcourse.

4.1 Exercise: Principles

Preparation None.
Running time Five minutes.
Resources Notebook or sheet of paper.
Frequency Once.

Time management systems can go mad with different levels of breakdown. You need a mission and objectives and goals and activities and tasks ... and wonder why you never do anything but fill in bits of paper. This exercise seems worrying, because it generates yet another category, but it's a very different one. Some time management gurus recommend having a mission statement, but they make me nauseous. Instead, I just want you to look for the underlying principles driving your activities. Why do you do them?

Be honest. Perhaps it's for power, or to spend more time with your children. Perhaps you want fame or an easy life. Perhaps it's love of God or belief in humanity. Principles don't have to be deep, though. You might have: 'Have fun every day' or 'Don't worry about things you can't influence'. Clichés? Maybe, but clichés and fallacies are different: clichés are often true. Most people have three to six major principles driving their activities. Spend a few minutes pulling together what drives you. Stick them at the front of your notebook or on the wall.

Feedback Putting your principles on view has most impact, but principles embarrass many people. It's an indictment of our society that we don't like to admit to such things. Hide them away, but understand what you are doing, and why.

Outcome Your principles provide a fixed reference. When reviewing your focal activities, when deciding your priorities, you don't need to read your principles every time, but they are there as a yardstick. They provide a great way to keep your time management meaningful.

Variations Although most principles are personal, a few apply to most people. See, for example, *Pareto* later in this unit. This is a sensible principle for practically everyone to apply.

Time management	✪✪✪✪
Stress management	✪✪✪✪
Negotiation skills	✪
General development	✪✪✪
Fun	✪✪

4.2 Exercise/Technique: Focus

Preparation Talents/desires exercises
Running time 10 minutes.
Resources Notebook.
Frequency Monthly.

A fundamental assumption of time management is that you allocate time to things you really want to do. In other activities, such as *Talent spotting* in Unit 1, you have the opportunity to identify your abilities and desires.

Look through your talents and personal goals. The aim is to pull together a handful of focal activities. Sometimes called key areas, these form the core of what you do, both at work and socially. There should be at least four of these and not more than eight. Beyond this they become unmanageable.

Don't go into detail. Focal activities can have an end-point in mind, but shouldn't be specific tasks. So, for instance, a focal activity could be 'Improve my tennis' or 'Launch a new product by next Spring', but not 'Buy a new racket' or 'Arrange for advertising'.

Feedback You may find it is difficult to pinpoint your focal activities. Take a first shot, and if you find important aspects of your life aren't covered, rearrange them. If you are worried about missing detail, you will find more in the rest of the unit. If you have lots of focal activities, you will lack direction. Ruthlessly select the most important seven or eight. Just because an activity isn't listed, it doesn't mean that it won't get done, just that it isn't fundamental.

Outcome Without focus you cannot sensibly allocate your time, and you are unlikely to complete major projects and activities. This is one of the most important exercises in the book.

Variations Your focal activities need revisiting at least annually, but for many a monthly review is more appropriate. It need not be a lengthy exercise, taking no more than five minutes. However, like all regular, infrequent tasks, it ought to be scheduled.

Time management	✪✪✪✪
Stress management	✪✪✪✪
Negotiation skills	✪✪
General development	✪✪✪✪
Fun	✪✪

4.3 Exercise/Technique: Priorities

Preparation Produce task list.
Running time Five minutes.
Resources Notebook.
Frequency Weekly.

Before trying this technique, jot down all the tasks you currently have in hand (or, at least, as many as you can remember). Usually there is too much to do: you need priorities. A first step is to work backwards from the completion date. If a task has to be finished by the end of March and takes a day to complete, it is low priority in December. Similarly, a task with an immovable deadline tomorrow comes higher up the list. However, important though timeliness is, it isn't the prime concern. Having established the low priority of distant tasks, top priority goes to tasks that are essential to achieving your focal activities. This may mean putting off an urgent but unimportant task to make sure that a focal activity is advanced.

A final consideration is knock-on. When you have a tightly timed series of tasks and the first over-runs, what do you do? Assuming it was right to over-run, it may be worth sacrificing the next task to keep the others on schedule, rather than have everything run late.

Feedback *Priorities* is valuable for tasks, but less practical for focal activities. How do you balance, for example, improving your tennis, getting a new product to market, improving staff morale and having fun at home? Sometimes you have to do this (and work wins too often), but it shouldn't be the norm. A more useful approach is a value list – see *What's it worth?* in Unit 2.

Outcome Prioritization is essential to getting the right tasks done: it's as simple as that.

Variations You will see different approaches to prioritization elsewhere. A top ten list, for instance, is complementary. Prioritization is essential when sorting out your schedule; the top ten list is better for communicating to the rest of the world, and for making on-the-spot schedule changes.

Time management	✪✪✪✪
Stress management	✪✪✪
Negotiation skills	✪✪
General development	✪✪✪✪
Fun	✪✪

4.4 Exercise: Pareto

Preparation None.
Running time Five minutes.
Resources None.
Frequency Once.

When I first heard of this technique it was given the grand title Pareto Analysis – now it's more often called the 80:20 rule. A 19th-century Italian economist called Vilfredo Pareto discovered that 80 per cent of the wealth was owned by 20 per cent of the people. Since then, this 80:20 rule has been found to apply in many circumstances.

The importance to managing your life better is recognizing that you can often achieve 80 per cent completion with 20 per cent of the effort. The final polishing takes a huge 80 per cent. Sometimes that remainder is vital. You don't want a nuclear power plant that's 80 per cent safe. However, for most tasks (could it be 80 per cent of them?) 80 per cent success is fine. The Pareto rule explains one of the reasons PCs can be such time wasters. It's tempting to use all those exciting features of your word processor to continue to refine the appearance of your letter (or form, or spreadsheet, or whatever) – with violently diminishing returns. When you are setting goals and milestones, wherever possible use an 80:20 target.

Feedback For some of us, Pareto is absolutely natural. We are happy with approximate solutions that do the job. For others it is a real wrench – a 'botched job'. This technique is not an excuse for sloppiness, but a plea for accepting a very good result rather than striving for perfection. Would this preclude the great works of art, the great theories of science ever being developed? Maybe, but lots of great thinkers and artists work very quickly – greatness isn't always about nit-picking.

Outcome The potential for freeing up time is enormous. If you moved everything from perfectionism to Pareto you would free up 80 per cent of your time. This isn't going to happen, but there is still a huge potential.

Variations Pareto could be one of your principles (see *Principles* above).

Time management	✪✪✪✪
Stress management	✪✪✪✪
Negotiation skills	✪✪✪
General development	✪✪✪✪
Fun	✪✪✪

4.5 Exercise/Technique: Drawn and quartered

Preparation None.
Running time Five minutes.
Resources Paper.
Frequency Weekly.

This is an alternative to *Priorities* (above) for choosing between tasks. Each is valid – try both and see which works best for you. Split a sheet of paper into four quarters. Label the top left 'Urgent, unimportant', the top right 'Urgent, important', the bottom left 'Not urgent, unimportant' and the bottom right 'Not urgent, important'. Assign each task to a box.

Tasks in the top right box are top priority; you must ensure that their time is protected. Tasks in the top left are time critical, but less important. They often get more time than they should, so get them out of the way as quickly as possible with a tight cut-off. Tasks in the bottom right gradually migrate to the top right as time becomes shorter. The ideal is to catch them early enough to avoid a crisis, but late enough to free up time for other activities. Finally, the bottom left is the area you want to give least time to. Don't let the fact that some of these tasks are enjoyable or easy to do overcome the fact that they are low priority. Give them minimum time.

Feedback A problem with a grid like this is that is not a fixed object. With time, some (but not all) tasks float upwards. Importance too can be time-dependent. Because of this you need to be prepared to redraw regularly – if you can put the diagram in a PC drawing package where you can move the items around the grid flexibly, it will probably prove a better long-term tool.

Outcome Achieving a good balance of priorities lies at the centre of time management. Don't shirk this activity.

Variations This approach can be used as four boxes or as a graph, plotting importance on the horizontal axis and urgency on the vertical axis, so that the further to the right a point appears, the more important it is, and so on.

Time management	✪✪✪✪
Stress management	✪✪✪
Negotiation skills	✪
General development	✪✪✪
Fun	✪

Unit 5: There's nowhere like home – work/life balance

Achieving the right balance between work and the rest of your life is an essential factor in managing stress and developing as an individual. For most of us having work to do (whether paid or not) is an important part of having a fulfilling life. But there needs to be enough time for other activities – and the ability to switch off from work and get on with relaxing or enjoying yourself in different ways.

There has never been a time when more work was expected of us as individuals, so getting this balance right takes some effort. Some while ago I wrote an article for *Professional Manager*, the magazine of the Institute of Management, in which I suggested that for most people the work/life balance was tilted too far towards work. This triggered a letter from a disgruntled reader who said that I had 'lost the perspective of today's business', after all 'who is going to do the job when I'm not there?' He concluded by saying that 'more commitment to work might be an answer.' He entirely missed the point. The idea is not to do a poor job, but to do it more effectively, freeing time to shift to other activities. Working better doesn't mean longer hours – that's concentrating on the time you spend sitting at the desk, rather than what you actually produce. I can't help but feel this manager spent most of his time in meetings, and produced nothing of value whatsoever. Perhaps I'm being unfair – but the important fact is that for most of us the balance is wrong and should be shifted – without compromising doing a good job of work.

Do try out the exercises as you go. Put them off until later and you probably won't ever do them. Read through the techniques. Make notes about how and when you can use them. And make sure you give them a try in the next appropriate forum.

Unit book

If your work/life balance is askew, look for a guide to some new and more pleasant places to have a meeting or just enjoy yourself. For the UK it's hard to beat *The Good Pub Guide*, edited by Alisdair Aird.

You can find more information on our unit books, or buy them, from our support site: www.cul.co.uk/crashcourse.

Web links

Sites with more information on work/life balance and on finding a good pub can be found at www.cul.co.uk/crashcourse.

5.1 Exercise: Scrap the briefcase

Preparation None.
Running time 10 minutes.
Resources Briefcase.
Frequency Once.

Compartmentalization is essential for good time management. This means being able to slice off a chunk of a task, get it done, then switch attention elsewhere. Nowhere is this more essential than in the division between business and social life. It's accepted that we shouldn't allow social life to intrude too far into work, yet the reverse is rarely true. This exercise involves setting up a beachhead against intrusion. In another exercise (*Banning homework*, later in the unit) we will build on the achievement.

If you haven't got a briefcase (or other means of carrying documents home), you can ignore this one. Otherwise, open that briefcase up. See what you carry around. How much makes several trips to and from home? Keep an eye on it over a week. See how much you use it, and what for.

Now substitute a bag that is more appropriate for your specific needs. For instance, a shoulder bag is better if you have to carry any weight. Or a carrier bag might be better for your sandwiches. Whatever the requirement, make sure you change to a very different bag. Prompted by the new bag, be conscious of putting things into it. Beyond basics like a pen, only put something in if you are going to use it that day.

Feedback This isn't about reducing the weight you carry around, it's about a change of attitude.

Outcome This exercise is the first step to making an effective division between business and social time. It also helps ensure the right priorities are given to documents.

Variations It's sometimes difficult to be honest. You put some papers in to read tonight, then there are better things to do and the papers stay there for days. Try this: each morning, throw away anything in your briefcase without an action attached. Too drastic? Okay, put anything that isn't read the night you take it home on your desk – but this is nowhere near as effective.

Time management	✪✪✪✪
Stress management	✪✪✪✪
Negotiation skills	✪
General development	✪✪✪✪
Fun	✪✪✪

5.2 Exercise: How long?

Preparation None.
Running time Five minutes.
Resources Diary.
Frequency Once.

The purpose of this activity is to set a target for dividing your time between work and personal activities. Using your diary if it's helpful, get an idea how many hours in a week you spend on work activities (if you've already done the activity *Where did it go?* in Unit 1 you should have your information already). Include any work you take home. Taking out sleeping time, check what that leaves for personal activities (there are 168 hours in a week, so with a seven-hour sleep, you have around 115 to 120 usable hours a week).

Is that balance what you'd really like? Be honest – don't try to match the expectations of your company or your family – what would you really like to do? Look at the difference on a daily basis. How many hours a day would you like to move from work to personal, or personal to work? Perhaps you've got the balance just right, in which case there is no more to do. More often than not, you haven't. Consider making it one of your focal activities to move this balance in your preferred direction.

Feedback Few people can make changes like this overnight, but it doesn't make the change any less desirable or possible. Changing might mean changing the way you work – more and more people are opting for flexible careers with a portfolio of tasks; more and more companies use consultants and contractors – or it may simply mean using different values when you decide when to go home. But remember, you've only got one attempt to get your life right: don't waste it.

Outcome This activity doesn't have an immediate effect, but sets an agenda item. It is, however, important.

Variations Work and personal is the most obvious split, but you might consider different splits like paying/non-paying work, work at different levels of pay, working from home versus commuting and so on.

Time management	✪✪✪✪
Stress management	✪✪✪✪
Negotiation skills	✪
General development	✪✪✪✪
Fun	✪✪

5.3 Exercise: Reading up

Preparation None.
Running time Five minutes.
Resources None.
Frequency Once.

Reading is an important activity in almost all contexts, yet it is often given a low worth. To be seen sitting at your desk reading a book or a magazine (even a business book or magazine) is generally considered to be only one step above being asleep. Yet whether your intention is to be more effective at your job, to know more about a hobby or to expand your personal creativity, reading is essential.

Because of the disparity between actual value and perceived value, reading needs special treatment. Spend a couple of minutes going through your typical reading matter for a week. Consider non-fiction and fiction, books, magazines and newspapers. Now try to put together a picture of your ideal reading content. Set some realistic targets, like a novel a week, a business book a week etc.

Finally allocate appropriate slots to reading. Because of the perceived low value, it will be necessary to make these in your less exposed time (unless you work in a particularly enlightened business) – but there should be no excuse for putting reading off. Reading can fit into a lower energy slot than some activities (we'll look further at your energy levels in *Hot Spots* in Unit 21), but don't choose a time when it will put you to sleep.

Feedback The disparity is an odd one, which you may find it valuable to discuss with your boss. Why is it that we are quite prepared to send someone off on a course for days at a time, but don't like to see someone reading a business book for half an hour? In fact, such a discussion may even result in legitimizing a business reading slot.

Outcome If you can pull reading on to a par with administration in priorities you will be achieving more than most people, and ensuring that you gain a personal edge.

Variations Look at different sources of reading material: libraries, bookshops, Internet bookshops, learning centres within the company.

Time management	✪✪✪
Stress management	✪✪✪✪
Negotiation skills	✪
General development	✪✪✪✪
Fun	✪✪✪

5.4 *Exercise/Technique: Banning homework*

Preparation Scrap the briefcase.
Running time Five minutes.
Resources None.
Frequency Regularly.

This exercise follows *Scrap the briefcase*, unless you don't have a bag for taking things home in. Compartmentalization is essential for good time management. With *Scrap the briefcase*, we opened the war on the drift of time from social to work. Now we're going to draw a line. Taking work home is a real enemy of time management. The aim is to avoid it.

In theory this is trivial, just don't take any work home. Full stop. Stay at work until you've finished. If you need to work at the weekend, go into the office. In fact, it's worth going in occasionally at the weekend for the experience; the office atmosphere is usually very different.

Feedback Taking work home has a negative impact on your family and social life and reduces the quality of your work. Don't do it.

Outcome This is vital to overcome. When you work at home, work is in control of your time. Unfortunately it's like stopping smoking. It may take a number of tries.

Variations Taking work home is different from home working. Home workers 'go to the office', it just happens to be a 20-second commute away. There's nothing wrong with working on the train, but make sure that the tasks are easy to switch off so you aren't tempted to continue at home.

Sometimes you have to work in the evening. Perhaps you want to get home and see the children, then do some work. Surely you can take work home then? If possible, no. Return to the workplace. If commuting time makes this impractical, have a specific work environment in the home. Don't go in there as soon as you get home. Have your social time, then make it clear you are 'going to work'. If you must work in the evening and can't get in to the office, convert to home working.

Time management	✪✪✪✪
Stress management	✪✪✪✪
Negotiation skills	✪✪
General development	✪✪✪✪
Fun	✪✪✪

5.5 *Exercise: Because I'm worth it*

Preparation None.
Running time Five minutes.
Resources None.
Frequency Once.

As we saw in the first unit, self-esteem is vital to be able to manage stress. Believing that you are worthwhile and giving yourself some time and space counters the hugely stressful position many people find themselves in through lack of control. It's particularly important if you have other people who are strongly dependent on you – children, close family, friends.

Spend five minutes thinking about how your week is divided between doing things for others and doing things that *you* really want to do. You may find a frightening lack of time for you. Partly this is time management – but also it's about valuing yourself. Make sure you get some time in your week that is yours to do with as you wish. This is particularly important if you are self-employed.

Feedback One caveat: the tendency in the latter half of the 20th century was to move increasingly to a self-centred world. People left their families to 'find themselves' or ignored responsibilities in pursuit of pleasure. There is something of a backlash now, because the cost of this cult of the individual has been misery from a breakdown of social values and a realization that the pursuit of success for its own sake isn't particularly rewarding. In looking for stress relief you need to get some space for yourself, but you also need to look outwards as well as inwards. What's needed here, as so often in stress relief, is not placing yourself above everything else, but achieving a balance.

Outcome Finding some time to be you, and to do what you want, is a great opportunity for stress relief. Most of us are out of balance in this respect. But remember the need to look outside yourself as well.

Variations It's easy to put off finding some time for yourself – you are such a busy person, after all. Don't put it off.

Time management	✪✪✪✪
Stress management	✪✪✪✪
Negotiation skills	✪✪
General development	✪✪✪✪
Fun	✪✪✪

Unit 6:
I can't concentrate – handling distractions

Distractions and time wasters can eat away at the limited stock of time you have available. Sometimes you can simply fob them off by using clear signals that you are not to be disturbed. At other times you need to hide away. The most insidious type of time wasters are those you indulge in yourself – often a matter of putting off the things you ought to be doing in favour of something that's more fun. All these distractions can be handled – you'll find more on them in later units – but it's probably one of the hardest steps to take.

Do try out the exercises as you go. Put them off until later and you probably won't ever do them. Read through the techniques. Make notes about how and when you can use them. And make sure you give them a try in the next appropriate forum.

Unit books

For a simple guide to avoiding your own tendency to do anything but what you should be doing, see *The Procrastinator's Handbook*, subtitled *Mastering the art of doing it now*, by Rita Emmett.

Bear in mind, though, that avoiding distractions and procrastination doesn't mean not enjoying yourself. As we saw in the previous unit, balance is important, so alongside avoiding unwanted distractions, make sure you programme in some distractions when the time is right. I'd strongly recommend H. E. Bates wonderful series of books starting with *The Darling Buds of May* – both as wonderful entertainment and also for a role model of truly enjoying what you do. If you've only encountered the TV series, try the books – they're so much better.

You can find more information on our unit books, or buy them, from our support site: www.cul.co.uk/crashcourse.

6.1 *Technique: The red hat*

Preparation Obtain a red baseball cap.
Running time Two minutes.
Resources No special requirements.
Frequency Regularly.

Unnecessary interruptions are a common problem when attempting to manage your time better. You have spent half an hour getting an idea together in your head, when someone asks if you saw *The X-Files* on TV the other night, or wants the telephone number of a print company. Any other time, you'd be happy to talk, but right now you need to concentrate.

The technique is simple. Get hold of a red baseball cap. Let it be widely known that when you are wearing the cap, you are not available for comment. Anything less than emergencies should wait. Don't over-use this technique. You shouldn't normally have the cap on more than half a day, or it becomes just another barrier to communication.

Feedback It will take a while for the message to sink in. Initially you will still get interruptions. Respond politely, but point out why you've got the hat on. The word will quickly get around.

Outcome If you handle interruptions when you've got the cap on very positively, you'll find red hats spring up all over; do it badly and you'll lose a lot of friends. This technique is particularly valuable in open-plan offices, where the temptation to call across the room is very strong. A side effect of this approach can be to help concentrate your mind on a task – the act of putting on the cap keeps your own attention focused.

Variations It needn't be a baseball cap. Try a flag on your desk or a bright red jacket. Whatever you use must be clearly visible from a distance, as the requirement is to stop an interruption from ever starting. It's too late when the person involved is standing by your desk. Some companies allow the use of personal stereos – provided the headphones are obvious (put red ends on them), these too can act as a warning that you do not want to be disturbed.

Time management	✪✪✪✪
Stress management	✪✪✪
Negotiation skills	✪✪✪
General development	✪✪
Fun	✪✪

6.2 Technique: Deflecting distraction

Preparation None.
Running time Two minutes.
Resources None.
Frequency Regularly.

However much you want to concentrate on what you are doing, there will be people who consider it their right to wander in and chat. In the *Red hat* we looked at signalling 'I don't want to be disturbed', but sometimes the person gets through. There are a number of techniques to deflect the distraction.

Some activities make you less likely to be disturbed. If you see a potential distraction on the way, you can start a phone conversation (real or imaginary), hunch over your keyboard or pad and start to write frantically, or grab someone and engage in an obviously personal conversation. Other mechanisms like taking your clothes off or blatantly picking your nose will work, but won't help your reputation.

You can remove yourself from the equation by leaving ('Sorry, must rush, urgent meeting') and slip into the toilet or work somewhere other than your desk.

Feedback If the distractor doesn't take the hint, shorten the distraction by reducing your responsiveness (avoid eye contact, reply with a single word or grunts. frequently look at your watch). If this fails, resort to the polite but explicit: 'Sorry, I'm going to have to cut this short now, I've got something to finish for the boss and I'm dead meat if I don't get started.'

Outcome Interruptions have a greater impact on your work than their length implies. Any significant task requires a fair amount of stacking up of thoughts before getting started – a significant interruption can totally shatter your house of cards. These techniques should be used sparingly, but will help reduce painful interruptions.

Variations A useful approach if conversation can't be avoided is to take the politician's approach of turning everything round to what you want to say. Whatever other people come to talk about, make sure you end up offloading work on them. They may soon take the hint.

Time management	✪✪✪✪
Stress management	✪✪✪
Negotiation skills	✪✪✪
General development	✪✪
Fun	✪✪

6.3 *Exercise: Jump-start*

Preparation None.
Running time Five minutes.
Resources None.
Frequency Once.

For this exercise we are going to spend a couple of minutes thinking about the preparation for your productive day. Jot down the characteristics of an average start. How much sleep do you get? Is it undisturbed? How do you wake? What happens before you leave the house? What happens on the way to work?

Often these preparatory hours are a mess. We don't get enough sleep. We rush around, shouting at the children or tripping over the cat. We eat a slice of toast as we go out, then spend an hour hitting the steering wheel and shouting at the idiot in front. This isn't great preparation for the day. If you can introduce more calm and better sleep, if you can turn the start of your day into a pleasure rather than a nightmare, you will set yourself up for a more effective day.

Spend the remaining few minutes deciding on a few quick actions to make things different. Don't expect overnight change; try feeding changes in gradually. They might include making sure you get to bed early enough, getting a reasonable breakfast (at home or out) and making the journey to work less stressful.

Feedback It's easy to think that there's nothing to be done about this area of life. Maybe there isn't a pleasant way of getting to work (unless you get there before eight or after ten ... is that totally impossible?), but there will always be some aspect that you can improve.

Outcome Starting a task with a positive attitude helps get it completed more effectively.

Variations You can use the positive approach in the evening too. On the way home, think about positive aspects of the evening. That way, when you get back, you don't arrive gloomy about the day you've had (making for a miserable evening), but looking forward to the pleasant time that you will have.

Time management	✪✪✪
Stress management	✪✪✪✪
Negotiation skills	✪✪✪
General development	✪✪✪✪
Fun	✪✪✪

6.4 Technique: Waiting room

Preparation None.
Running time Five minutes.
Resources Bag or briefcase.
Frequency Regularly.

Most of us spend too long waiting for others. You turn up three minutes early and sit in your boss's outer office for twenty minutes before the previous meeting finishes. So you read a business magazine or chat. This same scenario is played out in many other locations. Whether you are sitting in reception or waiting for a seminar to start, time is slipping away.

Some time management experts suggest that you leave a message to say you will be in your office getting some work done, and could the relevant person call you when the meeting is about to start. Unfortunately, this is impractical off-site and dangerous on-site. Either you end up playing call-me tag, waiting for everyone to finish a task, or you seriously irritate your boss. Instead, carry a package of portable tasks. Things you can get on with while you wait. It could be your mail, or writing a memo – anything you can do using only the contents of your bag. Make sure you have your task list with you, so you can pick off something appropriate.

Feedback You may be regarded as a little strange if others are waiting in the same place. If they don't have tasks to get on with, they might expect you to contribute to their chat. There isn't a right or wrong answer to whether you should chat to them – it depends on who they are and the relevance of the conversation.

Outcome Making use of such unplanned snippets of time is a great way of chipping away at background activities. You are, in effect, generating time from nowhere.

Variations A laptop or palmtop computer makes an ideal mobile task kit. If you are waiting for someone else to arrive, undertake a task that can be stopped at a moment's notice. It doesn't get the meeting off to a good start if your visitor has to watch you finish something off for 10 minutes.

Time management	✪✪✪✪
Stress management	✪✪✪
Negotiation skills	✪✪✪
General development	✪✪✪
Fun	✪✪✪

6.5 Exercise: Caught in the Web

Preparation None.
Running time Five minutes.
Resources Internet connection.
Frequency Once.

A lot has been written about the dangers of the World Wide Web. Much of this concerns pornography or time wasted exploring. In fact, the problems of time wasting are exaggerated. After all, just become someone isn't surfing the Net doesn't mean they would otherwise be fully productive. And no value is given to the information culled this way. However, you won't want to waste your own time on the Web.

Put together an Internet strategy. Have a cut-off time, perhaps half an hour, after which you will come off-line and give some thought to what you have retrieved. This may need to be reinforced with a kitchen timer. Secondly, have a single, clear objective. If something else comes up, make a note of it, but don't be distracted. Finally, make use of tools that allow you to revisit the pages you have seen offline, and of tools to search and summarize sites. This way you can condense the search effort and come back to your results at a later date.

Feedback Part of the reason for the Web's ability to eat time is its eclectic nature. This strategy is aimed at getting a straight answer to a specific requirement – but do allow yourself occasional free-access sessions. These could give you surprising insights.

Outcome The Internet is a powerful tool, but like any powerful tool can be dangerous if misused. This exercise provides a way of getting value from the Web while reducing the danger.

Variations If you have a number of topics, it is generally better to research each separately, but if you find significant overlaps, go with the flow – just make sure that you can separate the outputs after the event. Check out the unit book for Unit 22, *The Professional's Guide to Mining the Internet* for more information about getting it right.

Time management	✪✪✪✪
Stress management	✪✪
Negotiation skills	✪
General development	✪✪✪✪
Fun	✪✪✪

Unit 7: Chunking it up – breaking down your goals into manageable items

This is probably the most nitty-gritty part of time management – breaking down what you want to do into manageable chunks. What the Time Manager™ people refer to as 'eating the elephant' (ie you can't eat one all at once, but you can in suitable portions). Because it is so fundamental to time management, and is what all those companies making organizer diaries and software tend to build everything around, this part of the process can be seen as little more than bureaucracy, fiddling with lists for the sake of it. It's not though – it's the bread and butter mechanics of making things happen, and you aren't going to achieve personal development if you aren't making things happen.

Do try out the exercises as you go. Put them off until later and you probably won't ever do them. Read through the techniques. Make notes about how and when you can use them. And make sure you give them a try in the next appropriate forum.

Unit book

One of the best selling 'sort yourself out' books is Stephen Covey's *The Seven Habits of Highly Effective People*. For some this is a set of self-evident truths, but for others it has been a real breakthrough in taking control. Although it's good stuff, there isn't a huge volume of material here, and I recommend getting the audio book version, which is shorter and can be listened to in the car.

You can find more information on our unit books, or buy them, from our support site: www.cul.co.uk/crashcourse.

Web links

Links to the Web sites of commercial organizations offering products to help with chunking up your work and organizing yourself can be found at www.cul.co.uk/crashcourse.

7.1 Exercise/Technique: Chunking

Preparation *Focus* exercise (Unit 4).
Running time Five minutes.
Resources Notebook.
Frequency Weekly.

We all have activities that can't be completed in a single session, day or even year. This is true of most focal activities (see *Focus* in Unit 4) – they need to be broken down into manageable chunks. This is a fundamental part of good time management (and why the style of this book is so appropriate). Take each focal activity and break it into segments or tasks. Each task should have a clear outcome and completion date. It doesn't matter whether or not the activity has an end date – the chunks should have clear timing.

For example, taking the two example activities in *Focus*, 'Improve my tennis' might include 'Start tennis lessons by 1st March' and 'Buy a new racquet by 14th March'. Similarly 'Launch a new product by next Spring' might have tasks like 'Hold idea generation sessions by 1st October', 'Select and polish product concept by 18th October'.

Feedback It is important that you set dates and deliverables, but remember that the dates are guesswork. Your task list should be revised weekly, throwing off completed tasks, reassessing dates and adding new ones.

Outcome It is a mistake that is often made to think that good time management consists only of focus and chunking. Without the awareness of your personal priorities they are useless – but based on priorities they are an essential component.

Variations You may need more detail. Some chunks might be broken into sub-chunks. A task may involve others, so you may need to indicate who is involved and get their feedback. Electronic time management products often allow you to allocate tasks to others, then capture the results. This is fine as long as maintenance of task information doesn't become a major task in its own right. If you have a long list of tasks, you will need to bring in *Priorities* (see Unit 4).

Time management	✪✪✪✪
Stress management	✪✪✪
Negotiation skills	✪
General development	✪✪✪
Fun	✪✪

7.2 Exercise/Technique: Tasks, tasks

Preparation None.
Running time Five minutes.
Resources Notebook.
Frequency Daily/weekly.

In *Chunking* (above) we see how focal activities are broken down into tasks. One section of your notebook should be a task list. This is a clear list of things to do. Each should have a short description and a completion date. It is useful but not essential to link each task to a focal activity – certainly many tasks will be derived from them. Once a week it is sensible to check the focal activities and your task list to make sure there aren't new items to add.

Sometimes tasks are sensibly split up. For instance, one task in my focal activity of becoming a best-selling author might be writing this book. But writing a book is a lengthy task, so it can be broken down into components like writing the surrounding chapters, writing the exercises, checking the proofs and so on. Don't take tasks to too high a level of detail – it would be overkill to have a separate task for each of the exercises in this book – but ideally tasks should take no more than a week. I can break down writing the exercises into chunks, saying '10 completed by 10th November' or whatever.

Feedback The task list is driven by other sources too, like meeting action points. Don't waste time by turning the task list into a project management exercise, marking the percentage completed each day.

Outcome The task list is an excellent overview. It is an essential tool in managing your work, and should contain social activities too, to make sure there is a fair balance.

Variations I am using the term notebook loosely. It could be a conventional notebook, a ring binder, a time management system, an electronic personal organizer or a PIM. Electronic versions are particularly handy, as they can have alarms against key dates to make sure a task doesn't get forgotten. But the important thing is that your notebook suits you.

Time management	✪✪✪✪
Stress management	✪✪✪
Negotiation skills	✪
General development	✪✪✪
Fun	✪✪

7.3 Exercise/Technique: Task list stragglers

Preparation None.
Running time Two minutes.
Resources Diary.
Frequency Weekly.

We all have tasks that don't get completed when we first planned them. It's inevitable. So they get carried forward to the next day or week. But some tasks seem to live in a permanent limbo, never quite making it into the light. When you create a new schedule and task list for the next week, take the opportunity to do something about these stragglers. There are two alternatives: make a task high priority and get it done right away, or drop it from the list. If you choose the first, make sure it is genuinely high priority – if it isn't underway after a day or two, revert to dropping it.

In fact there's a third option, which can be used with a task which is low priority and unpleasant, but has a time dependence that will eventually make it high priority. Often we schedule something like filling in our tax return too early and it becomes one of these stragglers. In this case, it is probably better to schedule it nearer its last possible date and drop it from the task list until then.

Feedback It can be quite difficult to drop an item – after all, you put it in, so it must be worth doing. Just remember the 80:20 rule (see *Pareto* in Unit 4). You can't do everything. In fact, there are an infinite number of tasks you aren't going to do. What's wrong with having one more? Obviously it depends on why you kept dropping it, but a surprising number can be dropped without consequence.

Outcome Task lists can be killed by stragglers. If your list is full of familiar items that never seem to shift, it is easy to let your eyes skip over it without really taking in what is essential. Pruning the stragglers is essential to keep the list alive.

Variations No real variants.

Time management	✪✪✪✪
Stress management	✪✪
Negotiation skills	✪
General development	✪✪✪
Fun	✪

7.4 Exercise: We don't deliver

Preparation None.
Running time Five minutes.
Resources None.
Frequency Once.

A lot of people don't deliver on time. They say they will do something by a date. They may even sign a piece of paper to this effect. Then they seem surprised when they don't deliver – or even worse, they don't seem to care. If you regularly fail to deliver on time, your time management has failed and you are going to suffer as a result. What's more, it will continue to fail because uncompleted tasks will impact on the next things you planned to do.

If you believe delivering, and being seen to deliver, is important, you need to make realistic estimates. We shorten estimates to be competitive and to please – but it's better to estimate 10 per cent over and come in on time. Even if your estimates are good, things will go wrong. That's where you can make a big difference. By putting 150 per cent effort into recovering from an over-run, and keeping your stakeholders aware of what is going on, you will gain recognition and retain control of your time. It will mean the occasional change of priorities at late notice, but will be worth it. Check the timings of your current priority tasks. Are they realistic? Should you change anything? How about the timing of recent failures and successes?

Feedback This technique is not about living from crisis to crisis. If you are always pulling out the stops to fix problems, you've got the estimating wrong.

Outcome Surprising though it may seem in a consumer-driven society, delivering the goods on time is a rarity. Succeed and you will not only have good time management, you shouldn't go short of a job either.

Variations How you manage your estimates is outside the remit of this book, but bear in mind that forecasting is guesswork. Don't estimate something you know approximately to three decimal places. Planning works better with ballpark figures and a few milestones than grinding detail, and such plans are much easier to change at a moment's notice too.

Time management	✪✪✪✪
Stress management	✪✪✪
Negotiation skills	✪✪
General development	✪✪✪
Fun	✪✪

7.5 Exercise/Technique: Against the buffers

Preparation None.
Running time Two minutes.
Resources Diary.
Frequency Weekly.

This is about making sure you've time in your diary for nothing. In a perfect world, you could schedule each meeting, each activity with its follow-on travel time so that each runs into the other (actually, it wouldn't be perfect, it would be hell, but you know what I mean). In reality, things over-run or are underestimated and we need buffers. Gaps to allow for variation.

Just spend a minute thinking back over the last couple of weeks. How often did you find that something didn't run to time? Perhaps you were delayed by a traffic jam, or someone else turned up late, or everything took a bit longer than expected … or one of a million other random interferences with precision. Either you go through the day getting later and later, or you build in some slack – ie buffers.

For near complete safety you probably need around 50 per cent buffer time in your schedule, but with your enhanced time management you could probably get away with applying *Pareto* (see Unit 4) and only having a 20 per cent buffer. Try allowing 20 per cent unplanned time, but be prepared to increase the margin if it's proving effective.

Feedback Unused buffers aren't a waste of time. You can use them to catch up on lower priority activities which wouldn't otherwise get done.

Outcome Excessive use of buffers can ruin your scheduling, but by keeping a more realistic allocation your time management can be made more effective.

Variations You can make buffers vary considerably in length depending on the nature of the activity. Meetings with certain individuals will always over-run. Some journeys are particularly bad when it comes to delays. Use common sense in allocating buffers, rather than a fixed percentage.

Time management	✪✪✪✪
Stress management	✪✪✪
Negotiation skills	✪
General development	✪✪
Fun	✪

Unit 8: Stopping – saying 'No' and throwing things out

This isn't a problem for everyone, but for many people, managing to say 'No' is very difficult. Logical or not, they are responding to a feeling that they are somehow being rude if they refuse to take on a task. Yet we all have limits, we all need to say 'No' sometimes.

Similarly it can very difficult to stop doing something – whether it's fruitlessly reading a newspaper every day or attending a meeting you've attended every week for the last three years without getting anything out of it. As I write there's a flurry of TV shows where 'experts' help people dispose of some of the clutter in their lives. In a way this is a very similar process. You need to clear out some of the commitment clutter you have built up, or that others are trying to force on you, if you are going to be in control and get things done.

Do try out the exercises as you go. Put them off until later and you probably won't ever do them. Read through the techniques. Make notes about how and when you can use them. And make sure you give them a try in the next appropriate forum.

Unit book

Travel writer Bill Bryson may be an unlikely aid to saying 'No', but his superb series of columns, captured in *Notes from a Big Country*, on returning to live in the United States after many years of living in England provide some wonderful examples of the small but plentiful pressures we are all under to do things we don't necessarily want to do. Bryson's acerbic humour is a delightful pointer to our errors, and what's more, reading this kind of book combines an excellent stress reliever with an opportunity to travel vicariously and develop a world view, if slightly second hand.

You can find more information on our unit books, or buy them, from our support site: www.cul.co.uk/crashcourse.

8.1 Exercise: Why not 'No'?

Preparation None.
Running time Five minutes.
Resources Diary.
Frequency Once.

There are few more powerful time management tools than being able to say 'No'. It's a difficult thing to do, though, partly because we want to be polite and partly because we don't want to miss out, whether it's on some fun, some payment or a chance to improve our image.

This is a two-stage technique, which is completed in *No, I can* below. The first step is understanding why you say 'No'. Take a couple of minutes thinking through your own response to being asked to do something. Why don't you say 'No' more often?

Now spend a couple of minutes looking at recent appointments in your diary, and thinking through the tasks you have taken on in the last week or so. Are there meetings you have attended or work you've done (include leisure activities) which have not had a high value output to you or your family or your company? Why didn't you say 'No'? Make two short lists: Things I take on unnecessarily and Why I don't say 'No'.

Feedback Keep these lists to one side for the second saying 'No' activity. Meanwhile, when you take on new tasks and appointments, bear them in mind. You needn't act yet (though feel free to if you want to), but be aware of what you are doing.

Outcome Finding out why you don't say 'No' more is an essential step on the road to controlling when you want to reject. Simply being aware of what you are doing is often enough to make a significant change to your behaviour.

Variations Alternatives for exploring why you don't say 'No' are thinking about the people you interact with (business and social) and why you don't say 'No' to them, and thinking about the ways you get involved in something – face-to-face request, letter, e-mail, recurring meeting etc.

Time management	✪✪✪✪
Stress management	✪✪✪
Negotiation skills	✪✪
General development	✪✪✪
Fun	✪✪

8.2 Exercise: No, I can

Preparation *Why not 'No'*?
Running time 10 minutes.
Resources Diary.
Frequency Once.

This activity follows on from *Why not 'No'?* First look at your reasons for not saying 'No'. For each one, think of at least two counter reasons for saying 'No'. For instance, if your argument was 'Because I might offend the person', counter arguments might be 'If I don't say No, I'll offend someone else' or 'I don't mind offending them'.

Now look at the things that you probably don't need to do. For each draw up a short set of pros and cons to undertaking the task. What do you get out of it? What does the company/family get out of it? What will happen if you don't do it? Why should you not do it? Who else could do it? Put a summary of what you have discovered somewhere readily visible. Next time you get a request, measure the activity against your summary. If it's covered, unless there is a strong argument for it, say 'No'. With practice it becomes easier.

Feedback There's a common misconception that saying 'No' is rude. But you aren't helping by saying 'Yes', then not delivering. Try to say 'No' with a helpful suggestion and a reason. For example, 'Sorry, I can't do that for you because I'm finishing this report for the boss. Have you tried Lucy?'

Outcome Overdo saying 'No' and you will labelled unhelpful. But going too far the other way is equally dangerous. Say 'No' in the right way and people will still think of you positively, but they won't impose.

Variations Don't prevaricate. 'I'll think about it' might be easier, but it's damaging both to yourself and the person asking for help. If you are having difficulty saying 'No', try counter-loading. Say 'Yes, but you'll have to help me by doing X, Y and Z' where they are the tasks you would have been doing otherwise.

Time management	✪✪✪✪
Stress management	✪✪✪
Negotiation skills	✪✪✪
General development	✪✪✪
Fun	✪✪

8.3 Exercise/Technique: Meet yourself half way

Preparation Have a diary.
Running time Two minutes.
Resources None.
Frequency Weekly.

Open your diary and look through this week. There will be meetings and special events. And there will probably be gaps, when you intend to get things done. Now imagine that you get a phone call. Someone asks 'What are you doing tomorrow afternoon?'. 'I've nothing on,' you reply. So in goes another meeting. Unconsciously you have said that the meeting, even if it was the paper recycling committee, was more important than any other work you might do. It's horribly easy for scheduled events to hog your time.

There's only one answer; you've got to schedule meetings with yourself. Don't say this is what you are doing – it sounds terrible – but it's what you need. Each week, block off some slots. You might like a short slot each morning for admin, communications slots for e-mail and calls, and most of all, production slots to get things done. When you put a meeting in, be aware that you are cancelling something else, not putting it into free time.

Feedback Using this technique requires a modicum of cheek. But remember, there is no deception involved; you are simply making sure that things are arranged according to your priorities. If you have trouble remembering to undertake weekly exercises like this, consider a recurring start-the-week event of carving up your diary. This isn't the same as the buffers we looked at in the previous unit. Those were slots for doing nothing – these are slots for doing your work (or having fun).

Outcome This is a powerful technique that is essential if you suffer from too many meetings. It isn't right to give meetings the priority we do. By putting other activities in your schedule, you can achieve a better balance.

Variations A weekly approach suits most people, but you may find you need to look further ahead. Consider taking this approach with your personal time too. You can be much more broad brush, but slotting in some time for personal projects can help avoid them being subsumed by never-ending domestic chores.

Time management	✪✪✪✪
Stress management	✪✪✪
Negotiation skills	✪
General development	✪
Fun	✪✪

8.4 Technique: No action, no report

Preparation None
Running time Five minutes.
Resources For people with staff.
Frequency Ongoing.

Reports waste a lot of time. It takes time to generate them. It takes time to read them. All too often, they are an exercise in generating output that no one really wants. This exercise requires you to be slightly despotic, but in a good cause.

Put out an edict to your staff. From now on, no report is to be generated without associated actions. If they can't think of actions that are required as a result of the report being generated, it isn't to be produced. There are obvious exceptions where reports are required for legal reasons – but, even then, an attempt should be made to add actions.

Feedback The whole point of producing reports is to generate action. Otherwise they're a huge waste of time and money. If it seems impossible in your particular department, I'd like to point out that this was a tip passed on to me by Brian Thomas, Finance Director of financial services giant Zurich Bank. If a finance department, the ultimate report junkies, could operate a scheme where no report is generated without associated actions, so can any department.

Outcome There is an immense feeling of relief when unnecessary reports are no longer generated, both for those who have to produce them, and those who feel the need to look at them even if they are meaningless. This is a real all-round winner. If you feel a report does generate actions, but actions for someone else, they ought to be discussed with that someone else. That way, there will be more consensus between issuers and recipients after the event.

Variations If you are reasonably senior in your company, consider expanding this outside your particular department. When you receive reports from elsewhere without actions, send them back immediately with a covering note explaining that they have not been read, and will not unless they come back with appropriate action points.

Time management	✪✪✪✪
Stress management	✪✪
Negotiation skills	✪
General development	✪
Fun	✪✪

8.5 *Exercise: No news is good news*

Preparation None
Running time 10 minutes.
Resources None.
Frequency Once.

A constant diet of depressing news is stressful. We like balance, but rarely get it. In the 1990s a BBC newscaster made the controversial statement that there isn't enough good news – that reporters and editors don't balance the news content. It didn't help his career, but it's true. Spend a few minutes assessing your weekly news input. Consider all media. Now try to break it into rough categories, like business, home news, foreign news, sport etc. For each, get a feel for the media you use, and the value it has to your work and social life.

Finally, consider a few experiments to get a better fit to your personal requirements. Your needs will vary, but here are a few possible approaches:

- Cancel your daily newspaper. Only buy a paper when you have leisure time and want to do something different. If you usually read a newspaper when commuting, read a range of books instead.
- Don't watch more than one TV bulletin a day. Shop around to find the one that best suits you on content and approach rather than your habitual one.
- Have at least one day a week when you don't take in any news other than by word of mouth.
- Replace other forms of news with an Internet news summary.
- Have several longer news holidays (a week to a month) during the year.

Feedback An immediate response is 'I can't possibly do that'. In fact it's amazing how little news you really *need*, and most of that is either business or leisure specific. For the rest, select what you enjoy, not what is expected.

Outcome One reason that news can be particularly stressful is that you are being given lots of danger signals with no possibility for action. By reducing the constant flow of news you can reduce this impact. As a bonus, you will free up wasted time too.

Variations None.

Time management	✪✪
Stress management	✪✪✪✪
Negotiation skills	✪
General development	✪✪✪
Fun	✪✪✪

Unit 9: Managing meetings – don't let them rule your life

Meetings are valuable tools for running practically anything, but all too often we let the system take over. The meeting becomes an end in its own right, and whatever it was trying to achieve is forgotten.

When I give seminars, I often say to the group 'Of course none of you ever attends meetings that go on too long, but ...' by now there will always be laughter. Rueful laughter. Because practically everyone spends too long in meetings, knows that they spend too long in meetings, and still continues blindly filling up their diaries – with meetings. It's almost like an addiction.

The techniques in this unit will make meetings less of a problem – but only if you are prepared to use them.

Do try out the exercises as you go. Put them off until later and you probably won't ever do them. Read through the techniques. Make notes about how and when you can use them. And make sure you give them a try in the next appropriate forum.

Unit books

Another remark that always seems to get a laugh in seminars is asking the apparently harmless question 'Are the meetings you attend fun?' Of course they're not fun, seems to be the feeling. After all, we're not at work to have fun, and even if we were, we'd have to switch off the expectation in meetings, because meetings are DULL with capital letters.

Two books that aim to do something about fun at work are David Firth's *How to Make Work Fun* and *301 Ways to Have Fun at Work* by David Hemsath and Leslie Yerkes (Hemsath wrote a sequel, originally titled *301 More Ways to Have Fun at Work*). These books should be unnecessary, but they're not, because fun and work still rarely mix. Try them out.

You can find more information on our unit books, or buy them, from our support site: www.cul.co.uk/crashcourse.

Web links

Links to Web sites about meetings and having fun at work can be found at www.cul.co.uk/crashcourse.

9.1 Technique: Agenda bender

Preparation Must be performed in advance.
Running time Two minutes.
Resources Meeting, notebook.
Frequency Regularly.

Without agendas it is easy to hold a meeting without a clear purpose, and it is possible to spend a long time discussing irrelevant matters. Try this technique with the next meeting you organize. First, ensure that the agenda goes out at least a week in advance. If this is not possible because of short notice, at least get the agenda out with the invitation. Next, ensure that the agenda is clear. Don't use unnecessary jargon, and make each item action oriented with a time allocation. A bad agenda item might be: 'BSC', made slightly better as 'balanced score card' and much better as 'Deciding if the balanced score card should be used by finance division next year. (10 minutes)'. If it is likely that attendees are not experts (eg don't know what a Balanced Score Card is), include a background reference so they can read up.

Keep agendas short; a meeting can't cover too many subjects effectively. And ruthlessly omit 'any other business'. This can cause howls of protest. It isn't always possible to know all topics in advance. Fine – so have an opportunity at the start of the meeting to add agenda items. If this makes the agenda too long, drop or postpone something else. Stick to the timings unless the meeting negotiates extra time for a subject, in which case be prepared to push something else out.

Feedback Agendas can be unnecessarily bureaucratic. By sticking to this checklist you can transform agendas without going over the top.

Outcome Good agendas make for shorter, better focused meetings that actually get something done.

Variations It is easiest to apply agenda management to your own meetings, but if someone else's meeting doesn't have a clear agenda, try to establish one at the start. All you need is a whiteboard or a sheet of paper on the table with the key headings written on it.

Time management	✪✪✪✪
Stress management	✪✪✪
Negotiation skills	✪✪
General development	✪
Fun	✪✪

9.2 Technique: Garbage in, garbage out

Preparation None.
Running time Variable.
Resources Meeting, notebook.
Frequency Regularly.

Meetings are only as good as the output they generate. The purpose of this exercise is to maximize the valuable output of your next meeting, and to minimize the time-wasting output. Firstly, dispose of formal minutes. There is nothing more tedious to read. If you are required to keep a record for legal reasons, explore the practicalities of using audio tape. If even that is not possible, there is still no need to waste time and resources by sending out copies of minutes – just take them and file them.

In place of the formal minutes, generate action notes. These should state concisely what is to be done under whose charge by when. It may also say who is responsible for monitoring the action. It should be an exceptional meeting that generates more than one side of paper as action notes.

If your meeting is one of a series, there should be a running agenda item to feed back on the last action plan. This is not the same as a 'minutes of the last meeting' agenda item which is all about nit-picking the minutes. The point is to establish what action has actually taken place and what remains to be done.

Feedback You might not have minutes, but don't think this means you can get away without action notes – that's a recipe for meetings which go nowhere.

Outcome This approach cuts down on the time spent generating, reading and filing minutes and reduces the danger of having meetings that result in no clear actions. If your action notes are blank for two meetings in a row, perhaps it's time to shut down that meeting.

Variations Action notes can be personalized (ie just giving those actions you are responsible for) or for everyone. Usually it is worth giving them to everyone, as it acts as something of spur to ensure that things get done.

Time management	✪✪✪✪
Stress management	✪✪✪
Negotiation skills	✪✪
General development	✪
Fun	✪✪

9.3 Technique: Crowd control

Preparation Must be performed in advance.
Running time Two minutes.
Resources Meeting, notebook.
Frequency Regularly.

In *Agenda Bender* (above) we look at the meeting agenda. Equally important is the invitee list. Treat this as an exercise for the next meeting you organize and the next meeting you attend. All too often meetings consist of the wrong people, and quite frequently there are too many bodies present.

If you are arranging a meeting, consider who needs to be present. Who is a key stakeholder? Who has necessary expertise? Use these considerations to build an initial list. For a meeting that is intended to decide something (as opposed to an information dissemination meeting), it is desirable to keep numbers in single figures – between two and eight is ideal. Be aware that ongoing meetings almost always grow. People want to get involved, to find out what is going on, to make sure that they are represented or to enhance personal power. Be firm with your meetings – take someone off if another person is added.

If you attend a meeting, ask yourself 'Why?' Could someone else go instead? Does anyone from your area need to go at all? Are there better ways to get the input or information you need from the meeting? Need there be a meeting at all?

Feedback Start by questioning the existence of a meeting. If it has to exist, give serious thought to who should attend, and why you attend any meetings you go to.

Outcome Less people at less meetings means more individual time available for productive work, and more effective meetings that don't get bogged down in the interplay of so many people.

Variations Consider replacing meetings with electronic discussion groups. Beware the argument that says such an approach is bad, as it degrades face-to-face contact. You can still have plenty of face-to-face contact, but it needn't take up anywhere near so much time, and can be more socially beneficial.

Time management	✪✪✪✪
Stress management	✪✪
Negotiation skills	✪✪
General development	✪
Fun	✪✪

9.4 Technique: Go casual

Preparation Meeting organized.
Running time Variable.
Resources None.
Frequency Once.

Meetings eat up time and often don't produce results. Yet meetings are an essential part of business. A high proportion of important decisions and ideas come out of informal meetings. Not a group sat around a board table in a stuffy office, but casual get-togethers around the coffee machine, or chance meetings in the corridor.

Here's a challenge then. Take a meeting you are due to have in the next couple of weeks and move it to a casual location. It might be a coffee bar or a park. I've had one in a car park, but ideally it should be somewhere you can get comfortable but not have the formal, stuffy surroundings of a meeting room. It should be a meeting that doesn't require lots of technical support like electronic whiteboards or computers. See how it feels. In most cases you will have a much better, more productive meeting.

Feedback Meetings of this sort tend to be shorter than a traditional meeting (the one I had in a car park only lasted 10 minutes, where the usual ones were 90 minutes). They get through more, yet improve interpersonal relations – all to the good both for your business and personal goals. And they make meetings more enjoyable. Surely, anything that can make meetings more enjoyable is worthwhile.

Outcome This isn't a technique you will use for every meeting, but it is worth bringing out in certain cases. For meetings that tend to get bogged down and over-run, for meetings that need a different sort of input, this approach is ideal.

Variations The possible locations can be very varied. To keep it really short, have the meeting standing up – it sounds bizarre, but it is possible. It might mean taking down actions on a pocket recorder and transcribing them later, but it could be worth it if you have a time-keeping problem.

Time management	✪✪✪✪
Stress management	✪✪✪
Negotiation skills	✪✪
General development	✪✪✪
Fun	✪✪✪

9.5 Technique: Coherent discussion

Preparation None.
Running time Five minutes.
Resources None.
Frequency Regularly.

Traditional discussion is like the output of a light bulb – rays head off in all sorts of directions with no focus or unanimity. By contrast, the rays of a laser's coherent light are in step and the result is a much more powerful beam. Similarly, if it is possible to pull together a discussion so you are all working the same way, you will get a more effective result, with less stress for all concerned.

Before running a meeting, whoever is managing the agenda should consider how to structure the discussion. The trick is to separate off different approaches, so that you are all working together, rather than fighting each other. A meeting structure might be something like:

- Review what the meeting intends to achieve.
- Discuss background information.
- Brainstorm (or use other creativity techniques to generate) some new ideas.
- Select the most appealing idea on gut feel.
- Get feedback on the group's feelings.
- Spend a few minutes looking at what is good about the idea, and how the good points can be made even better.
- Spend a few minutes looking at what is bad with the idea, and how the negative points can be fixed.
- Devise a handful of milestones and timescales for action.

Feedback How you assemble the items (and whether or not you include them at all) is up to you and the group. The importance is in getting people working coherently rather than destructively. When engaged in one activity, try to keep off the others. For example, when coming up with ideas don't say what you feel about them, and when assessing good points, don't let any 'buts' creep in.

Outcome Much of the stress from bad meetings comes out of badly managed discussion. Coherence helps everyone.

Variations The classic approach to coherent discussion, which is still very popular, is Edward de Bono's Six Thinking Hats, described in the book of the same name.

Time management	✪✪✪
Stress management	✪✪✪
Negotiation skills	✪✪✪
General development	✪✪✪
Fun	✪✪

Unit 10: A pat on the back – self reward

It's easy to get carried away with being inward looking and self-centred. It's arguable that many of our current world difficulties can be put at the door of the concept of 'human rights'. If, rather than speaking of the inward looking, self-seeking 'human rights' we had devised the outward looking 'human responsibilities' we might have done more to alleviate suffering and poverty than we have.

Having said that, and having recognized the dangers of the cult of 'me', it is something that actually needs encouraging in a small way. Self-esteem is essential for personal development. If you want to manage your time effectively, you need to value your time. If you want to control stress you need to have a reasonable level of self value. If you want to succeed in negotiations, it's important to believe in your own arguments.

What this unit focuses on is providing small self-rewards, essential defences against the mess that the world throws at you.

Do try out the exercises as you go. Put them off until later and you probably won't ever do them. Read through the techniques. Make notes about how and when you can use them. And make sure you give them a try in the next appropriate forum.

Unit books

A reward doesn't have to be big – in fact almost all the rewards in this unit are small – but the reward has to match the requirement. It's hard to find a reward that works better and more instantly than a concentrated dose of humour – try any one of Gary Larson's superb *Far Side* cartoon collections – I'm especially fond of *Last Chapter and Worse*.

You can find more information on our unit books, or buy them, from our support site: www.cul.co.uk/crashcourse.

Web links

Links to humorous Web sites to give yourself a little reward can be found at www.cul.co.uk/crashcourse.

10.1 Technique: Cherry-picking

Preparation None.
Running time Five minutes.
Resources None.
Frequency Once.

A criticism of consultants is that they are always cherry-picking, finding easy hits with a quick return so they look good. Cherry-picking is something we all indulge in. Given a list of tasks, which do you choose to do first? The natural inclination is to the things we enjoy and are comfortable with, and the tasks which are quick to finish with instant gratification. This can mean that important or time-dependent tasks get put off until it's too late.

Like many people, I don't like ringing up someone cold. Yet this is sometimes required for an interview. My natural tendency is to put off this call until the last possible moment. The trouble is, it can often take a week or two to get through. So leaving the calls to the day before the deadline can be a recipe for disaster. When it comes to choosing tasks to do first, always have the two essential criteria in mind. Is this task central to a focal activity (see *Focus* in Unit 4), and is it time critical?

Feedback While it is essential to use the two criteria mentioned above, it is also a good thing to have a steady flow of quick hits. They have two benefits – they boost your self-esteem, and you are seen to be someone who delivers. As long as quick hits don't take up a high proportion of your time, they're beneficial.

Outcome Another exercise (*Priorities*, also in Unit 4) helps choose the right tasks. This is more about avoiding the dangers of prevarication. Try writing 'No cherry-picking' at the top of your task list.

Variations If you use an electronic task list with a prioritization feature you could set values of one for time critical and focal, two for time critical or focal and three for quick hits – but if this takes too long, don't bother – monitor cherry-picking by eye.

Time management	✪✪✪✪
Stress management	✪✪✪
Negotiation skills	✪
General development	✪✪
Fun	✪✪✪

10.2 Technique: Little treats

Preparation None.
Running time Five minutes.
Resources Notebook.
Frequency Regularly.

Sometimes it makes good time management sense to stop working. No one can do brain work for hours on end and maintain efficiency – 90 minutes is about the limit before serious degradation sets in. A first step can be a change of air and position. Get up, perhaps go outside for a couple of minutes – air conditioning and heating sap your energy. Get yourself a cup of coffee or look at a magazine.

If you are engaged in an all-day task you will need more diverting breaks. Keep a list of bite-sized mini-projects in your notebook. These should take up little time, and be diverting but not urgent. To be effective, you should be able to complete something in a few minutes. When you are working on a lengthy, high-pressure project, divert into a treat for a few minutes every couple of hours.

Feedback It can be difficult to do this. Under pressure, you want to spend every minute on the subject at hand. But this will lead to inefficient use of your time as you lose concentration. Force yourself to take a few minutes out. Of course, there will be circumstances when you are on a roll, everything is flowing and you really don't need a break, so don't follow this approach slavishly, but do bring it in when needed.

Outcome Five minutes' diversion will be repaid with a much greater equivalent increase in effectiveness. An essential ingredient is that the treat tasks are things that you enjoy doing (however menial) and that there is a clear completion in a few minutes. There is something wonderful about completion.

Variations Turn this exercise upside down to capture treats when they aren't appropriate. If you find yourself thinking 'Oh, I wish I could just do X' and you know it is prevarication, jot it down in on your treats list, knowing that you will do it in due time.

Time management	✪✪✪✪
Stress management	✪✪✪✪
Negotiation skills	✪
General development	✪
Fun	✪✪✪✪

10.3 Technique: Doggie chocs

Preparation None.
Running time Two minutes.
Resources None.
Frequency Regularly.

Some tasks are necessary but difficult to start. Some are *Task list stragglers* (see Unit 7) which are always being bumped down the chain. Others are essential drudgery, or a sort of negative *Cherry-picking* (see above). Faced with such tasks, it helps to employ a touch of psychology. Just as animals are encouraged with a titbit to do things they have no natural urge to do, you can give yourself the promise of a small reward if you get a task done.

It might be the opportunity to do a fun, low priority activity (see *Little treats*, above). It might be going out that evening, or literally a titbit – a cake with your coffee or a chocolate bar. Whatever the reward, make sure you use the same techniques as an animal trainer (or parent). The reward must be immediate, beginning as soon as possible after the task is completed. And size doesn't matter; a chocolate bar is as effective for these purposes as an expensive watch.

Feedback This technique sounds ridiculous, because you know what you are doing, so surely it won't work. Not at all. The impact isn't reduced by the knowledge of your actions; the promise of an immediate reward will help you get something done.

Outcome This technique is great for attacking the ragged edges of your time management. It helps trim away those tasks that you just can't bring yourself to get on with.

Variations To be effective, the reward has to come soon. This means that a big task needs to be split up into daily deliverables so that you can achieve something every day. You may like to have a slightly larger reward for the overall completion, but shouldn't replace the milestone rewards. You can help other people by giving them similar rewards – and if your boss gives you a reward, you won't have to do it yourself.

Time management	✪✪✪✪
Stress management	✪✪✪✪
Negotiation skills	✪
General development	✪✪
Fun	✪✪✪✪

10.4 Technique: Pat on the back

Preparation None.
Running time Two minutes.
Resources None.
Frequency Regularly.

Some of us are very good at giving other people a pat on the back when they've done something right – and that's an excellent thing to do, because with any luck they will return the compliment. Receiving regular small pats on the back stops the build up of the feeling that you aren't appreciated, and hence stress.

Sometimes, though, no one is going to do the back-patting for you. It might be that those who should be doing it are too busy, or simply aren't very good at telling people what a good job they've done (if that's the case, try to find ways to pat them on the back as a stimulus). It might be that there isn't anyone there to do it for you. If so, don't be shy about giving yourself a pat on the back.

When something goes well, shout 'Yes!' and punch the air, take yourself on a quick guided tour of the benefits, bask a brief while in the glory, perhaps buy yourself a little treat – anything from a chocolate bar, through a nice lunch, to the sort of toy that appeals to you.

Feedback Many of us are held back by the consideration that we can't be objective, and that anyway we shouldn't be blowing our own trumpet. When there's no one else to do the trumpet blowing, don't be shy – much stress is conquered by being in control, and control includes the ability to enjoy your successes.

Outcome This needn't be more than saying to yourself 'That went rather well' and indulging in the luxury of a big grin, but psychologically the impact is considerable. Give yourself a pat more often – you know you deserve it.

Variations None.

Time management	✪✪✪✪
Stress management	✪✪✪✪
Negotiation skills	✪
General development	✪✪
Fun	✪✪✪✪

10.5 Exercise: I did that

Preparation None.
Running time 10 minutes.
Resources Notepad.
Frequency Once.

As we've seen in various other techniques, there is a strong link between self-esteem and ability to manage stress adequately. This exercise is all about self-esteem.

Sit down with a notepad and note down some of the occasions when you've had a real success in your life. Things that are important to you or things that are important to the world. It could be success in exams and education, getting a job, getting married, having children, the first time you did something successfully that had been hard to achieve (driving a car or beating someone at chess). In one sense these achievements don't have to be large, at least in not in the earth-shattering sense, but they need to be significant to you. Little successes are useful too – see *Little successes* in Unit 1 for more details.

Feedback When you've got together a list of successes – it doesn't matter if it's one or two or a great string – spend some time thinking through what it felt like at the time. Relive the moment when you realized you'd succeeded. Don't feel guilty about enjoying your success; you deserve it. Remembering a moment of success has a surprisingly strong influence on your current feeling of well-being.

Outcome By working on your self-esteem you can add hugely to your ability to stand up to stress and to deflect it. All the evidence is that those with high self-esteem are better able to cope with stress – here's a simple way to reinforce your self-esteem. Don't worry if it sounds artificial, it still works.

Variations You could repeat this exercise, perhaps yearly, looking back over your achievements of the last year.

Time management	✪
Stress management	✪✪✪✪
Negotiation skills	✪
General development	✪✪✪
Fun	✪✪✪

Unit 11: Look around you – dealing with the environment

Despite the title, this isn't a unit about going green, but rather is a matter of looking at the impact that the environment in which you work has on the way you feel and your ability to cope with stress. Sometimes very small environmental changes can be enough to give the impression (however fragile) that you are in control, that you have some influence – and that is an essential for stress management.

One particular environmental concern is the effect of change. We live in a rapidly changing world where the pace of change itself is accelerating. Coping well with change, and if possible enjoying it, will make all the difference.

Do try out the exercises as you go. Put them off until later and you probably won't ever do them. Read through the techniques. Make notes about how and when you can use them. And make sure you give them a try in the next appropriate forum.

Unit book

One of the most frequent examples of environmental stress is that caused by flying. Of all the modes of transport it is the most unnatural, and everything from the slow passage through the airport to the low air pressure in cabins and the frightening disturbances of turbulence contributes to extremes of stress. In *The Complete Flier's Handbook* I look at what it's possible to do to get the most out of the air travel experience and to minimize stress.

You can find more information on our unit books, or buy them, from our support site: www.cul.co.uk/crashcourse.

Web links

Links to environmental change Web sites and *The Complete Flier's Handbook* site can be found at www.cul.co.uk/crashcourse.

11.1 Technique: Quiet corners

Preparation None.
Running time Five minutes.
Resources None.
Frequency Regularly.

Getting on with something that needs your full attention is impossible if you are constantly interrupted. Consider hunting out a quiet corner. Thanks to laptop computers, many more work activities can now be done away from the desk. Even without a laptop, you can use that classic mobile solution, a pad and paper.

Where you get to depends on you and your environment. If your workplace has hot-desking, or guest worker spaces, try finding a space in a different part of the building. If there are small meeting rooms book one for a meeting with yourself. Quite often on a large site there will be unoccupied offices. Take one over for the afternoon.

If none of these is practical, there are quiet corners which you can subvert. If your company has a library or management study centre, try hiding there. Alternatively, venture out into the world, to a public library or even (weather and location permitting) a field or a beach.

Feedback Bear in mind the need to be perceived as hard working as well as actually being hard working. Leaving the company site would only work with a flexible employer (or if you are relatively senior). If it is likely to be a problem, make sure that there is a prominent notice on your desk saying that you are in a meeting, and when you will be back.

Outcome Finding a quiet retreat is increasingly important in a world where communications and open-plan offices open us up to constant interruption. If retreating like this shows signs of becoming a way of life, work hard on something like working from home; otherwise it's a great way of protecting a time slot for productive work.

Variations There is no point seeking out a quiet corner if you take your mobile phone, your pager and wireless e-mail. Turn them off or leave them behind.

Time management	✪✪✪✪
Stress management	✪✪✪
Negotiation skills	✪
General development	✪✪
Fun	✪✪✪

11.2 Exercise: How wide is your door?

Preparation None.
Running time Five minutes.
Resources None.
Frequency Once.

Having an 'open door' policy has been a popular management technique for quite a while. In fact, many modern offices don't even have doors. But a policy like this is not really about furniture, it's about an attitude or frame of mind.

Spend a minute thinking about your own policy on accessibility. Include work and home – even if you don't go to work, think about the way you provide accessibility to family and friends. Do you have an ever-open door? Can anyone approach you? Or is your door welded solidly closed? Does someone need an appointment just to get sight of your PA? Where would you put yourself on the spectrum between open and closed?

If you haven't actually completed the previous step, go back and do it. Now.

There's no doubt that a closed door policy is a disaster. The message is that you don't care, the practicality is that you can't be brought into processes and decisions, so things take place despite you and you will become marginalized. Unfortunately a totally open door, while better, isn't much better, because it is too easy for you to get swamped with approaches.

Feedback The ideal is that you are readily accessible, but not necessarily all the time. This doesn't sound easy, but is quite practical, provided you work at it. It isn't an objective that can be achieved overnight as it will involve education of others, but it is entirely practical.

Outcome This exercise isn't designed to control your accessibility. Its importance is gaining an understanding of just what you do and how you seem to others. This will have a strong impact on how they react to you.

Variations Ask some of your stakeholders – staff, customers, peers, bosses – about your accessibility: see what they think. Think also about the effect on your time that your current policy has. Is your level of accessibility using up a high percentage of your time?

Time management	✪✪✪✪
Stress management	✪✪
Negotiation skills	✪✪
General development	✪✪✪
Fun	✪✪

11.3 Exercise: Home, sweet home

Preparation None.
Running time 10 minutes.
Resources None.
Frequency Once.

If you already work from home, consider this exercise complete. This is a planning exercise – you aren't going to change your working pattern in 10 minutes. Working in an office has big advantages, but it is also loaded with distractions. It can be very helpful to spend some time working from home, not taking work home outside office hours, but being at home in working time.

Spend a few minutes thinking about the benefits of home working. For most people this might be one to three days a week, not the whole time. Think of the advantages for you and for the company. They might include less distraction, less commuting time, better productivity, more comfort, more contact with the family. Then spend a couple of minutes thinking of the disadvantages. They might include unsuitable premises, your boss not knowing what you are doing, having more family distraction, being harder to contact.

Put this together as a balance sheet. If the outcome is strongly positive, make the move to home working a focal activity (see *Focus* in Unit 4).

Feedback Mostly due to a lack of trust, implementation of home working has been agonizingly slow. Unless your company supports it, your options are to change company, to become self-employed or to support any initiatives (and volunteer for any pilot schemes). For the company to achieve maximum financial benefit, it may combine home-working with hot-desking, where desks are not personally owned, reducing office space. This forces an orderly approach, but does have an administrative overhead.

Outcome This exercise should explore your valuation of home working. Depending on the outcome you may start pushing in this direction – those who have done so voluntarily usually feel it makes a huge difference to their personal productivity and time management.

Variations There are a variety of alternative schemes, like small local satellite offices, with a similar effect to home working, but usually with less time management benefit.

Time management	✪✪✪✪
Stress management	✪✪✪
Negotiation skills	✪
General development	✪✪✪
Fun	✪✪✪

11.4 Exercise: Environmental stuff

Preparation Meeting.
Running time 30 minutes.
Resources Notepad.
Frequency Once.

Most people spend between 30 and 60 hours a week in their working environment. That's a long time – it's probably more, for instance, than you spend in your lounge at home. Consider the relative amount of effort you put into making your lounge a pleasant environment, and into making your workplace pleasant.

Get together the people who work in a separable chunk of your workplace – or simply do the exercise on your own. Put up two flip charts. On one list everything that's wrong with your present workplace environment – small and large. On the other list anything you feel makes for a pleasant environment – again cover small detail as much as large-scale considerations.

Now, combining the two, come up with the top ten things you can do in terms of 'bangs per buck' that would make the environment more pleasant. These can be individually or across the group. Finally, consider where you can get the money from, and put together a timetable for making them happen.

Feedback The money bit can be a stumbling block. The company will probably contribute, but consider whether the employees should contribute too – wouldn't it be worth it? Often a bigger problem is bureaucracy that, for example, doesn't allow individual decoration or changes to the workplace. Consider the options of defeating the bureaucracy, cheating or ignoring the rules (subject to safety considerations) – but get something done.

Outcome The conditions in which you work influence your stress levels, positively or negatively. Most employers are clued up enough about stress to realize this and be supportive. Be prepared to fight designer uniformity to get a pleasant working environment.

Variations If you don't work with others, perform the exercise anyway – your environmental concerns are just as great. You have the advantage of less need to agree with others over what you do, but may find it harder to get funding.

Time management	✪
Stress management	✪✪✪✪
Negotiation skills	✪
General development	✪✪
Fun	✪✪✪

11.5 Technique: Coping with change

Preparation None.
Running time 10 minutes.
Resources Notepad.
Frequency Occasionally.

Change can be the bane of our life, or the only thing that makes life worth living. Everyone has a change continuum from the level they enjoy to the level that makes them highly stressed. As the pace of change accelerates – and there is no sign of it slowing down – we are all in danger of being moved out of our comfort zone.

Every now and then, particularly when change is in the air, spend a few minutes building a change map. To do this, you will have to think about how you resist change-based stress. There are two primary weapons involved in coping with change without being stressed. The first is your anchors. What do you have to return to that remains constant? Write your anchors on the map with circles round them. They could be your family, your friends (or one special friend), your home, your religion, your pet – the things you turn to when everything else is in turmoil.

The second weapon is learning to love change. Not espousing change for change's sake, but taking a particular change, understanding the benefits it can bring and making a conscious effort to buy into it. This is possible much more than we normally allow. Draw the prime areas of change on your map, highlighting those where the change is distressing. For those change elements, note down what's good about them. Tie them back, where relevant, to your anchors. Try to focus on those positives rather than your negative feelings.

Feedback Resistance to change isn't inherently bad, but carry out this exercise first. If you still find the benefits unconvincing, consider action you can take to fight the change. But make sure you are fighting change because you don't like its implications, not just because you don't like change full stop.

Outcome Change is ever-present and always stressful. Learning to cope with it is a major stress relief skill.

Variations None.

Time management	✪
Stress management	✪✪✪✪
Negotiation skills	✪
General development	✪✪✪✪
Fun	✪✪

Unit 12: Giving it away – sharing your burdens

Personal development isn't all about starting new things – sometimes it's about letting go. For many of us, delegation proves surprisingly difficult. You might find it difficult to delegate a pet project that you feel you have to see through to the end – or it could be your business has grown to the extent you can't do everything yourself, but you feel that you have to. Face it – you can't do everything.

Another aspect of sharing your burden is having someone to talk things through with, someone who can give impartial advice – we can all benefit from having a mentor.

Do try out the exercises as you go. Put them off until later and you probably won't ever do them. Read through the techniques. Make notes about how and when you can use them. And make sure you give them a try in the next appropriate forum.

Unit book

This unit's recommended book is *Barbarians Led by Bill Gates*, by Jennifer Edstrom and Marlin Eller. It's a fascinating insight into the dark side of working for an organization like Microsoft, and a great illustration of the way apparent conspiracies are often more down to incompetence. It also shows how some individuals find it very difficult to let go.

You can find more information on our unit books, or buy them, from our support site: www.cul.co.uk/crashcourse.

Web links

Web references on delegation can be found at www.cul.co.uk/crashcourse.

12.1 Exercise/Technique: Letting go

Preparation None.
Running time 10 minutes.
Resources None.
Frequency Monthly.

A big problem of time management is trying to do everything yourself. Almost everyone has some opportunity for delegation, yet many of us are reluctant to do it. Mostly it's a matter of trust. Will the other person get the job done? If they do it well, will they show us up? They can't win.

You won't pick up effective delegation from a single exercise, but this technique will start you in the right direction. About once a month, think about what you actually do. How well do your actions fit with what you ought to be doing and what you do best? Your focal activities (see *Focus* in Unit 4) and talent list (*Talent spotting* in Unit 2) will help. Highlight anything that deviates significantly, especially if it is time-consuming.

Now spend a couple of minutes thinking of potential delegates. Obvious candidates are your reports, your peers and your boss. There may be specific functions within your organization that could take on a job. Also think of external agencies, contractors and consultants. We live in an age of extended business structures – don't be parochial. Finally, aim to delegate at least one task or activity. You may manage several, but make sure something is given away.

Feedback A contract helps overcome difficulties with trust. This may just be desired outcomes and completion dates, but with more complex tasks or unknown delegates, it is sensible to include milestones. Many people find delegation a problem – see *Delegation difficulties* below for more help.

Outcome Provided you aren't giving responsibility without authority, you have a clear contract and you keep your hands off, delegation will free up plenty of time. If you prove good at it, you will also be considered a good manager, and will increase the respect of your staff.

Variations Delegation sideways and upwards has to be handled carefully if you aren't to be regarded as work-shy. It requires the positive agreement of those involved. However, this does not mean that peer delegation and delegation to your bosses should be avoided.

Look for an opportunity to unload something onto one of your peers that is of no interest or benefit to you, but will bring him or her pleasure. Similarly find things to delegate upwards that will be enjoyed or give your boss an element of recognition.

Time management	✪✪✪✪
Stress management	✪✪
Negotiation skills	✪✪
General development	✪✪✪
Fun	✪✪

12.2 Exercise: Be prepared

Preparation None.
Running time 10 minutes.
Resources Staff.
Frequency Once.

This exercise assumes you have staff reporting to you – if you don't you can skip it. The Boy Scout motto is going to be used in some time management, once-removed. Communication with your staff is vital – in fact it's one of the most important parts of your job. Nevertheless, such communication can become obtrusive. Other techniques look at deflecting interruptions or channelling them – it's even better to train your staff to interrupt more efficiently.

Next time you have a team meeting, assign 10 minutes to this issue. Explain your problem and give them a couple of minutes to come up with possible ways of making their communication with you more effective. Take the best ideas and add in any of the following which aren't already there.

- Send low priority information by e-mail.
- Keep everything but high priority communication for an agreed time of day.
- Package your communication to get across any necessary information, then present the need for action or a decision.
- Have some recommendations, rather than expecting you to come up with solutions on the spot.
- Have a realistic idea of how long the interruption will take, and check it up front.
- Produce a mini-agenda for the discussion.

Feedback This has to be handled diplomatically. Everyone may know that your time is important and in short supply, but there's nothing to gain from rubbing their noses in it. Expect to issue gentle reminders to begin with – running in to say something is a habit and needs some breaking.

Emphasize that the benefits can work two ways. By thinking before running to you it may be that your staff members can achieve something, show some initiative in a way that can be recognized next time their performance can be assessed. And remind them that you *want* communication, but effectively filtered communication.

Outcome Anything you can do to encourage others to manage their interruptions for you is a superb piece of time management, because you are delegating the management task. Also the conscious effort of structuring the interruption will cause a fair number of low priority disruptions never to occur.

Variations This technique can be put across by edict rather than the quasi-democratic approach here, but it will have less impact.

Time management	✪✪✪✪
Stress management	✪✪
Negotiation skills	✪✪
General development	✪✪✪
Fun	✪✪

12.3 Exercise: Delegation difficulties

Preparation None.
Running time Five minutes.
Resources People to delegate to.
Frequency Once.

Many of us find delegation difficult (note by the way, this exercise applies even if you don't have staff – you still delegate, whether by asking a peer to do something for you or paying a cleaner to tidy your house). In this short exercise we will start to address difficulties with delegation.

Spend a couple of minutes writing down why you find delegation difficult. If you think you don't, write down why others might. Only then check the list below.

- You know you can do it better.
- It's your job to keep a tight rein.
- You are insecure.
- You aren't sure of your own role.
- The other people have enough to do.
- The job needs a recognized figure.

Each of these reasons – and any others you may have come up with – has a counter. Spend the remaining time thinking of specific counters to each reason.

Feedback Only you can really counter your own objections: this one goes beyond logic. Some answers will be as simple as 'So what?'. This is a good response, for example to 'You know you can do it better' – as long as the person you delegate to can do a satisfactory job, so what? Others will require you to find something out or take a risk with people. Unless you can, you aren't going to gain their trust or their full input. In the end, if they aren't good enough to delegate to, why do you work with them?

Outcome Delegation is essential to effective time management – there are very few roles which you can truly undertake alone. In the end, delegation is only learned by doing it. Take the risk and see what happens.

Variations Instead of coming at the problems of delegation by examining the arguments against it, list the advantages of delegation. Then use these as arguments for doing it. A few starters to get you going:

- Frees up your time.
- Develops others.
- What is of minor interest to you may be of burning interest to someone else.
- You can't be in two places at once.

Time management	✪✪✪✪
Stress management	✪✪✪
Negotiation skills	✪
General development	✪✪
Fun	✪✪✪

12.4 Exercise: It's mine

Preparation None.
Running time Five minutes.
Resources None.
Frequency Once.

This exercise looks at a delegation problem that is particularly strong in the social arena. There all sorts of tasks which tradition allocates to the householder. He or she is expected to do the decorating and minor repairs, and to keep the garden looking good. Similarly a car owner is expected to sort out minor problems, and so on. This emotional pressure, often associated with sexual stereotyping ('What sort of man can't put up a shelf/change a spark plug?', 'What sort of woman can't cook a meal/iron?') is surprisingly strong. Spend a couple of minutes listing the typical chores in your social life – include the activities of everyone in your close family.

Now split them up into those you enjoy doing (don't ask me why, but I like going to the supermarket, for instance) or feel you get personal benefit from, and those you hate. Against each 'Hate' put a high, medium or low cost mark. Use an average hourly rate for your pay as medium, anything significantly more as high, and significantly less as low. Consider paying someone to do any low cost tasks. There are a lot better uses of your time.

Feedback Delegating is different in the domestic environment. It's clearer that you are moving a scarce time resource from a chore to something you'd like to be doing, but the emotional pressures are stronger too. Make sure you do something specific with the time you free up – that way you can really appreciate the benefit.

Outcome Shifting chunks of social time away from unwanted chores generates real benefit for your time management. And gives someone a job too – can't be bad.

Variations Although this technique is specifically designed for social time management, it is applicable at work too. An alternative approach is turning a chore into something you enjoy doing by having the right tools, training or motivation.

Time management	✪✪✪✪
Stress management	✪✪✪✪
Negotiation skills	✪✪
General development	✪✪✪
Fun	✪✪

12.5 Exercise: Mentor mine

Preparation None.
Running time 15 minutes.
Resources Notepad.
Frequency Once.

There's lots you can do alone to manage stress, but sometimes you need a hand. This doesn't necessarily mean a therapist, though. Just having someone to talk through your problems and aspirations with is immensely valuable.

First spend five minutes thinking about your life, at work and at home. Jot down the most significant things that take up your time, your energy and your worrying. Try to project forward to future concerns. Then think through your contacts. An ideal mentor is:

- Absolutely trustworthy – you want to be able to discuss confidential matters and have them go no further.
- Someone you know well…
- …but not a close friend.
- Someone who is good at listening.
- Someone you have regular contact with.

Choose someone for a mentor. Don't approach them and say 'I want you to be my mentor', just start to get together with them infrequently but regularly and chat about what concerns you.

Feedback For mentoring to be effective, you will need regular chats with your mentor – maybe weekly. This can be over lunch or coffee or out of office hours. Don't try to make it formal. The whole point of a mentoring session is that it can cover anything and everything. Note, by the way, you have an unwritten obligation to act as a mentor for someone else. It probably won't be your mentor, but there's someone out there who needs you to listen to them.

One warning: not infrequently a patient develops affection for an analyst, and because you are forcing yourself to be relatively intimate with your mentor, there is a danger of getting mixed up emotionally if you are dealing with someone you might find attractive. This isn't an out-and-out ban on such people, but bear it in mind.

Over time you may find you need to change your mentor. I naturally moved from one individual to another as my job emphasis changed from consultancy to writing. If contact with your mentor becomes an irritation or difficult to fix up, it's time to move on.

Outcome The mentor's role is uniquely powerful in helping you get to terms with stressing situations. Get one as soon as possible.

Variations None.

Time management	✪✪✪
Stress management	✪✪✪
Negotiation skills	✪
General development	✪✪✪✪
Fun	✪✪✪

Unit 13: Making communications work for you – rather than for them

Communications are important on a number of levels. Business gurus like Tom Peters will tell you how valuable a good contact list is if you want to succeed in the new world of virtual corporations and shifting alliances. At a deeper level, communication with other human beings is something we all cherish – it's a very significant part of what makes us human. But…

And it's a big 'but'. But uncontrolled communication can be a real pain when you are trying to get something done. With phones, fax, mobile phones and e-mail we are in danger of constant bombardment with electronic messages and conversations. Don't get me wrong – I'm not against these things. When my e-mail connection goes down during working hours I get twitchy very quickly. Even so, these tools need appropriate control – as does that older communication monster, paper – if you, rather than they, are to be in control.

Do try out the exercises as you go. Put them off until later and you probably won't ever do them. Read through the techniques. Make notes about how and when you can use them. And make sure you give them a try in the next appropriate forum.

Unit book

Tom Peters not only comments on the value of your contacts, but a whole host of other areas that are important to building a business life around *you* rather than around an employer in his excellent book *The Tom Peters Seminar – Crazy Times call for Crazy Organizations*.

You can find more information on our unit books, or buy them, from our support site: www.cul.co.uk/crashcourse.

13.1 Technique: The e-mail of the species

Preparation None.
Running time Five minutes.
Resources E-mail software.
Frequency Regularly.

E-mail has revolutionized business communications and is making rapid inroads into the social world. However, it comes with a price. Reading and responding to e-mail takes time, and the immediacy can provide a constant distraction. Keeping e-mail in its place is a three-stage process.

Firstly, turn off notification. Stop your e-mail package from telling you when e-mail arrives. Secondly, have between one and four e-mail slots in your schedule. These needn't be explicitly in your diary, though it may help. They should be the only time you read e-mail. (This doesn't mean they are the only times to send e-mail – check *E-mail it away* below to see how sending e-mails instantly can benefit you.)

Finally, be brutal about time. Fix a maximum time – perhaps 30 minutes, certainly no more than an hour – to spend on e-mails. Stick to this by skimming through your in-tray first, reading key messages and responding, then working through low-priority mail. Don't feel you have to read all of a low priority message: bin it as soon as you are sure it's irrelevant. Whatever you do, don't let unread mail build up in your in-tray. Similarly, if you have to reply, try to do so immediately.

Feedback Have a standard 'Sorry I haven't time' (or 'No thanks') message for unimportant e-mails requiring a reply. If the sender doesn't get anything, he or she may keep resending the mail. This isn't helpful to anyone.

Don't reply at all to any obvious junk mail, even when it offers to let you 'unsubscribe' – this is often used to confirm that you exist.

What about the occasional really important mail? You can always set your e-mail software to notify you when mail comes in with the urgent flag set, or from key contacts.

Outcome Freedom from notification is a big relief. Once you see a mail has arrived, it will continue to nag. Is it important? Who is it from? It's much better not to know it has arrived. By managing e-mail reading into sensible chunks it remains a valuable resource, but won't take over your life.

Variations Consider using mail filters to organize incoming mail. When you have made a hot spots chart (coming up in Unit 21), fit e-mail reading into lower energy times.

Time management	✪✪✪✪
Stress management	✪✪✪
Negotiation skills	✪
General development	✪✪
Fun	✪✪

13.2 Technique: E-mail it away

Preparation None.
Running time Two minutes.
Resources E-mail.
Frequency Regularly.

E-mail can be a great tool for managing stress. Imagine that you were in the middle of writing an important report. The pressure is on; you have very little time. Suddenly you remember that you haven't organized the materials for tomorrow's meeting. That's important, but you still need to get your report done, so you carry on, while trying to remember to do something about the materials. This exerts stress all along the way – doubly so if you finally forget and don't do anything about it.

One way to relieve that stress is to write yourself a note – but there's still a problem. You have to remember to read the note. Again, there's a nagging memory, continually disrupting your thoughts and adding stress. However, if you've got e-mail always ready to send, in a few seconds you can pull up your e-mail package, write a note to someone to get the job done and send it off. Then you can get back to your report with nothing causing additional stress.

Keep your e-mail running at all times and when such a requirement occurs to you, pop quickly in, send the mail and clear the worry.

Feedback If you want e-mail to alleviate stress rather than cause it, you have to be in control of your e-mail. Many people in corporate environments have e-mail packages set to alert them when a mail comes in. This is a recipe for stress, as each arriving mail breaks into your concentration. When you then find out it is junk mail you are doubly stressed by the anticipation and the disappointment.

Some companies still have e-mail systems that can't be activated in a second or two. If yours is one, make a fuss – you need something better.

Outcome It's popular to rubbish e-mail, but used in this way it's a great tool for relieving the stress of sudden thoughts of something that needs doing.

Variations None.

Time management	✪✪✪
Stress management	✪✪✪✪
Negotiation skills	✪
General development	✪✪
Fun	✪✪

13.3 Technique: Calling by numbers

Preparation None.
Running time Five minutes.
Resources Telephone.
Frequency Daily.

Many days you will make phone calls. Some are known about in advance, others crop up through the day. This technique reduces the tendency of outgoing calls to fragment your activities.

Where much time management is about breaking activities down, this is about chunking up, pulling together small tasks that would otherwise waste time. In a business context, you can normally restrict outgoing calls to two chunks, mid-morning and mid-afternoon. This reduces time wasting, and maximizes the chance of a reply by using core business hours. Making it happen is simply a matter of keeping a call list. At the start of the day, put any planned calls on the list. As the need arises, add new items – don't be tempted to make the call unless timing is critical.

Feedback There will be exceptions – good time management is about principles, not rules – but most calls can be handled this way.

Outcome This technique cuts interruptions to your work flow, and maximizes the chance of getting through first time. For those who dislike using the phone it also minimizes the pain, and forces the issue – it's easier to put off an individual call than a list.

Variations Some personal information manager software lets you build a call list that dials automatically – so much the better. Make sure the list is in a single place. If you have a 'mess of paper' system, keep to a single sheet – yellow sticky notes are too easy to misplace. On hearing an engaged tone, press 5 (or equivalent) to get an automatic callback when the number is free. This won't work with all exchanges, but is very effective if it does. If you have callbacks outstanding when the period is over, cancel them, making sure the individual is still on your call list.

Time management	✪✪✪✪
Stress management	✪✪
Negotiation skills	✪
General development	✪
Fun	✪✪

13.4 Technique: Fluffy phones

Preparation None.
Running time Two minutes.
Resources Telephone, notebook.
Frequency Regularly.

Phone calls can eat up large amounts of time. In *Calling by numbers* you are encouraged to chunk up your outgoing calls. Here, we look at the content. If you make a call, identify what you want to get out of it. Note the key points and keep them in front of you. You won't work through the points in order – to do so would make the call very stilted – but it will be a guide to what is left to do.

You can use your key points as a checklist or develop branching notes from each point. Most usefully, you can ensure that everything is covered, and be aware when you drift from the point. Social convention requires some deviation. One of the valuable aspects of phone calls is reinforcing your network of contacts, and you cannot afford to be brusque. However, you should be aware of deviation, and bring the conversation back when practical. On the phone you lack many non-verbal cues. Giving short, one-word answers may shut down a topic; otherwise you will have to actively move the subject back into line.

Feedback It may seem artificial, but this approach doesn't interfere with the flow of conversation.

Outcome Applied properly, this technique cuts down on time spent chatting or going over old ground, using your time more effectively.

Variations For incoming calls you have less opportunity to prepare. If your caller doesn't state his or her intentions, ask – as long as it's done politely it won't cause offence and it will enable you to keep the conversation on track. In principle this technique can be used in a social context, and it is useful to make sure important subjects are covered, but bear in mind that the peripheral content is often the main point of a social call, and needs to be given a higher priority.

Time management	✪✪✪✪
Stress management	✪✪
Negotiation skills	✪
General development	✪✪
Fun	✪✪

13.5 Technique: Paper mountains

Preparation None.
Running time Five minutes.
Resources Incoming documents.
Frequency Daily.

We all receive plenty of reading matter – letters, memos, magazines and so on. Like e-mails, paper needs chunking. Don't read each item as it hits your desk, but pull them together at sensible intervals – perhaps once or twice a day – to fit your working pattern.

Take a couple of minutes over a first pass. Sort paper into three types. Junk, items requiring action and items requiring reading. Practise making this decision within a few seconds. Check the heading and the first paragraph – you ought to have made a decision by then. Commercial junk is probably best trashed, but reports and other internal documents are different. Write in large, red letters at the top (even better, get a stamp – it's very satisfying) 'Returned unread' and send it back. This is particularly valuable in a culture where you may be criticized for not taking action – here you have taken a very clear action.

Feedback You may get people contacting you who assume you have read a document. You can try honesty ('It didn't look relevant so I didn't read it' or 'I don't know.'), distraction ('Remind me what it was about') or deception ('Yes'). Each is valid – see which suits you best.

Outcome The principle aim is to avoid wasting time, but there are secondary benefits. By putting reading matter like magazines in a separate pile, you can chunk them up sensibly. And sending back items marked 'Returned unread' may make the sender consider stopping the production of the offending article – provided you aren't going to cause unwanted friction.

Variations Don't be tempted to split reading matter into categories – that's the level of detail where time management takes more time than it saves. However, you might find it useful to divide action items into 'Today', 'This week' and 'This month'.

Time management	✪✪✪✪
Stress management	✪✪✪
Negotiation skills	✪
General development	✪✪
Fun	✪✪

Unit 14: Filling the gaps – using your spare time

This isn't a guide to finding a hobby, it's more about the general activities that you undertake – some as basic as eating – that have an influence on your stress levels and development.

Do try out the exercises as you go. Put them off until later and you probably won't ever do them. Read through the techniques. Make notes about how and when you can use them. And make sure you give them a try in the next appropriate forum.

Unit books

As we've suggested elsewhere, one of the important things to do in your spare time is to read outside your 'obvious' reading matter connected with your job. Not only is this better for stress relief, it makes a positive contribution to your personal creativity level, as the wider the scope of your reading, the wider the pool of concepts you have to draw on when you need to solve a problem or come up with a new idea.

I recommend very different books in this unit. *Light Years* by Brian Clegg is a tour through the history of our understanding of what light is, from the ancient Greeks to the present day. Light is one of the most significant parts of our life – we couldn't exist without the sun's light – yet it's something we tend to take for granted. Exploring what light's all about – and the remarkable new possibilities with 21st-century light technology – is an excellent diversion.

The other recommendation is any of Margery Allingham's Campion books – try, perhaps, *Sweet Danger* – theoretically these are murder mysteries, but with Allingham's strange twist that makes them so much more, yet wonderfully light and stress-free.

You can find more information on our unit books, or buy them, from our support site: www.cul.co.uk/crashcourse.

Web links

Spare time links for the Web, including more on popular science and Margery Allingham can be found at www.cul.co.uk/crashcourse.

14.1 Technique: TV turn-off

Preparation None.
Running time Two minutes.
Resources TV.
Frequency Regularly.

The television is probably the biggest waster of your social time. This isn't a criticism of TV – it is a simple fact. Few people list watching TV as a focal activity, yet most of us spend 5–20 hours a week watching it – a fair percentage of the time that isn't allocated to work or sleep.

I am not advocating giving up the television set. However, if you do find that your time to build on your social activities is limited, consider a few simple actions. Limit yourself to a single programme a day – if necessary, use a video recorder to time shift everything else. Limit your viewing time most days, with one 'splurge' day when you can watch a whole film or feature-length programme.

If you find this difficult, give your viewing a rough ranking and drop some of the lowest rated programmes. Be honest about this ranking – it's only for you. Don't use the traditional 'cultured' view that puts news ahead of arts programmes ahead of documentaries, then the rest – if you like soap operas, they get the highest ranking.

Feedback We all have days when we are totally worn out and want to slump in front of the TV. There's nothing wrong with this at all, provided it is some days, rather than all days.

Outcome If time freed up from TV viewing is used well – by making sure that it is concentrated on the social activities that you have decided are among your focal activities – it is a superb source of extra time.

Variations Some people find it helpful to record all the TV programmes they might watch, finding that in practice they don't watch nearly so many this way. This has limitations when it comes to live broadcasts, but can otherwise be very useful.

Time management	✪✪✪✪
Stress management	✪✪✪
Negotiation skills	✪
General development	✪✪
Fun	✪✪✪

14.2 Exercise: You are what you eat

Preparation None.
Running time 15 minutes.
Resources None.
Frequency Once.

There's no magic link between food and stress relief, but being broadly healthy is a positive factor in stress management, and diet is a contributory factor to health. While there are constant arguments about some specifics of diet – Do eggs increase cholesterol? Are vegetables better raw or heavily boiled? – some aspects are very clear. The fact that most of us should reduce intake of saturated fat and salt, while eating more vegetables, fruit, fish, fibre and (surprising to some) carbohydrates is hard to dispute. Similarly most of us ought to drink more water, especially if we are under stress when we are more likely to become dehydrated.

Spend a few minutes thinking about your diet. Identify a handful of changes that would improve your diet. Think about how you could implement these changes. For example, if you wanted to eat more fruit and vegetables, could you take a carrot and an apple to work for when you get peckish? Often the reason we don't eat 'better' food is that it's too much trouble – so make it easy instead.

Feedback Being careful about your diet can actually be stressful. Most of us don't find dieting particularly enjoyable, and at times it is a definite pain. Unless you have medical reasons for sticking to a diet, be prepared to break infrequently but quite regularly as a treat, to celebrate and to unwind. Similarly, a regular if controlled amount of alcohol, particularly red wine, isn't a bad idea unless you have associated medical problems. Although alcohol is actually a stimulant, many people find a moderate amount of alcoholic drink helpful in the process unwinding.

Outcome An improvement in diet (and hence physical condition) and a reduction in the stress caused by worrying about health issues should be the twin outcomes here.

Variations None.

Time management	✪✪
Stress management	✪✪✪
Negotiation skills	✪
General development	✪✪✪✪
Fun	✪✪

14.3 Technique: Play!

Preparation None.
Running time 10 minutes.
Resources None.
Frequency Regularly.

Play is a valuable technique that eases stress very naturally. It's sad that we lose a lot of our ability to play as we grow up, when we need it in this respect more than ever. This exercise is not about sport – in fact, most sport isn't play in the sense of being fun and unstructured. Play certainly can be about laughter, but here laughter is a secondary component of what is happening.

Find some form of play in which you can totally lose yourself. It might be playing PC games or board games or silly party games. It might be conjuring up a fantasy world on the tube, or trying not to step on the cracks in the pavement, or even saying 'Boing' every time you pass someone with red hair. Just play.

Feedback Such play can be undertaken pretty well any time of day (especially the types than don't involve technology) and can last a few minutes or hours. The great thing about play is not only are you putting aside all your everyday stressors, but the activity you are involved in is deliberately not important. It doesn't matter what happens, it is just play.

Some find it difficult to see how playing a computer game fits with this picture. The right sort of game is an excellent candidate. It has to be something you enjoy and, most importantly, must be for a single player. Yes, you can get involved, even excited while playing such a game, but underneath you know it does not matter in the slightest. This is why this a very different technique to sport, which is valuable as physical exercise but can provide stress of its own because the outcome is more important. Similarly, multiplayer games are not so effective because other people depend on you and can see how you perform.

Outcome We should all indulge in play more often. It's a great stress reliever.

Variations None.

Time management	✪
Stress management	✪✪✪✪
Negotiation skills	✪
General development	✪✪✪✪
Fun	✪✪✪✪

14.4 Exercise: The spiritual path

Preparation None.
Running time 15 minutes.
Resources None.
Frequency Once.

Achieving spiritual enlightenment in only 15 minutes is unlikely, but this exercise is about examining your options. The rest will take longer, quite possibly the rest of your life, but making a start can have an instant impact.

Having a spiritual rock to rely on is very valuable in stress management. It puts the problems causing the stress in context and acts as a source of inner strength. This won't help everyone, but given the statistics showing that most people have some religious belief, however unformed, it may be that you have a resource that you aren't using. Spend a few quiet minutes thinking about what you do believe, or would like to know more about. Most religions provide information and courses – consider looking into one or more approaches to spiritual stress management.

Feedback Spiritual matters are difficult to cover in a course like this. Apart from anything else, the media convention is to assume that religions are entirely non-factual, while a subject like astrology is given the benefit of the doubt. This contrasts surprisingly with the approach taken by scientists, who pretty well unanimously regard astrology to be without basis, but frequently have a religious belief, or are willing to consider the subject unproven. Until a few years ago it was often assumed that achieving peace spiritually involved following a Far-Eastern practice, but the Western/Middle Eastern religions offer better stress management by combining an external focus with equally strong traditions of meditation. If in doubt, the best guidance is probably to start by finding out more about the religion prevalent in your own culture, rather than searching out the exotic.

Outcome No one is going to join a religion just to achieve stress management. However, by giving the spiritual inquisitiveness most of us feel a chance to get off the rationalist reins for a while, there is an opportunity to explore the stress-relieving benefits of a religious belief.

Variations None.

Time management	✪
Stress management	✪✪✪✪
Negotiation skills	✪
General development	✪✪✪✪
Fun	✪✪

14.5 Exercise: Different values

Preparation None
Running time Five minutes.
Resources None.
Frequency Once.

This is a thought exercise. First consider the following research. A 1999 edition of *Demography Magazine* carried a study based on survey data from 1987 on 28,000 individuals. Around 2,000 of these people had died between the survey being taken and the 1999 study. In general terms, it turned out that people who attended religious services of any kind at least once a week lived, on average, seven years longer than those who did not. The comment of someone involved in the study was: 'People who attend church have friends to count on and a sense of their importance in the scheme of things.'

This exercise is not about attending religious services, but about considering how the difference in approach to life and personal values seems to have influenced the stress levels of those concerned. Spend a few minutes thinking about how you use your life. Are there opportunities to take a step back from frantic pursuits? It might be worth finding something that is your equivalent of being part of a religious group.

Feedback There is a always a danger in statistics of confusing correlation and causality. Two facts can have a matching pattern (correlation) without any direct link between them. For example, for a number of years after the Second World War, there was a strong correlation between banana imports and pregnancies, but no one suggests that bananas caused the pregnancies. Similarly, it is possible that there isn't a causal link between attending regular religious services and the extended lifespan. However, it seems likely that a combination of a local support network and the opportunity to step back from stress were major contributory factors.

Outcome There may be no outcome at all, but giving some consideration to the benefits of finding a support network and a way to put your life into context is worth the investment of a few minutes.

Variations None.

Time management	✪
Stress management	✪✪✪✪
Negotiation skills	✪
General development	✪✪✪✪
Fun	✪✪

Unit 15:
Devils and angels – anger and laughter

Getting angry can be useful as a release, but it's a double stress manufacturer. Unless you are totally isolated it generates stress in others, and it usually involves a loss of control – we all say and do things we don't really mean when we're angry – and as we've established, loss of control is at the heart of stress.

Laughter, by contrast (unless it's malicious) is always a stress reliever, a welcome release when under too much pressure. It might seem strange focusing a whole unit on a mere emotional response, but this merely reflects the convention that we don't act in an emotional way in a working environment – this doesn't mean, though, that emotions are constantly at play in what we do.

Do try out the exercises as you go. Put them off until later and you probably won't ever do them. Read through the techniques. Make notes about how and when you can use them. And make sure you give them a try in the next appropriate forum.

Unit book

I'm recommending a straightforward stress book in this unit. Although *Conquer your Stress* by Cary L. Cooper and Stephen Palmer covers some of the same ground as parts of this course it's useful background reading and can go into some aspects in more depth.

You can find more information on our unit books, or buy them, from our support site: www.cul.co.uk/crashcourse.

Web links

Links to Web sites on anger and laughter, and a series of columns from the magazine *PC Week* illustrating the funny side of consultancy can be found at www.cul.co.uk/crashcourse.

15.1 Exercise: Handling confrontation

Preparation None.
Running time 10 minutes.
Resources None.
Frequency Once.

Several techniques and exercises in the course relate to assertiveness and confrontation. This is probably the simplest but the most generally applicable. Having an argument is fine, but when neither side is listening to the other you end up with pointless confrontation. There are often better ways of reaching an outcome, but once you have got to confrontation, action is necessary.

Spend a couple of minutes jotting down what your first steps would be in these two confrontational positions. What would you say? How would you react, both physically and verbally?

A colleague comes in and starts prodding you, saying you've stolen her best member of staff.

A customer is complaining that your product or service has delayed him so he has missed an important meeting and what are you going to do about it? He is shouting.

Feedback It's tempting to ask the other person to calm down, but this often results in more anger. Don't tense up, and avoid the body language of tension. Don't laugh or smile (a common nervous reaction) – look sympathetic. Nod a lot. Keep your body open (don't fold your arms across your chest or scrunch down away from the person). Your first piece of speech should be in agreement. There will usually be some fact you can sympathize with. Continue positively but unthreateningly to say why you can't actually deliver entirely on the person's expectation. If you left it here, the person would simply return to the attack. So finish instead by saying 'and I'm sure we can…' or whatever. End with an action that might be acceptable to both of you, using the linking 'and' to make sure it's building on what has gone before, not arguing with it.

Confrontation is stressful to all concerned (including onlookers) and rarely results in a satisfactory outcome. This sort of exercise seems artificial to begin with, but you need practice to be able to speak naturally in this positive, inclusive way. Note, by the way, that many of us enjoy managed confrontation. There's something about feeling the adrenaline flowing and launching into the attack that can be very appealing. Just consider that this is not a great way to achieve results – leave it to fun activities, especially where there's physical exercise, to work off the adrenaline.

Outcome Defusing confrontation is a valuable management tool and a good defence against stress. Try it out.

Variations Look out for other techniques in books on motivation and assertiveness.

Time management	✪✪
Stress management	✪✪✪✪
Negotiation skills	✪✪✪✪
General development	✪✪✪✪
Fun	✪✪

15.2 *Exercise: Laugh!*

Preparation None.
Running time Five minutes.
Resources Notebook.
Frequency Once.

Stress can get into a feedback loop. The more stressed you are, the more unhappy you become. This unhappiness then results in further stress. A fundamental requirement is to break out of that loop, and a very powerful tool for managing this is laughter.

Spend a few minutes putting together a laughter lifeline pack. Note down everything you can think of that makes you laugh. Not a snide, put-down sort of laugh. In fact, not any nasty or calculated sort of laughter, but sheer, uncontrolled hilarity. It could be certain books, cartoon strips, films, comedians, TV programmes – or just a good evening out with your friends. Once you've got your list, see if you can have one or two laughter lifeline elements on call for when you feel down.

Feedback We don't find it at all strange that we are required by law to keep first-aid kits on hand in case someone needs some minor physical repairs, so it's rather odd that we don't give any consideration to our mental well being. Humour and laughter tends to be frowned on in a business context. Apparently we aren't supposed to enjoy ourselves when we are working. This sheer madness seems to derive from some Victorian work ethic, or the strange concept that humour and laughter is somehow not professional. Whatever the cause, it needs fighting.

Outcome Laughter is a multiple stress reliever, helping on the mental, physical and spiritual level. There are actual chemical processes at work that partly explain this, but a lot of it is down to the benefits of sheer enjoyment. Indulge!

Variations This is a particularly good technique to apply when others are suffering from stress. Get them involved in an evening of laughter. A trip to see a top rate comedian performing is probably best of all. There's something very refreshing about laughing with a group of other people.

Time management	✪
Stress management	✪✪✪✪
Negotiation skills	✪
General development	✪✪✪
Fun	✪✪✪✪

15.3 *Technique: Rage*

Preparation None.
Running time Two minutes.
Resources None.
Frequency Occasionally.

Rage is everywhere in the media. It might be that old favourite road rage, or newer manifestations like PC rage or airport rage. In fact, according to recent studies, rage is nothing new, but something insidious is happening. The media's use of these labels has made us all conscious of the existence of the phenomenon. And like it or not, the labels have given rage a certain legitimacy. These outbursts are somehow more acceptable because we know what rage is.

Generally rage results from over-stimulation. Driving is a classic example, where there is a constant underlying stress brought about by the need to concentrate on the road and cope with busy traffic. This leaves the driver 'too near the edge', ready to be pushed into a major stress reaction by a small incident.

Such rage is bad for both your health and your performance. If you feel anger welling up, take a couple of slow breaths and put the matter into context. For instance, when someone pulls in front of you while driving, think how trivial this would be on the pavement – why is it different in a car? Don't get angry, laugh at the other driver. Imagine that person sitting on the toilet. Mock his or her vehicle. Alternatively, put yourself in the other person's position. This can be particularly useful in circumstances like delays at an airport. The poor person at the information desk hasn't caused the delay – why get angry with him or her? Think how he or she must feel. Finally think of your own benefit. You'll get a better response if you are nice – don't rage, smile. Smiles are the enemies of thoughtless rage.

Feedback It's easy enough to write these logical steps, and another to use them when you want to tear someone's head off, or smash your PC. It takes determination and staying power to beat rage.

Outcome The benefits to your blood pressure and general stress levels far outweigh the cost of being disciplined enough to conquer rage.

Variations None.

Time management	✪
Stress Management	✪✪✪✪
Negotiation skills	✪✪✪
General development	✪✪✪✪
Fun	✪✪

15.4 Technique: Don't do that

Preparation None.
Running time Five minutes.
Resources None.
Frequency Several times.

This one sounds bizarre, but give it a chance. Being negative is stress inducing. The more you shoot things down, criticize (in a destructive way) and put across negatives, the more you induce stress in yourself. It seems that the brain is pretty dumb and has difficulty distinguishing between mental and physical processes. The more you think and communicate in a negative manner, the more you will stress up.

Next time you are having an energetic conversation, take a step back and monitor those words. It's the obvious negatives (don't, no, stop), the commands (must, will, should, do this) and the put-downs (idiotic, stupid, brainless) that you need to trap. The more you use them, the more your brain becomes convinced you are moving into threat and activates the mechanisms of stress. This doesn't mean that you should agree with everything, but try to phrase and think in a more open way. Don't tell people that they can't do X, ask them if they've thought of doing Y. Don't tell them they *should* do A, instead point that they *could* do A. Find things to compliment rather than to criticize.

Feedback Of course, you can't always avoid the negative. Apart from anything, phrasing everything positively would waste the richness of the English language. This exercise has a negatively phrased title – but I was prepared to take the stress for you. The point is rather to move the general feeling away from the negative into the positive. If it seems that this is being too soft on the other person involved, remember whose benefit this is for – yours. But you never know, you may get a more constructive outcome.

Outcome Negativity is a great way to stress yourself. By moving over to a more positive approach you can reduce this self-stressing – and probably get better results too.

Variations This exercise is worth repeating several times until it becomes more natural.

Time management	✪
Stress management	✪✪✪✪
Negotiation skills	✪✪✪
General development	✪✪✪
Fun	✪✪

15.5 Exercise: When you lose your temper

Preparation None.
Running time Five minutes.
Resources Pen and paper.
Frequency Once.

Think back to the last time you *really* lost your temper. What were the first warning signs that you were getting angry? What did you say? How did you act? Were the things about the incident that you regretted later?

Having thought through the incident, put together a checklist of actions you could take to counter uncontrolled anger.

Feedback Losing your temper in a negotiation wipes out any possibility of a win–win outcome until there has been a lot of work to undo the damage. It is much better if you don't lose your temper at all. Unfortunately, we are all human and many of us find that our tempers slip out of control before there's a chance to stop them, even if we are consciously trying to be restrained.

A good action plan might be:

- Get a five minute timeout. Get physically away from the others.
- Do a quick breathing exercise (see *Breathing is good for you* in Unit 16).
- Think through what made you angry and try to put it into perspective, compared with the importance of the whole negotiation, or even the bigger perspectives of life.
- Focus on the outcome, not the process.
- Go back looking for ways to get around the problem, rather than just reacting to it.

You need a plan that fits your temper and personality, so mix and match any ideas that seem to fit. Note, by the way, that controlling your temper does not mean you have to be soft with the other stakeholders all the time. It's like dealing with a child – you can tell them off and sound angry, but you shouldn't do it in a temper or you've lost control.

Outcome You will still lose your temper occasionally, but this sort of preparation will give you the best chance of controlling your temper before negotiations are damaged.

Variations None.

Time management	✪
Stress management	✪✪✪
Negotiation skills	✪✪✪
General development	✪✪✪
Fun	✪✪

Unit 16: Easing off – relaxation

It seems that these days we all find it harder to switch off. It's fine to give your all to your work, or your outside interests, but there comes a time when you need a break. Relaxation techniques can help make that detachment. They're also useful (particularly the less visually obvious ones) when you're in a stressful situation you can't escape from. The need for relaxation and the format of the techniques is based on physiological reality – it's not just a nice option, or a cranky alternative therapy.

Do try out the exercises as you go. Put them off until later and you probably won't ever do them. Read through the techniques. Make notes about how and when you can use them. And make sure you give them a try in the next appropriate forum.

Unit books

One of the techniques involves using the right kind of book. For many people, John Mortimer's wonderful Rumpole series, featuring his battered Old Bailey hack and defence council extraordinaire, is ideal relaxation material. Rumpole is funny, yet there's more than humour – the Rumpole series is feel-good writing at its best. I'd recommend the omnibus editions, such as *The First Rumpole Omnibus* as the most effective way to get a strong dose of Rumpole.

You can find more information on our unit books, or buy them, from our support site: www.cul.co.uk/crashcourse.

Web links

Links to relaxation Web sites can be found at www.cul.co.uk/crashcourse.

16.1 Technique: Touchy-smelly

Preparation None.
Running time 15 minutes.
Resources None.
Frequency Occasionally.

Massage has long been seen as a way of soothing stress. Whether used on its own or in combination with aromatherapy, it has a lot going for it. Like exercise, it helps the blood flow and relaxes over-tightened muscles. How you get your massage is up to you. You can give yourself some basic massages – scalp, neck, shoulders – while bringing in a friend with a suitable book should enable you to go considerably further. There's no doubt, though, that having a massage from a professional will produce the best results, especially as experienced hands will often be able to feel where the muscles are most in need of work.

Aromatherapy does not require massage, though the two work together well. Just breathing in the appropriate essence, or perhaps taking an appropriately scented warm (but not hot) bath can be effective on its own. You should be safe in do-it-yourself mode with commercial aromatherapy products, but it's worth taking advice if you venture into the heavy-duty oils used by professionals.

Feedback Like most alternative methods, aromatherapy has a mixed press. There certainly seems to be something in it. For example, British Airways is now providing lavender oil in its First Class wash bags. There seems some evidence that a quick squirt of this on the pillow aids sleep – a very direct help in stress management. Other claims are less well supported, but this has to be an area where the recommendation is try it and see. Stress is such a complex mix of the mental and the physical that what works for you is what matters, whether or not this is for physical or psychological reasons.

Outcome There's an essence of pure relaxation about massage, and aromatherapy for some makes it even more effective. If you are having trouble relieving stress, especially with associated physical tenseness, it is well worth trying either or both.

Variations None.

Time management	✪
Stress management	✪✪✪✪
Negotiation skills	✪
General development	✪
Fun	✪✪✪

16.2 Exercise: Ritual relaxation

Preparation None.
Running time Five minutes.
Resources None.
Frequency Once.

Ritual, a regular practice, is a powerful bulwark against stress. An established ritual for a small portion of each day provides an anchor for a fast-changing life.

In itself, the ritual doesn't have to be big or significant. And there are times when you will have to abandon it with good grace. But the norm should be that your ritual exists. Evenings are generally the best time, as the ritual helps you refocus after the workday. It might be having 10 minutes with a glass of red wine, or reading a story to the children, or watching *Coronation Street* or attending Evensong – the activity is less important than the nature of the ritual.

Sit down for five minutes and think about your life. What elements are potential rituals? How can you protect them? Try to give yourself something daily, preferably in the evening. You might also like to establish a weekly ritual at the weekend – here the evening setting is less important, but again it needn't take up too much time. Try it for a few weeks to get in the swing.

Feedback Ritual has got a bad name. If you say 'It's a ritual with him', the tone is condescending. The implication is that having a regular pattern of doing things means being stuck in a rut. There's a germ of truth there. If everything you do has to fit a pattern, then you are doomed in today's ultra-paced, fast changing, scintillating world. But it's not that simple. No matter how flexible you are, you can benefit from a small core of ritual. Like the family and the home it provides stability in an otherwise chaotic environment. Rituals mustn't dominate, but there should be a thread of them in your life.

Outcome Many of us already have a ritual but don't recognize it, and certainly don't give it the importance it deserves. Others currently lack an anchor and will benefit even more from this exercise.

Variations None.

Time management	✪
Stress management	✪✪✪✪
Negotiation skills	✪
General development	✪✪✪
Fun	✪✪✪

16.3 Exercise/Technique: Breathing is good for you

Preparation Find a quiet place.
Running time Five minutes.
Resources None.
Frequency Regularly.

It's a self-evident truth that breathing is a good thing – but there's breathing and there's breathing. Firstly, as all singers know, there are two types of breathing – with the chest muscles and with the diaphragm. The latter is more controlled and gives you a much deeper breath, yet it tends to be under-used, particularly by those under stress.

First try to feel that diaphragmatic breathing. Stand up, straight but not tense. Take a deep breath and hold it for a second. Your chest will rise. Now try to keep your chest in the 'up position' while breathing in and out. You should feel a tensing and relaxing around the stomach area. Rest a hand gently on your stomach to feel it in action.

Now lie on the floor or sit comfortably in a chair. Close your eyes. Begin to breathe regularly: count up to five (in your head!) as you breathe in through your nose. Hold it for a second, then breathe out through your mouth, again counting to five. Rest a hand on your stomach. Don't consciously force your rib cage to stay up now, but concentrate on movement of the diaphragm. Your stomach should gently rise as you breathe in and fall as you breathe out.

Feedback One of the great things about breathing exercises like this is that they can be performed pretty well anywhere. For instance, although while driving a car isn't the ideal position, you can still indulge in deep breathing.

Outcome A regular five minute session of breathing properly will provide the foundation for many other stress management techniques. It is simple and very effective. What's more it will help with your breath control if you sing or play a wind instrument.

Variations Don't miss out on this one – it involves little effort and it is very valuable. Ideally you should do it daily – some recommend breathing exercises as much as three times a day.

Time management	✪
Stress management	✪✪✪✪
Negotiation skills	✪✪✪
General development	✪✪✪
Fun	✪✪

16.4 Exercise/Technique: Pushing waves

Preparation Find a quiet place.
Running time Five minutes.
Resources None.
Frequency Occasionally.

It might be that the simple breathing exercise is enough for you – but try this too.

Stand with your legs slightly apart and your knees unlocked (lock your knees in the vertical and then just relax them slightly out of this). Push your bottom backwards as if you had a large kangaroo tail that you were resting on behind you. Make sure that your back and shoulders are straight. Now imagine a cord from the centre of your head to the ceiling. Let this pull your head up a little. Relax. Okay, that's the standing sorted out.

Now hold your hands in front of you, fingers pointing upwards and palms away from you, with the backs of your hands against your chest and your elbows by your hips. Keeping your hands vertical, slowly push them away from you until your arms are almost outstretched but so that your elbows don't lock. Once they are out there, slowly pull them back towards you with your hands horizontal and the palms pointing downwards. Try this a few times until the movement is slow, graceful and wave-like. Make the transition at each end of the movement as smooth as you can.

Now for the breathing. As you move your hands away from you, breathe out through your mouth. As you move your hands towards you, breathe in through your nose. Slow down the whole process so that your movements are as slow as your breathing can become. Close your eyes and continue with slow, graceful movements and slow deep breaths.

Feedback This is a Chi Gung exercise that is often used for relaxation in Tai Chi classes. It is mind-bogglingly simple, but extremely effective. Do try it; you will be surprised at how relaxed you feel. If this one doesn't work for you though – for some, watching the slow motion, concentrated effort of such exercises is both hilarious and excruciating, on a par with mime, so they feel silly themselves when undertaking the exercises – fall back on simple breathing.

Outcome Relaxation helps you drain the physical impact of stress and to give a chance to balance out the mental impact.

Variations Try different forms of relaxation to see which suits you best. Make sure that you assemble a portfolio of different styles and approaches to be able to cope with the range of pressures and stresses you are likely to encounter. Some should be capable of use invisibly in public situations. Others can be for private moments.

Time management	✪✪
Stress management	✪✪✪✪
Negotiation skills	✪
General development	✪✪
Fun	✪✪

16.5 *Exercise/Technique: Medicinal reading*

Preparation None.
Running time 15 minutes.
Resources Books.
Frequency Daily.

I sometimes think books should be labelled 'To be taken twice a day, or when stress arises.' Under the right circumstances, reading books is very calming. This isn't a prescription to deal with peak stress. If you are extremely worried about something, or bursting for action, you will not be able to get into a book. But books are ideal for chronic stress, when the little things in life wear you down.

In Unit 5 we looked at setting targets and slots for reading. Most of us don't read enough – in breadth or quantity. Have you started using those slots yet? If not, find two slots a day to do some reading. Then look at your choice of books. You need something that will take you away from everyday pressures. Don't go for a 'quality' novel about depressing people and their agonizing lives. The book doesn't have to be upbeat, but the last thing you want is to be depressed. Often genre fiction can be effective. After all, a fantasy or a murder is unlikely to reflect your everyday problems. Equally, readable non-fiction can work well. Look at areas like travel fiction, chatty business books (narrative books, rather than an action book like this) and business biographies, popular science or history.

Feedback There are many reasons for reading. Stress management is only one component. Sometimes, perhaps standing up on a crowded commuter train, reading passes the time without really doing anything about stress. To get the best stress relief you ought to be sitting in a comfortable chair with no disturbances.

If you are not certain where to start, check the Creativity Unleashed online bookshop at www.cul.co.uk/books, which has a combination of creativity, business, personal development, popular science and science fiction books to get you going.

Outcome Just because this technique is only applicable to the everyday accumulation of small stresses does not mean that it is trivial. Keep up that reading.

Variations Other media can be effective. Don't dismiss the TV and movies because they're down-market. Similarly, computer games can be good for stress relief. Adventure games have a similar effect to a novel, while an action game might push up the adrenaline levels temporarily, but will be cathartic in taking out your stress on a clear, identifiable enemy. (See our DVD recommendations at www.cul.co.uk/dvd for some suggestions on DVDs to stretch the mind.)

Time management	✪
Stress management	✪✪✪✪
Negotiation skills	✪
General development	✪✪✪✪
Fun	✪✪✪✪

Unit 17: Dealing with a troublemaker – de-stressing the interaction

Mostly the techniques in this unit are about dealing with a situation where someone else is causing trouble. It may be by sulking, it may be by being aggressive. It's essential to be able to deal with such circumstances as they hit both your time management and your stress control. Of course, because you are dealing with others you can't guarantee a result, but these techniques will help make things easier.

The final technique is slightly different. It is still looking at the interaction with others, and it's a technique that can reduce stress on you (though it can cause stress to others) – but the essence is to change the pace.

Do try out the exercises as you go. Put them off until later and you probably won't ever do them. Read through the techniques. Make notes about how and when you can use them. And make sure you give them a try in the next appropriate forum.

Unit book

Stressful interactions are usually made worse under difficult physical circumstances. We've all got angry out of sheer frustration with someone who has no connection with something that's gone wrong. In Frances Ashcroft's *Life at the Extremes*, we see the impact on the human being of the ultimate in difficult physical circumstances. It makes fascinating, if not always pleasant, reading.

You can find more information on our unit books, or buy them, from our support site: www.cul.co.uk/crashcourse.

Web links

Links on dealing with aggression can be found at www.cul.co.uk/crashcourse.

17.1 Exercise: Sulkers

Preparation None.
Running time Five minutes.
Resources Notepad, pen.
Frequency Once.

Sulking is a human reaction. We all do it to a degree. But some people can make it more than a few minutes of irritation. At the extreme, there are individuals who can bear a grudge for years. Such behaviour is less immediately stressful than aggression, but over time it will wear you down until it seems unbearable.

Spend five minutes jotting down what action you'd take if you had to deal with a sulker. If you actually work (or live) with someone like this, so much the better. Just having a plan can make a significant difference; because each thing the sulker does is very minor, it's easy to leave them in control otherwise. Here are a few tips that you might consider if they aren't already in your plan:

Sulking is childish behaviour. Just as you would with a child, don't let anger take over, or sulk back at the sulker. Ignore the sulks; be positive when the person doesn't sulk.

If you don't know why someone is sulking, try to find out. It will take several tries, as a traditional component of sulking is denying there's anything wrong. Use *Broken record* in Unit 18.

If you don't succeed in getting a reason out of the sulker, explain that you can't help if he or she won't talk to you, so you'll just have to carry on as usual, but you are very willing to discuss it as and when the person wants to. Really do carry on regardless.

Feedback If you let sulkers get away with it for a long period of time, you are playing into their hands. They can, apparently reasonably, argue that you are over-reacting if you are being driven to distraction by little more than a subtlety of tone. Don't give them the weaponry.

Outcome Sulking seems trivial but can evoke considerable stress if you are subjected to it over a long time. Counter it.

Variations None.

Time management	✪
Stress management	✪✪✪✪
Negotiation skills	✪✪✪
General development	✪✪
Fun	✪✪

17.2 Exercise: Nemesis

Preparation None
Running time 10 minutes.
Resources None.
Frequency Once.

This technique is only relevant if there's someone you have regular contact with who is a major stressor in his or her own right. Spend a few minutes thinking about the people you deal with. Is there someone who has a physical effect on your well-being? After being with this person, do you feel ill, are you dizzy, does your head or heart pound? How about damp palms or a dry mouth? If there isn't, fine. If there is, you need to do something. Consider these two major options.

In a surprising number of work cases, the answer can be to terminate the relationship. Actively avoid the person. Keep out of his or her way. Avoid stress. If necessary, make changes to one of your jobs to make this more likely. But this isn't always the answer, especially where the person might be part of your family. If you decide that the answer is to stay in the relationship, though, you can't leave things as they are. Try to stand back and observe a confrontation. What is about the other person that causes the reaction in you? Try to understand it, and look for ways of circumventing it.

Only you can observe your feelings, but it would help, if there's someone you really trust, to get his or her views on what is happening too.

Feedback It is tempting to think that we should be able to brush over any personal difficulties because we're 'professional people' or because personalities aren't important in business. In fact, personal aspects have much more influence than we admit. If there is a major clash that is stressing you, action is necessary.

Outcome If you are in regular contact with someone who causes you stress just through that contact, it is essential you do something about it, whether it is to sever the contact or to deflect the stress. Otherwise it can be a dangerously persistent stressor.

Variations None.

Time management	✪
Stress management	✪✪✪✪
Negotiation skills	✪✪
General development	✪✪✪
Fun	✪

17.3 Exercise: Bully off

Preparation None.
Running time One week.
Resources None.
Frequency Once.

We are all familiar with the classroom advice: 'You should stand up to bullies, they are cowards, really'. And perhaps we also remember the way that this advice seemed dubious when the bully responded by wittily punching us on the nose. Bullying doesn't stop at school. It is common in the workplace (and out of it). The difference is that threats and abused power usually replace violence.

It should be easier to face up to a bully as an adult, but the social pressure not to do so is often strong; even so, the advice stands. In some circumstances it will be enough to point out that it isn't polite or acceptable to act or speak in a certain way. If this doesn't work, calmly threaten to use whatever channels are available to get something done about it. If there is still no change, resort to formal means – it might seem overkill for bullying, but this practice can keep the bullied person in continuous stress.

For this exercise, spend a week consciously looking out for bullying in the workplace. Watch how you and others act. Observe how you are treated and how others are treated. Take action if necessary.

Feedback Perhaps you are fortunate and there is no bullying in your working environment, but even so, it will have been worth undertaking the exercise. It shouldn't have taken up much time, hence it's still reasonably instant, despite taking a week.

Outcome An awareness of bullying and the basic steps you can take to do something about it can help relieve your own stress and that of your colleagues.

Variations If you are involved on either end of the bullying and can't take an objective view it might be worth bringing in an external person to untangle things, but you are the only one who can assert yourself against a bully – someone else can't do it for you.

Time management	✪
Stress management	✪✪✪✪
Negotiation skills	✪✪✪
General development	✪✪✪
Fun	✪

17.4 Exercise: Cut the aggro

Preparation None.
Running time Five minutes.
Resources Pen and paper.
Frequency Once.

Emotion has a very positive part to play in your dealings and negotiations with others. However, when emotion shades into aggression your chances of achieving win–win go out of the window.

Imagine you are in a negotiation. The other party has a sudden outburst of aggression, thumping the table and shouting. What do you do? Spend a couple of minutes thinking about real circumstances where this has happened. Jot down a few things that have helped. Try to associate these fixes (and the suggestions below) with aggression so they come back to you automatically. Because you are countering a natural fight/flight reaction you need to make the responses pop into your mind immediately when you encounter aggression. Revisit them on a regular basis.

Feedback Generally it's useful to take a quick breather – attempting to do anything in the heat of the moment can fuel the anger. Then, a very useful technique is to divert the focus from people to the problem. However much the other stakeholders push in the direction of anger, stay calm and show how the obstacle to progress is the problem, not the people around the table.

As is often the case with emotional conflict, it can help to make the situation explicit. Explain that you don't like the atmosphere – that it isn't helping progress. Allow a few minutes time out. If necessary be firm and assertive (but not aggressive) about not taking this sort of abuse. Surprisingly often the aggressive stakeholder doesn't realize that he or she is doing anything other than having an intense discussion. Making your feelings explicit can defuse the situation.

Outcome If you can substitute a calm response for the natural reaction to aggression you are well on the way to recovering the negotiation.

Variations Try acting out this situation with a friend. Get him or her to become angry with you. It's hard not to feel the emotional response even in this artificial circumstance. Then practise your response.

Time management	✪
Stress management	✪✪✪✪
Negotiation skills	✪✪✪
General development	✪✪✪
Fun	✪

17.5 Exercise: Slowing the pace

Preparation None.
Running time Five minutes.
Resources None.
Frequency Once.

In undertaking a negotiation you are normally aiming for a particular goal. It's only human to want to reach that goal as soon as possible. In fact, you want it *now*. So it's a natural tendency to rush things to get finished. Unless there's an overriding time pressure, resist this urge. Slow down. This has two beneficial effects. It gives you a chance to get your facts right, to ensure that you say and do the right things. The more you are rushed, the more likely you are to make a mistake. And also slowing down will put the pressure to move on the other stakeholders. Seeing that you aren't in any hurry might force their hands.

For this exercise, spend five minutes thinking about how you control the pace of a negotiation or other discussion. You can explicitly slow things down, or introduce secondary factors that result in a more measured pace. You can pause to think. You can arrange breaks and timeouts. That's just a sample. Get together a 'slowing down' toolkit that you can have alongside you. All you need do now is observe the pace of negotiation when it is taking place, and be prepared to employ that toolkit.

Feedback Sometimes there is a real time pressure, but often timing is a much more arbitrary input to the process than might seem to be the case. Identify where time pressures are coming from and separate the immovable from the other stakeholders' desires.

There's something strange happening here. After all, the argument is that slowing things down gives you a chance to be more considered – but it seems to have the opposite effect on the stakeholders, who will come under pressure as a result of the timing. The reason for this paradoxical outcome is that the slowing down is under your control – so can simultaneously help you and hinder others.

Outcome Slowing things down will give you a chance to put your input in safely and may push other stakeholders into movement.

Variations None.

Time management	✪✪
Stress management	✪✪
Negotiation skills	✪✪✪✪
General development	✪✪✪
Fun	✪✪

Unit 18: Getting what you want – assertive behaviour

Being in control. It's a lovely goal, but all too often the outside world conspires to ignore your attempts to have things your way. It's easy then to react by becoming aggressive, trying to impose your will. At this point you are acting like a pack animal, where the dominant individuals can force acceptance. Sometimes this will work – but often the result in a human interaction will be the reverse of that desired – the other person will become less helpful, will actively attempt to frustrate what you want to happen.

That's people for you. It's much better, then, to move away from aggression and use assertion – holding onto your intention and putting it across firmly and unwaveringly, but without ever resorting to aggression. Always reasonable, always controlled, always *in* control.

Do try out the exercises as you go. Put them off until later and you probably won't ever do them. Read through the techniques. Make notes about how and when you can use them. And make sure you give them a try in the next appropriate forum.

Unit book

Assertiveness is a classic example of doing things differently – of putting what you want at the heart of the action, rather than the knee-jerk reaction. In Andy Law's book on the St. Luke's advertising agency, *Open Minds*, you can see the result of applying a similar approach to running a business. St. Luke's hasn't got the traditional aggressive management – it uses a very different style of assertion based on trust. Its people are its business, full stop.

You can find more information on our unit books, or buy them, from our support site: www.cul.co.uk/crashcourse.

Web links

Web references on assertiveness can be found at www.cul.co.uk/crashcourse.

18.1 Exercise: Are you assertive?

Preparation None.
Running time Five minutes.
Resources Notepad.
Frequency Once.

Being assertive is a great defence against stress. Imagine yourself in three positions. In each case, jot down what you would do.

- You are in the middle of a queue, having waited for half an hour. A young couple come along and casually walk into the queue right in front of you.
- You have just bought a new CD player. It didn't work, so you took it back. The replacement broke after the first week. When you take that back, the shop says it won't replace the player but will send it off to be repaired.
- A child you are looking after for the afternoon demands some sweets, but you have been asked not to give him any.

Feedback There were a number of options in each case. You could fail to stand up for yourself, as so many British people tend to do, pretending that the situation hasn't happened. Or you can steam in aggressively and demand to get your way. Or you can be assertive, making it plain what is right without being threatening.

Often an assertive person wears away opposition, not getting emotional but not budging from their position. For example, in the second scenario above, an assertive person would refuse to accept anything other than a replacement, but with good grace and without losing his or her temper. In fact, there's also a fourth way that children are particularly good at – sly indirection. In taking this approach, you get someone else to take the blame, or manipulate those involved without actually demanding anything. Although this approach can get results it can be damaging long-term to your reputation.

Note the distinction between assertiveness and aggression. Assertiveness may push the bounds of conventional politeness, but it is a calculated practical approach to reach an end. Aggression is an emotional response that usually has a negative effect on reaching a conclusion. Imagine that someone has just pushed in front of you in a queue. Contrast the assertive 'I'm sorry, you've accidentally taken my place' (combined with gently but firmly pushing back into position), with the aggressive 'Get out of the way you queue-jumping morons' (combined with a punch on the nose).

Look back at each of the three scenarios. Put together the 'best' aggressive approach you can come up with (best means most likely to get what you want here) and the best assertive response. Look at the differences. In each case, what action would you need to take to move from aggression to assertion?

Outcome Some of the techniques later in the unit will build assertiveness as part of your defence against stress – the point now is simply to decide how assertive you already are.

Variations None.

Time management	✪
Stress management	✪✪✪
Negotiation skills	✪✪✪✪
General development	✪✪✪✪
Fun	✪

18.2 Technique: Broken record

Preparation None.
Running time Five minutes.
Resources None.
Frequency As required.

We've all been there. You know you're right, but the person you are talking to just won't give in. You can almost feel the steam coming out from under your collar. Imagine a situation in which you have to complain about something. For example, you could be taking back a broken product and demanding a replacement, or asking for a refund in a restaurant. In such circumstances, use the traditional assertion technique of 'broken record'. Simply repeat your request whatever the other person says.

Feedback This technique is slightly risky, as there is the possibility of making the other person angry, and hence generating rather than reducing stress. Make sure that you keep your repeated request for the information low key and friendly. Nod, agree, say 'Yes, I see,' to the other person's reasons for not coming up with the goods – then ask again. This technique is best used face-to-face; it is too easy for the other person to just put the phone down. If you find it very difficult, practise some more – it becomes relatively easy and can even be enjoyable.

Outcome It is surprising how often this technique will whittle away resistance and get a result. It's not one you want to use too often, or somewhere you are a regular visitor, but it can sometimes be very effective.

Variations If there is a genuine reason to practise the technique, so much the better. This could either be in the sort of scenario used here (complaint) or when you are trying to get information from a reluctant source. A close variant is to keep up the same request, but phrase it differently each time.

Time management	✪
Stress management	✪✪✪✪
Negotiation skills	✪✪✪✪
General development	✪✪✪
Fun	✪✪

18.3 Exercise/Technique: Broken CD

Preparation Invent scenario.
Running time Five minutes.
Resources A stooge.
Frequency As required.

This is a variation on broken record – get a friend act as a stooge to try this one out as an exercise, as well as using it when you need to be assertive. Imagine a situation in which you have a point to put across in negotiation that you simply have to succeed with. The stooge is to counter your requirement. For example, you could be saying you need an order of at least a hundred items, or that you can't work at weekends. Think of at least half a dozen different ways of asking to have the same point accepted. They should be as different as possible without actually varying the outcome. Try different phrasing. Probe the other person for aspects of the point that he or she doesn't understand or has trouble with.

Feedback Sometimes when you are making a perfectly reasonable point you will be resisted. This exercise gives some practice in dealing with such a possibility by being assertive. Make sure that you keep your repeated requests low key and friendly. Nod, agree, say 'Yes, I see,' to the other person's reasons for not coming up with the goods – then ask the same thing again in a different way. Like most negotiation techniques, this is best used face to face; it's too easy for the other person to just put the phone down. If you find it very difficult, practise some more – it becomes relatively easy and even enjoyable.

Feedback It is surprising how often this technique will whittle away resistance and get a result, and it can be less irritating than the pure broken record technique of repeating yourself without variation.

Feedback If there is a genuine negotiation in which you can practise the technique, so much the better. You could also practise the technique when complaining about something or when you are trying to get information from reluctant source.

Time management	✪
Stress management	✪✪✪✪
Negotiation skills	✪✪✪✪
General development	✪✪✪
Fun	✪✪

18.4 Technique: Setbacks

Preparation None
Running time Five minutes.
Resources None.
Frequency Regularly.

Sometimes an apparently trivial setback can really hurt. Like most writers I have a thick pile of rejection letters from my early attempts to get published. Having a book rejected seems pretty low in the scheme of things, but when it's an idea you poured your heart into, rejection is very painful. The same goes for any setback. To make matters worse, failures sometimes come in clumps. It's not fate or being jinxed – if you think about it, a series of problems wouldn't be random if they were all nicely spread out. By the time you've hit your third setback in a row you can be feeling very low and very stressed.

The technique here is ancient, but it still works. If a child is learning to ride a bike we encourage it to get straight back on after a fall. Similarly, when hit by a setback, launch another initiative as soon as possible. This could involve a small change, be loosely related or be totally different. So, for instance, when I get a rejection on a book I might send the same proposal to a different publisher, or rework the proposal, or send out a totally different proposal addressing a different market. If you get a real downer, you can increase the reinforcement by doubling the response. If a rejection really upsets me, I send out not one proposal but two.

Feedback Timing is important. React quickly, ideally within a few hours. The knowledge of impending action will cut out a lot of the impact straight away.

This technique demonstrates the power of anticipation. Anticipation is often better than reality. If you can set up a positive anticipation of something that equals or betters the setback, you can largely counter its impact.

Outcome Some setbacks are so big that nothing will counter them effectively. But for the vast majority this technique will push you back into a positive frame of mind, not giving stress a chance to take a hold.

Variations None.

Time management	✪
Stress management	✪✪✪✪
Negotiation skills	✪
General development	✪✪✪✪
Fun	✪✪

18.5 Personality types

Preparation None.
Running time Five minutes.
Resources None.
Frequency Once.

People fall into a number of personality types. The exact number is open to debate – Myers Briggs, one of the best-known type profiles based on Jung's theories, recognizes 16 – but the important thing for the negotiator is to be aware of how you tend to act, and how others do. Consider your answers to these questions:

- Do you prefer the big picture or getting down to detail?
- Do you prefer to work alone, or in a team?
- Are you motivated more by personal satisfaction or the praise of others?
- Do you find a regular progress check helpful or irritating?
- Do you draw up priorities or to-do lists for the week, or would you rather have broad objectives?
- Are you better at coming up with new ideas or developing and refining existing ones?
- What is more important – using the right process or getting to the result most expediently?
- Are you more comfortable with an 80 per cent solution or striving for perfection?

Feedback You answered these questions a particular way. Others around the negotiating table would go for different answers. If other stakeholders are naturally inclined another way, you will probably think they are being difficult – in fact they are responding normally for someone of their type. Once you are aware of this being the case it's surprising how much easier it is to deal with others effectively. Their behaviour becomes natural rather than provocative. You can work together rather than in conflict.

If you can, take a full profile, like Myers Briggs or Insight. Get a feel for the different personality types and how you react to them. Be prepared to counter your natural reaction in a negotiation.

To get a better feel for what it is possible to achieve with an analysis of personality types, visit the Web site of the Insights Consulting Group at www.insightsworld.com. Explore the different parts of the site. Although it is primarily intended to sell Insights products it gives very useful background.

Outcome By being aware of your own inclinations you can avoid getting irritated because someone else is different, and hence stop negotiations snarling up over personality differences.

Variations It's rarely possible for everyone in a negotiation to take a profile, but you could see if the other stakeholders are aware of their own profile.

Time management	✪
Stress management	✪✪✪
Negotiation skills	✪✪✪✪
General development	✪✪✪
Fun	✪✪

Unit 19: Make the break – getting away from it all

Mostly this unit is about physically getting away. Sometimes we need to make a physical move – whether it's just going out for a drink of coffee or taking a holiday. And that holiday isn't just from business. Sometimes it can help just to be by yourself.

We begin, though, with a rather different sort of break, an inverted break – making a break from procrastination. Finding out what it is that we're putting off and why. Because you are never going to get away from it all unless you can first get away from the problems that are hanging over you.

Do try out the exercises as you go. Put them off until later and you probably won't ever do them. Read through the techniques. Make notes about how and when you can use them. And make sure you give them a try in the next appropriate forum.

Unit book

A very direct and simple recommendation here – *The Time Out Book of Country Walks*, edited by Nicholas Albery. Getting a regular walk, ideally in a country setting is a wonderfully effective way to get away from it all (provided you turn off your mobile phone). You don't need a book of walks to get out there and do it – but it can help in keeping you out of a rut.

You can find more information on our unit books, or buy them, from our support site: www.cul.co.uk/crashcourse.

Web links

Links to Web sites on getting away from it all can be found at www.cul.co.uk/crashcourse.

19.1 Exercise: Don't bury yourself

Preparation None.
Running time 10 minutes.
Resources Diary.
Frequency Once.

Almost everyone is guilty of procrastination. We put off the evil day when we have to make a decision. We put to one side the problem that is hanging over us because it is too unpleasant to deal with. We avoid giving someone bad news. The result is that we have a constant, nagging worry, stressing us from within. Because of the way the brain works, any such nagging concern is likely to keep resurfacing, disrupting the other things that you need to do.

Spend a few minutes thinking through your personal goals and requirements. Do you have any nagging worries at the moment? Are there decisions you really need to make, or actions that simply have to be taken? You can't do all these in 10 minutes, but you can decide when you are going to do them and make a note to remind yourself. Just the action of planning when you will do something removes a lot of the associated stress.

Feedback Do not confuse procrastination with living for today. Although, of course, you need to plan, and there's nothing wrong with enjoying your past, the only point at which you can actually live is now. If you are constantly thinking of the future you are totally missing out – and building up stress. Living for today implies that you don't worry about lots of things that might be. Yes, make plans, but then forget the future until it is necessary to take action. This is quite different from procrastination, where you are constantly worrying about which action to take, but never actually doing anything.

Outcome Avoid procrastination and the stress that is its inevitable baggage – but remember to live for the day.

Variations None.

Time management	✪✪✪✪
Stress management	✪✪✪
Negotiation skills	✪✪
General development	✪✪✪
Fun	✪✪

19.2 Technique: Café life

Preparation None.
Running time 15 minutes.
Resources None.
Frequency Occasionally.

A favourite quotation of mine, from that most philosophical of cartoon characters Wellington in the old *Daily Mirror* 'Perishers' cartoon, was 'What is this life if, full of care, we have no time to stand and stare?'. This little snippet from the W. H. Davies poem *Leisure* is not a bad motto for this particular exercise.

Every now and then take yourself off to a café – preferably one with tables on the pavement. Sit down with a cup of your favourite beverage and watch the world go by. Switch off your mobile, don't let your work or home life intrude, just soak up your environment and indulge in some people-watching.

This exercise will not take long, and will amply repay the time, so be prepared to do it during working hours if your boss doesn't mind. If you can take a coffee break away from your desk, do it.

Feedback This technique requires a degree of immediacy. If you have to get in a car and drive to the café, you have reduced the effectiveness. Ideally the location should be within five minutes' walk. If this isn't practical when you are at work, try to fit it in occasionally when you are doing the shopping. If you are lucky enough to work in a building that has built-in pavement coffee bars, so much the better.

To get the value out of this exercise you need to be alone. If you are working near the café (or if it's in your workplace) you may get people joining you to chat – that's fine, don't send them away, but try again another time. Similarly you really need to do the shopping on your own to get the impact.

Outcome We aren't very good at relaxing, but this is one of the few circumstances when most of us can easily unwind. Try it.

Variations None.

Time management	✪
Stress management	✪✪✪✪
Negotiation skills	✪
General development	✪✪✪
Fun	✪✪✪

19.3 Technique: Get away

Preparation None.
Running time Five minutes.
Resources None.
Frequency As required.

You need to take holidays. Let's say that again in case you missed the point: you *need* to take holidays. If you usually say with grim delight 'I always carry my leave forward to the next year', you are not helping yourself or the company. It's rare that anyone is so indispensable that an absence of a few days will make a difference.

A good stress-relieving holiday should provide a total change of pace, of inputs (both mental and physical) and of stresses. Avoid holidays that are stressful themselves. If your job involves driving, don't think that a driving tour of the United States is the best holiday (though the lack of purpose helps). Ideal stress relief holidays are those where the pace is slowed down. For example, taking a narrow boat along a canal, where you can't go beyond a walking pace, is a great unwinding holiday. Make sure that you have at least a week off – you need that long to really detach yourself. Take a few minutes to think this one through, and schedule a week's break in the next six months. Then stick to it.

Feedback When you go on holiday, don't be tempted to take your mobile phone or your laptop with you. I recently got an e-mail from a colleague who was on holiday with his family. When I suggested he dumped his laptop, he said he was only using it while the rest of his family were reading in the hotel room. That's not good enough. Keep a physical link to the world of work and all the psychological pressures will come pouring down it. Don't use e-mail – read a book or explore or swim.

Outcome A total break is a guaranteed tonic to refresh those batteries. It sometimes feels like the benefits are lost as soon as you get back to work, but in terms of relieving stress you will have worked wonders.

Variations None.

Time management	✪✪
Stress management	✪✪✪✪
Negotiation skills	✪
General development	✪✪✪✪
Fun	✪✪✪✪

19.4 Technique: Walkies!

Preparation Find location.
Running time 15 minutes plus.
Resources Suitable footwear.
Frequency Regularly.

Go for a walk. End of technique.

Well, almost. Most physical exercise provides good stress relief, but walking scores highly on a number of counts. It isn't challenging – a majority of people can do it – it doesn't make you look odd, and it should appeal to those who find most exercise mind-numbingly boring.

If possible walk somewhere you can take in the natural stress relief of the countryside (or at least a park) – fresh air, greenery, lack of traffic. But if you can't get to the country-side, at least get outside and really take in what's around you. Remember to use suitable footwear – trainers might not be your usual style, but they're much better than typical office shoes.

Feedback There are two approaches to stress-relief walking. You can either deliberately keep all your thoughts at bay, or let them work through. In the first approach, focus on your surroundings. Don't let your thoughts wander back to the office. Imagine you were an artist or writer or composer and wanted to capture your surroundings – take them in, both in depth and in overview. If there are people around, take an interest in them (not too obviously) – everyone is interesting.

The alternative approach is to pick whatever's going through your mind most at the moment – the big problem at work or home. Just let the problem and any surrounding facts slosh about in your mind. Don't make a heavy effort to find a solution – let things happen at their own pace.

Outcome Walking gives you the triple benefit of exercise, fresh air and an opportunity for your mind to work in a very different way. As an added bonus it's a defence against stressors because you're usually out of reach (don't take your mobile). Make it happen.

Variations Several times a week you should be able to go for a walk for 15 minutes as a sensible minimum, although half an hour would be even better.

Time management	✪
Stress management	✪✪✪✪
Negotiation skills	✪
General development	✪✪✪
Fun	✪✪✪

19.5 Technique: Going solo

Preparation Plan location.
Running time Half day.
Resources Transport.
Frequency Occasionally.

We are sometimes so obsessed with socialization – being together with our friends, family, spouse, children – that we forget the benefits of a little time alone. Take half a day to have some time totally on your own. Do what you find relaxing. It might be walking in the country or taking in architecture. It might be serious shopping or just sitting somewhere peaceful with a good book. The most important thing is to be alone.

Feedback If half a day doesn't seem exactly instant, bear in mind that there doesn't have to be lots of planning involved.

This technique is only effective for stress relief if you don't feel guilty about doing it. After all, it seems somehow treacherous to admit that getting away from your family or friends can be good for you or enjoyable. The implication seems to be that you don't like to be with them. Yet everyone sometimes needs a little space to be alone and often the pressures of work and family life leave little time unless you make it. Don't feel guilty.

Sometimes the hardest part is describing this need to those who are close to you and might dislike the thought you want to be away from them. Explaining how you need 'space' may be considered pretentious. It could be easier simply to arrange circumstances so it happens this way, rather than trying to justify it. This isn't a matter of lying or being devious – just fit it in with some other activity that the others want to do but you don't.

Outcome By being alone for a little while you can sometimes achieve a peace that is difficult to achieve under normal circumstances.

Variations None.

Time management	✪
Stress management	✪✪✪
Negotiation skills	✪
General development	✪✪✪
Fun	✪✪✪

Unit 20:
Bumf bashing – dealing with bureaucracy and paperwork

There's a wonderful book by John Gall called *Systemantics* (New York Times Book Company, 1977). I haven't made it a unit book because it's difficult to get hold of these days, but its subtitle *How systems work and especially how they fail* is a good indicator of what it's about. Gall points to the way systems grow in complexity of their own accord, and that you sometimes need to start again from scratch, rather than try to cut a system down.

Bureaucracy is like that. It starts off as a sensible system to get something done – but it ends up growing and becoming more complex. Then the original reason for it goes away, but the system continues, now only existing for the purpose of continuing to exist. A small percentage of the bureaucracy we encounter is necessary. For these activities – often the chores we decide must be done – it is possible to make sure that they have minimal impact on your 'real' activities. The rest can and should be resisted – not only will this save time, it's very satisfying too.

None of these techniques can be done individually as an exercise, but do read through the techniques. Make notes about how and when you can use them. And make sure you give them a try in the next appropriate forum. For the moment, this an ideal opportunity to catch up on your unit books.

Unit books

Our legal system is a classic example of a system that has grown and grown to the extent that much of it is only their for its own benefit. This is painfully obvious in John Vidal's book, *McLibel*. This documents the trial of two activists who were alleged to have libelled McDonalds in a leaflet that condemned the multinational's activities. In part it's a fascinating David versus Goliath story – but equally fascinating (and horrifying) is the bureaucratic nightmare of dealing with the legal system in what turned out to be the longest case in English legal history.

Another quite different example of bureaucracy – in this case how to deal with it – is Ricardo Semler's *Maverick!* in which the author describes the transformation of his family firm.

You can find more information on our unit books, or buy them, from our support site: www.cul.co.uk/crashcourse.

20.1 Exercise/Technique: Penalizing pen-pushing

Preparation None.
Running time 10 minutes.
Resources None.
Frequency Annual.

This is an infrequent (once a year should be enough) but valuable exercise. Spend a few minutes thinking about the non-productive work you do. Filling in forms, admin, etc. Jot down a list of the main activities. Highlight those which happen very frequently or take a long time.

Now take the highlighted items. For each one consider three options. First, could you stop doing it all together? Would the world fall apart if you no longer filled in leave forms but simply dropped your boss an e-mail? Would your business fail if you bought a packet of paperclips next time you are at the supermarket, rather than requisitioning them by filling in three forms in triplicate then waiting six weeks? Note which you can stop altogether.

Next look at items you can get someone else to do. If you do have to have leave forms, can your staff process them themselves? If you must be involved, can you make your involvement less frequent, or do less? Could you authorize leave with a single signature, once a year? Do you really need to be involved in paperclip purchase? Could you (or someone else) buy paperclips by ticking a box on an online form?

Feedback Don't spend too long on this exercise. When you've got the principle culprits sorted, stop – there's no point proceeding to the nth degree. Similarly, don't do the exercise too frequently – bureaucracy is high in inertia, so it tends not to change too quickly.

Outcome Time recovered from bureaucracy is win–win time. You get less bored, and the company gains time when you are doing something more productive. It's satisfying too.

Variations If you are very senior in your company, you can openly remove the bureaucracy. If you are junior and don't want to rock the boat it may be more politic to get on with things quietly without making too much of a fuss about it.

Time management	✪✪✪✪
Stress management	✪✪✪
Negotiation skills	✪
General development	✪✪
Fun	✪✪✪

20.2 Exercise: A file in a cake

Preparation None.
Running time 15 minutes.
Resources None.
Frequency Once.

This one's about filing – but don't stop reading now, it won't be too painful. The essential tool is a good set of trays. These can be stacked trays, drawers, piles on the floor (bear in mind the warning in the Introduction about appearances – see page 11) – whatever suits you. The first part of this exercise is to set up the trays. Label a set of trays (if you haven't any, use an alternative and change later if required). Most people need In, Out, Read, Today, This Week, File. You may have other requirements. I have Expenses and Tax, because I operate a small business.

Now you need two disciplines. The first is to use the trays properly. When papers arrive, they go straight into the In tray. When you deal with paper (see *Paper Mountains*, below), make sure items go into one of the trays (or the bin). Don't let anything stay in the In tray, or go into limbo. Oh, and check daily if anything should move from This Week to Today. The second discipline is the filing. It should be regular, but not too often – perhaps weekly. As you pass through your File tray, attempt to throw things away – many lawsuits have proved the dangers of hanging onto paper – if you must file it, make sure there's an appropriate folder. If not, set one up. If you can't be bothered to set up a folder, bin it.

Feedback These trays sound a bureaucrat's dream. They're not; you are performing triage. By forcing everything into a tray, it's out of the way, leaving you to get on with real work.

Outcome This exercise is about freedom from the pressure of a pile of incoming items. It structures your input, making it easier to handle.

Variations If your filing needs are small, handle it directly, rather than having a File tray.

Time management	✪✪✪✪
Stress management	✪✪
Negotiation skills	✪
General development	✪✪
Fun	✪✪

20.3 Technique: Scheduling admin

Preparation *A file in a cake.*
Running time Five minutes.
Resources None.
Frequency Daily/weekly.

Admin needs a firm hand to keep it under control. Before doing this exercise, make sure you have completed *A file in a cake* (above). Having done so, you should have a neat system of trays. But what to do with them? Each day needs slots in your diary for dealing with paper, phone calls and e-mails. Remember also to have some slack time for reading. You can schedule this (I like lunchtime) or use it to distract yourself when you are losing impetus on a piece of work – but if you take the latter approach, make sure it doesn't disappear.

When everything is neatly sorted into trays, though, your day isn't over (unless you are a filing clerk). At the start or end of each week, get a rough plan for the week to come. Check your task list. Look through anything already in the This Week tray. Rough out appropriate slots in your diary. Each day, perhaps after your first quick pass through the paper and e-mails, firm up the day's plan, taking account of the Today tray and your task list. The aim should be to have disposed of appropriate items by the end of the day. You won't always succeed – planning is inherently guesswork – but you've got something to aim for.

Feedback This sounds more complicated than it is; try it.

Outcome A routine like this makes time management possible. Without it, admin takes over or doesn't get done and you have regular crises.

Variations Exactly how you arrange this is down to your personal approach. Try to schedule admin when you aren't particularly mentally effective (see *Hot spots* in the next unit).

Time management	✪✪✪
Stress management	✪✪
Negotiation skills	✪
General development	✪✪
Fun	✪✪

20.4 Technique: Bureaucratic bounce-back

Preparation None.
Running time 10 minutes.
Resources None.
Frequency Occasionally.

Bureaucracy is a regular cause of stress. Almost all bureaucracy started innocently, but the red tape strangles the purpose leaving a stress-inducing tangle. Try a bureaucracy bounce-back session. This can be on your own, or in a team meeting if you work with a team. Identify those items of bureaucracy that cause you most stress and see what you can do about it. The action you can take depends on your position in the company and what happens to the output of the bureaucracy. These are the principal options:

- Do nothing – often in bureaucratic systems, nothing is done with the output. What would happen if you simply did nothing?
- Do it your own way – it may be you can fulfil the output requirements of the bureaucracy without going through the required processes.
- Get someone else to do it – this is particularly useful if someone else is trying to impose bureaucracy on you. Push the hassle back onto that person.
- Work the system – get the results you want, rather than those the system was designed for.
- Raise awareness at high levels of the system's inadequacy.
- Suggest (or better, implement) less bureaucratic alternatives.

Of course, some bureaucracy is essential for legal or safety reasons – but most of it isn't.

Feedback It is possible to do away with bureaucracy on a large scale. In the unit book, Ricardo Semler's book *Maverick!*, he describes how much of his company's bureaucracy from issues concerning security badges to fixed travel expenses was dumped. Staff even set their own salaries – but as with the expenses, everyone knows what they're getting, so there's little misuse. The combination of freely available information and freedom to act knowing everyone is aware of what you are doing is the most powerful weapon for beating bureaucracy.

Imagine you were going to do this in your organization. Totally bin all the procedures and rules and forms. Try jotting down why this would not work. Then for each of your negative points find a counter. There will always be a way to make it happen if there is an imperative. Of course some bureaucracy is there for legal reasons or safety – but most of it isn't.

Outcome The sheer pointlessness of bureaucracy is depressing and stress-inducing. Bouncing back from bureaucracy is a valuable tool to surviving business stress.

Variations None.

Time management	✪✪✪
Stress management	✪✪✪✪
Negotiation skills	✪
General development	✪✪
Fun	✪✪✪

20.5 Technique: Sharing chores

Preparation None.
Running time Five minutes.
Resources None.
Frequency Occasionally.

Spend a minute or two thinking through a series of typical days. Look out for regular activities that you don't enjoy, but you always end up doing. These chores could be at home (getting up with the children in the morning, washing up, ironing, putting out the rubbish), or at work (collecting the mail, clearing up, watering the plants).

Look at ways that you can share these tasks around more. Sometimes it will be just a matter of swapping a chore – doing someone else's chores can be surprisingly pleasant compared with doing your own. It may be necessary to renegotiate your division of labour, but if this is the case, go into it positively and lightly. Any attempt to charge in demanding rights is liable to wind everyone up the wrong way.

Feedback The division of a particular chore doesn't have to be equal. It might be that you quite enjoy the job despite its mundane nature but don't want to do it every time. In such a case, being given a surprise break every few weeks can be just as beneficial as a rota, and much less bureaucratic.

Sometimes, if you are the only one doing a dirty job, it could be because your view of what is important doesn't fit in with everyone else's. If this is the case, try stopping doing it. If you find you can manage without it, fine. If other people miss it, encourage them to join in from now on.

Outcome Chores are small activities that don't seem particularly significant. However, if it's constantly assumed that you will do the dirty jobs, you will find it depressing and stressing. Sharing the chores around makes a lot of difference.

Variations You could use a rota, and sometimes this is inevitable, but try to operate without one first. Few people enjoy the rigidity of a rota. Keep it for situations where the task won't get covered otherwise.

Time management	✪✪
Stress management	✪✪✪
Negotiation skills	✪✪
General development	✪✪✪
Fun	✪✪

Unit 21: The inner you – dealing with physical issues

Stress, and your ability to achieve what you want to achieve, are not purely mental issues. They have significant physical components. This is particularly true for those of us who spend most of the day sitting at a desk, with hardly any physical effort involved beyond pounding a keyboard or lifting a phone. To get an all-round picture we need to include the physical issues.

Do try out the exercises as you go. Put them off until later and you probably won't ever do them. Read through the techniques. Make notes about how and when you can use them. And make sure you give them a try in the next appropriate forum.

Unit book

I wanted to include a fitness book, but find very few of them particularly helpful – they often seem more about selling a brand (some Hollywood star, or oddly pronounced special regime) than about getting your body in trim.

In a way, the book I've selected is about a brand, but at least it's a brand with a difference. The book is *Fit for Life* by the eccentric polar explorer Ranulph Fiennes. Most of the other fitness books are about fitness for its own sake, or for looks (or just to make money for the author) – this is about fitness to *achieve*.

You can find more information on our unit books, or buy them, from our support site: www.cul.co.uk/crashcourse.

Web links

Links to some of the more informative (and less branded) Web sites can be found at www.cul.co.uk/crashcourse.

21.1 Exercise: Hot spots

Preparation None.
Running time Five minutes.
Resources Paper and two coloured pens.
Frequency Once.

No one functions at top efficiency all the time. There will be particular times of day when you work particularly well or particularly poorly.

Turn a sheet of paper sideways. Draw three parallel lines across it. Label the top 'High', the next 'Medium' and the bottom 'Low'. List hours along the bottom, from your typical waking time to your typical bedtime. Think through your day. When are the times (typically two or three a day) that you are most effective? Using the second colour, draw a bar along the top line for each of these periods. Now think when you are particularly sluggish and unresponsive. Again there will typically be two or three periods. Highlight these on the bottom line. Fill in the remainder of the day on the middle line, then join the segments with vertical lines, so you have a chart of your personal energy levels.

Feedback When planning activities, try to fit in with your time graph. High times are best for developing new ideas, key meetings, creativity etc. Medium times are best for everyday work, non-essential communication and meetings, and reading which requires concentration. Low times should be reserved for the humdrum – admin, reading requiring little concentration and so forth. Keep your time chart easily visible so you can refer to it throughout the day. When you have no choice about timing, be aware of the need to make extra effort when your energy is low.

Outcome If you use your time chart when booking meetings and deciding what tasks you take on, you will find that you get the best results for high energy activities, and make best use of your less productive times. What's more you feel much less sense of frustration.

Variations If you have clear variations on cycles other than the day you might produce a chart for these also, but usually the daily variation is the strongest.

Time management	✪✪✪✪
Stress management	✪✪✪
Negotiation skills	✪
General development	✪✪✪
Fun	✪✪

21.2 Exercise: Stress workout

Preparation None.
Running time 15 minutes.
Resources Notepad.
Frequency Once.

Regular exercise is not just good for your health, it is an essential part of a stress reduction programme. This section isn't about exercising – that takes two or more sessions a week of at least half an hour – it's about planning. Most people who suddenly decide to take exercise don't keep it up. Try this three-point plan.

1. Self-motivation. Find a driving reason to exercise (go for the gut, like staying alive for your children). Make sure it is at the forefront of your mind when you decide how to use your time.
2. Choose something you enjoy. This may seem self-evident, but many people choose a form of exercise that's trendy (the gym) or that's career boosting (golf). Find something you really enjoy.
3. Add value. Get together with friends and make it a social event, or choose an activity where you can wear a Walkman and listen to music or speech radio or book tapes or learn a language.

Feedback Your activity should be aerobic, maximizing use of the body. Typical choices are swimming, cycling, running or gym routines – avoid sports that don't involve continuous activity. If, like me, you find these boring, don't ignore walking. We're used to walking as a gentle stroll to introduce people to exercise. In fact, walking quickly can be an effective exercise (especially if hills are involved) with less risk of damage than jogging. What's more, walking is practical. I hate exercise for its own sake – having a goal of getting somewhere doubles the value.

Plunging into heavy exercise is not good for you. Get some guidance if you are in any doubt.

If you are having trouble finding any exercise that you really want to do, turn it around and try to build the exercise around what you have to do anyway. Have to take the lift? Use the stairs instead. Need to cross town for a meeting? Try walking it or use a bike. See 21.5 for more suggestions.

Outcome Exercise reduces physical tension and brings down levels of stress chemicals. It also builds up the body, helping general fitness and ability to cope. The physical control of stress is the foundation on which everything else is built. You can't overlook this one.

Variations None.

Time management	✪
Stress management	✪✪✪✪
Negotiation skills	✪
General development	✪✪✪
Fun	✪✪

21.3 Exercise: Sleep!

Preparation None.
Running time Five minutes.
Resources None.
Frequency Once.

You only have to speak to someone who has had a baby for the first time to realize how stressful going without sleep can be. We're all conscious of the limited time there is to live a life and want to squeeze every last drop out. That's fine, but insufficient sleep is a sure-fire remedy for stress.

In this exercise you spend a little time thinking about your sleeping and what you can do about it. If you have regular variations in sleep patterns of more than about an hour a day, you are likely to suffer. But it's one thing to prescribe sleep (and only you can determine how much you need), and it's another to get it.

There are mental and physical techniques to help. Make sure you aren't trying to remember something as you go to sleep. If something you need to do next day is nagging at you, jot it down, even if it means getting out of bed. Don't try to go to sleep straight after a passionate discussion – wind down first. If something is going round and round in your head, sit up and pin it down, don't try to force sleep on yourself. When you do lie down, use a calming, tranquil mental image to help drift into sleep. Some people find a warm, non-stimulating drink helps. Also a warm bath, followed by getting straight into a warm bed – but make sure the bath isn't hot, as this will stimulate rather than wind down.

Feedback If you are having problems getting to sleep, try relaxation and mental exercises before resorting to drugs. Sleeping pills are rarely an effective answer.

Outcome Sleep deprivation piles stress on stress until you are almost driven mad. If you aim for the sleep you need to feel well, rather than the sleep you can get away with, you are going to underpin all your other efforts in managing stress.

Variations None.

Time management	✪
Stress management	✪✪✪✪
Negotiation skills	✪
General development	✪✪✪
Fun	✪✪

21.4 Exercise: Stimulants stink

Preparation None.
Running time Five minutes.
Resources None.
Frequency Once.

At least, stimulants stink from the stress-relief viewpoint. They are sometimes valuable and often enjoyable. This exercise isn't an attempt to get you to give up stimulants, just to raise awareness of the stimulants in regular use so you can cut them down when under pressure. Anything with significant caffeine content is an obvious contender (coffee, tea, chocolate products, colas etc). If you are feeling stressed, cut down your consumption. Particularly avoid them before going to bed or you can have a double dose of stress from sleep disruption.

Other less obvious stimulants are alcohol and smoking, both often considered calming. Unfortunately, alcohol *is* a stimulant, and the effect of excessive alcohol can be to encourage actions that will cause more stress when the drink has worn off. Similarly, nicotine pumps up the heart rate, not something you want when you are trying to be calm.

Feedback Try a few of the caffeine-free alternatives. Most people, for instance who 'need' a cup of coffee to get going in the morning find that decaffeinated coffee is just as effective. These days, herb teas are much more pleasant than they used to be. Consider them if you are a tea drinker. Many people who have removed caffeine entirely from their diet say that it has a very positive effect on their general feeling of well-being.

Giving up smoking is a no-brain decision (though certainly not easy), but moderate alcohol use is much less clear-cut. With some evidence that a regular glass of red wine is beneficial for the heart, and general appreciation of the benefits of controlled use of alcohol, it's hard to argue against it entirely – but consideration of amounts and timing makes a lot of sense.

Outcome A reduction in consumption of everyday stimulants will help you to keep calm and to wind down at the end of the day. Most of us could moderate our habitual stimulant consumption to some degree.

Variations None.

Time management	✪
Stress management	✪✪✪✪
Negotiation skills	✪
General development	✪✪✪
Fun	✪✪

21.5 Technique: Integral exercise

Preparation Plan route.
Running time 30 minutes.
Resources Appropriate clothing.
Frequency Regularly.

Most of us are aware that we don't do enough exercise, but somehow never quite get round to starting a fitness programme. You'll find several other possibilities for exercise elsewhere in this chapter, but perhaps you've been avoiding those too. Exercise is a crucial component of stress relief, so it's worth trying to find ways to integrate exercise into your daily routine.

The easiest way to do this is to walk to work. Abandon the bus, train or car. Get a pair of trainers and some comfortable clothes and walk. If walking to work is not practical, look at ways to get 15 minutes or more continuous exercise in some other way around the workplace. If you can't drag yourself off to do exercise, bring the exercise to where you are.

Feedback It's easy to argue against this one. You live too far away to walk to work. Okay, get off the train or bus a little earlier. Park remotely. Start with around half a mile and build up to a couple of miles. You might also argue that clothes are a problem, but you can carry a change with you or keep them at work.

The other big excuse is that you just don't have time. This doesn't really work as an argument. In some cases you'll actually save time by walking. Even if you don't, we're only talking about getting out of the house 15 to 30 minutes earlier – hardly an immense strain.

Outcome You get exercise, you get stress relief and you've helped the environment – all in one go!

Variations Try to make your walk through a pleasant environment (countryside or a park) if possible – but don't worry if you can't. If you are looking for alternatives to walking to work, look for places to walk around the workplace (including stairs).

Time management	✪✪
Stress management	✪✪✪✪
Negotiation skills	✪✪✪
General development	✪✪✪
Fun	✪✪✪

Unit 22: Development through knowledge – using information to your advantage

Most of this course features three key components of personal development – time management, stress control and ability to negotiate effectively. But it would be simplistic in the extreme to suggest that is all that personal development is about. This unit focuses on expanding your knowledge base. Sometimes this will mean actually learning, at other times simply knowing *how* to get hold of a particular piece of information when you need it.

Such knowledge has a double benefit – not only can you gain information that you can put directly to use, and incorporate in the pool you draw on when you need to be creative, but having the appropriate knowledge can help save time, reduce stress and succeed in negotiation. Knowledge may be an additional factor to our three main themes, but it supports all of them.

Do try out the exercises as you go. Put them off until later and you probably won't ever do them. Read through the techniques. Make notes about how and when you can use them. And make sure you give them a try in the next appropriate forum.

Unit book

Knowing people is an essential to being able to negotiate effectively with them, whether we are thinking of explicit knowledge of individuals or more general knowledge of how people work. Business biographies make excellent reading in this respect. Both for this reason, and also as a guide to some people who really have taken control of their life, see Charles and Elizabeth Handy's *The New Alchemists*, a powerful study of 20th-century entrepreneurs.

To get the complete picture on using the Internet as an information resource see our second unit book *The Professional's Guide to Mining the Internet* by Brian Clegg.

You can find more information on our unit books, or buy them, from our support site: www.cul.co.uk/crashcourse.

Web links

Some links to help build your knowledge library can be found at www.cul.co.uk/crashcourse.

22.1 Technique: Capture ideas

Preparation None.
Running time Two minutes.
Resources Notebook.
Frequency Regularly.

Ideas are strange things, popping up at the most unlikely times and places. People have them in the car, in the bath, while walking, while sitting dreaming in a field, on the toilet, in bed … but hardly ever at the desk (and certainly not under pressure).

Leaving ideas uncollected is a bad move. Not only do you miss out on your inspirational gems, it generates stress. You will try to hold the ideas in memory. So for the next few hours you will be muttering 'I just need to remember X', or 'What was that idea, now?' Because idea generation often happens in the mental state between waking and dreaming, it's easy for the detail of an idea to fade quickly. Leave it longer and you may still be trying to remember the idea as you go to sleep, disturbing your night. And you may forget it entirely.

Carry around a notebook, small enough to keep in your pocket. When an idea occurs, jot it down. On a regular basis – at least weekly – revisit your notebook and turn worthwhile ideas into tasks.

Feedback Inevitably ideas will strike when you haven't got your notebook, or can't use it. Leaving yourself a message can help. Call your voicemail (handy in the car if you've a hands-free phone), and leave a message about the idea. Or borrow someone's e-mail and send yourself a note.

Outcome Capturing ideas provides the triple benefits of the idea itself, of not clogging up mental resources trying to remember the idea (always stressful) and of not being frustrated by losing an idea.

Variations Some people find a pocket recorder more effective than a notebook. It certainly means that you can capture ideas easily while driving. I find the notebook better, because I'm more likely to do something with the output – but try a recorder if it seems sensible.

Time management	✪✪✪
Stress management	✪✪✪✪
Negotiation skills	✪
General development	✪✪✪
Fun	✪✪

22.2 Exercise: Lifetime value

Preparation None.
Running time Five minutes.
Resources Company information.
Frequency Once.

Identify your company's top three customers. It should be possible to find out who they are – however big your company, this is the sort of information you ought to know. If you think you don't have customers, think again about everything you do – the customers will come out of the woodwork. Work out, in round figures, their lifetime value to the company. That is the amount they are worth to you each year multiplied by the number of years you expect to do with business with them.

Feedback Think of your overall value for the lifetime of the relationship to the other stakeholders in a negotiation – and their value to you. Think also of the lifetime impact of your negotiation on that relationship. Some aspects of lifetime value are easier to calculate than others. It's easy for a supplier to get a ballpark figure for a customer. It's harder to establish a supplier's lifetime value to you. One contributing factor is any benefits gained from the supplier's products, plus the particular impact of the unique reasons why you should go for that supplier and not some other (the supplier should be happy to provide these).

Other negotiations may be even harder to get into this mindset – but try anyway. For instance, in a union negotiation, it's fairly easy to see the lifetime value of the relationship of worker and company both ways if you think about it. Whatever the negotiation, lifetime value is worth thinking of. It needn't take long. This is a crude approximation for guidance, not an accountant's forecast. A high lifetime value for a stakeholder may make you prepared to go for a loss leader, and to make sure that the stakeholder is given the impression that you care very much about them. Even 'small' customers can have a considerable lifetime value. Supermarkets, for instance, might be less cavalier about doing deals with individual customers if they considered a typical family lifetime value could easily be over £100,000 ($150,000).

Outcome Lifetime value is an extremely valuable tool when assessing how much weight to put on strategic and tactical considerations in a negotiation.

Variations None.

Time management	✪
Stress management	✪
Negotiation skills	✪✪✪✪
General development	✪✪
Fun	✪✪

22.3 Exercise: Web research

Preparation Familiarize yourself with Internet mining.
Running time 30 minutes.
Resources Web access.
Frequency Once.

The World Wide Web, and to some extent other aspects of the Internet, offers a whole new resource for finding out more about the other stakeholders in a negotiation and what their starting position will be. We've already looked at using the Web more efficiently: now's a chance to put that expertise into practice.

Pick a large company that you might need to do business with in the future, and also a key individual in that company. Check out the company and the individual in a range of search engines. Use business information sources to get more detail on what the company is up to. If you've time in the exercise (you would certainly do this in a real negotiation) don't stick to the single company. Look at its competitors and suppliers as well.

Feedback There has never been so much information so readily available as is now the case through the Web. If you aren't familiar with the skills required to get the best out of the Web, take the time to read the Unit book, *The Professional's Guide to Mining the Internet*.

Initially this exercise had another section on researching the other stakeholders by conventional means, but I realized that there wasn't much left to put in it. Yes, you might use (say) the Wall Street Journal – but the easiest way to get to it is via the Internet. Of course there is still conventional research to be done, but it's very much the mechanism to fill in the gaps, no longer the primary approach.

Outcome There is no doubt that information is vital to negotiation, whatever the style or importance of the exercise. To ignore the power of the Internet in this respect would be to waste a massive resource.

Variations None.

Time management	✪✪
Stress management	✪
Negotiation skills	✪✪✪
General development	✪✪✪
Fun	✪✪✪

22.4 *Exercise: Knowing the opposition*

Preparation None.
Running time 10 minutes.
Resources Pen and paper.
Frequency Once.

When you are undertaking a selling negotiation you will often be compared with your competitors. This exercise is only for those who have competitors – but realistically, that's most of us.

Spend two minutes noting down who your main competitors are (if necessary limit this to the competitors involved in a recent negotiation). Then list each competitor's main products and services. For each competitor, note also how your products and services are better, and how the competitor's products and services are better than yours.

Feedback You may well find that you know a lot more about your products' benefits than you do about those of your competitors. PR people and salesmen quite often use 'silver bullets', documents that list all the advantages their products have over the competition. However, realistically, there will be some ways that the competitors' products are better – and if you don't know what they are, you will appear ignorant in negotiation, or even worse it may seem as if you are trying to mislead the other stakeholders, destroying any trust you may have built up. Of course you don't need to brag about your shortcomings, but you shouldn't try to conceal them either. Instead, make them a feature. Point out how these are areas where it doesn't do to be at the bleeding edge, or emphasize how your new developments won't take you a little way ahead, as the competitors are, but leap over this generation entirely.

If you found that you didn't know a lot about your competitors' products and services, book time in your diary to find out about them now.

Outlook Knowing your competitors' products, and their strengths, will only help you in your negotiation. Think of a military campaign – intelligence is essential.

Variations None.

Time management	✪
Stress management	✪✪
Negotiation skills	✪✪✪✪
General development	✪✪✪
Fun	✪✪

22.5 Exercise: Knowing your products and services

Preparation None.
Running time 15 minutes.
Resources Pen and paper.
Frequency Once.

Sit down with a pen and paper, but none of your company's literature. On one sheet of paper, draw up a list of your key products and services. Group them into blocks, and for each block write a line or two that summarizes just what that group is about.

On a second piece of paper, pick out your company's highest money-making product or service. Make that single piece of paper a sales masterpiece. Describe the product or service and how it is used, but make the description as enticing as you can.

Feedback Many of us struggle with this exercise. We don't know enough without the sales literature to back us up. (Note, by the way, that this isn't just an exercise for salespeople, but for anyone who is going to negotiate for his or her company.) Ideally you ought to be able to produce one of those detailed, exciting fact sheets for every major product and service. Perhaps it's time to do a little homework.

Knowing your company's range isn't just about getting the best deal on a specific product. It also makes it practical to bring other products and services into the deal and to sell a whole system, not just a product. The other stakeholders will want to see information on paper, but they won't be impressed if you have to scramble through the printed material yourself to chase up a fact. It is also useful if you are buying as well as selling – after all, each vendor is also a potential customer.

Outlook Knowing your products and services is a fundamental requirement if you are to negotiate on behalf of your company.

Variations See *Knowing the opposition*, above, for the other side of the requirement.

Time management	✪
Stress management	✪✪✪
Negotiation skills	✪✪✪✪
General development	✪✪
Fun	✪✪

Unit 23: Seeing through the fog – understanding what they're really saying

We've already considered controlling the impact of communications and this unit is about getting value from the communications you receive from others. Listening is a skill that often seems less valued than being a good speaker, yet listening skills are essential if you are going to succeed in your interactions with others. The techniques here go into listening, and also ways of getting through the fog that is often thrown up – sometimes intentionally, sometimes not – when we communicate with others.

Do try out the exercises as you go. Put them off until later and you probably won't ever do them. Read through the techniques. Make notes about how and when you can use them. And make sure you give them a try in the next appropriate forum.

Unit books

Communication and listening are often at the heart of the misunderstandings in Jane Austen's perennially readable novels. Rather than pick up some manual on neuro-linguistic programming, or whatever the flavour of the month is in the communication world, immerse yourself in an Austen book – but be aware of the communication under-tones. If you've been over-exposed to certain titles, try *Northanger Abbey*, if anything more comic than many of the frequently filmed titles.

You can find more information on our unit books, or buy them, from our support site: www.cul.co.uk/crashcourse.

Web links

Web links on the art of listening and on Jane Austen can be found at www.cul.co.uk/crashcourse.

23.1 Technique: Listen well

Preparation None.
Running time Five minutes.
Resources None.
Frequency Regularly.

Poor communication is a relentless generator of stress, and the area of communication most of us are worst at is listening. To improve your listening skills, start taking a step back from your conversations. On a regular basis, try to monitor just what is going on. Firstly make sure you are listening – really listening, not thinking about something else or what you are going to say. Use non-verbal cues to emphasize that you are listening. Lean forward, use eye contact, acknowledge that you've heard with 'hmm-hmm' noises. Try not to fidget, move around and play with things as you listen.

Strangely it's also important to leave the person you are listening to with enough silence to fill. While he or she will benefit from your non-verbal cues, talking can sometimes get in the way. When there is a silence, don't rush in to fill it, however tempting it may be. Sometimes the person who is talking needs silence to assemble their thoughts. Give the person a chance.

Finally, use your words to bring out the person's story. Use open questions to give him or her a chance to develop the topic rather than closed questions that force a 'Yes' or 'No' answer. At appropriate points, echo what you think you've heard so that you can confirm that you really are communicating. And whatever you do, look interested.

Feedback This may seem artificial to begin with, which is why it needs regular practice, but before long you will be considered a good listener. Don't undervalue the non-verbal side. Aspects like eye contact make a huge difference to whether or not you are perceived as listening.

Outcome For both you and those you listen to, good listening skills cut down the stress generated by misunderstanding and poor communication. You will also give the other person the added benefit of feeling valued, building his or her defence against stress.

Variations None: listening well is an essential for personal development.

Time management	✪
Stress management	✪✪
Negotiation skills	✪✪✪✪
General development	✪✪✪✪
Fun	✪✪

23.2 Exercise: Are they telling the truth?

Preparation None.
Running time Five minutes.
Resources None.
Frequency Once.

Next time you are really negotiating, or just talking with other people, be on the lookout for the suspicion of untruth, and try to be more analytical in your response. Everyone can manage detachment, but it takes practice. In each of the examples below, take a couple of moments to see how you would react before reading the feedback:

- You are negotiating with a very small company. They claim to have resources far and above those you know they can afford.
- A stakeholder is telling you about his problems with delivery. He won't meet your eye, often looking at the floor. He shifts a lot in his seat.
- A foreign stakeholder is very expansive, boastful even, about her position.
- The numbers don't add up in a stakeholder's presentation.

Feedback Here are some possible realities behind the observations. In the first example the small company did have those resources, by calling on other companies. The shifty stakeholder was telling the truth, but was worried because he hadn't been involved in a high level negotiation before. The boastful stakeholder was mostly responding to a cultural norm that is different to yours. She was also trying to cover up a weakness in her pitch. In the final example there was a simple error, no attempt at deceit, but it did give you a position of superiority that may help in negotiation.

If you have suspicions, tread cautiously and ask yourself 'Why?' – you may have misread the situation. Encourage the stakeholders to give more information. Make it easy for them to back out – defensive pride can devastate a negotiation. If you haven't got anywhere, try being upfront. Ask what's wrong. Be honest about your concerns. And if there's still no response, make it clear the lengths you will go to in order to make sure everything is okay.

Before responding to anyone else's lies, be careful that you are happy that your own statements are perfectly factual. There's nothing worse as a blockage to getting anywhere in negotiation than settling into criticizing each other's doubtful veracity. Watch out for the 'beam in your own eye' syndrome.

Outcome This short exercise mostly concerns raising awareness of the difficulties of reading a lie or misrepresentation. If you can take charge when the truth is in doubt you are more likely to get a favourable outcome.

Variations None.

Time management	✪
Stress management	✪✪
Negotiation skills	✪✪✪✪
General development	✪✪✪
Fun	✪✪

23.3 Technique: Play that back

Preparation None.
Running time Five minutes.
Resources A stooge.
Frequency Several times.

Unless you can really take in what the other stakeholders are saying you are unlikely to get the best out of a deal. In *Listen well* above, we focus on ensuring that you give real attention to listening, but that alone is not enough. Language isn't always great at communicating what we really mean. If you are to really listen, you also need to make sure that what you heard is what the other stakeholder thought he or she said.

Get a friend or colleague to talk to you about something he or she feels passionately about, but that you know very little about. Every minute or two, feed back to them what you think they said. Try this several times over a few weeks.

Feedback Sounding back what you think you have heard is a primary tool of the communicator. Without it you can never be sure that there hasn't been a breakdown of understanding, leading to all the confusion possible in a game of Chinese Whispers. Make sure you use different words, don't just echo exactly what you heard (a parrot can do this). It's possible for this feeding-back process to seem threatening, as if it is a criticism of what has been said. If you feel that the other stakeholder is getting fed up with it, say something like 'I'm sorry, I'm just not with it today. Can I just make sure I've got this right. You want to …' This way, the blame for the implied misunderstanding is on you, not on the other person.

Outcome Listening well is the hardest part of communicating. Unless you listen well your communications will suffer, and so will your negotiation. Testing what you heard increases your chances of getting it right.

Variables Like most communication skills, this benefits from repeated practice. Look for other opportunities to play back conversations and check understanding.

Time management	✪
Stress management	✪✪
Negotiation skills	✪✪✪
General development	✪✪✪
Fun	✪✪

23.4 Exercise: Remote negotiation

Preparation None.
Running time Five minutes.
Resources E-mail, stooge.
Frequency Once.

Modern communications mean that it is possible to conduct a negotiation without ever seeing the other stakeholders. Generally speaking this is not a good idea for a major negotiation, but it is fine for many smaller scale negotiations.

The two prime possibilities are the telephone and e-mail. Phone-based negotiations are the weakest of all options. You lack much of the subtext of a face-to-face meeting, and it is simply too easy to hang up. E-mail, on the other hand, has some real benefits for low-value negotiation. It automatically introduces the authority of the written word, and can provide worldwide negotiation despite time zones. In an e-mail you can propose a movement and give all the supporting argument before the other stakeholder gets a chance to counter-propose.

Get a colleague to help out in an e-mail negotiation exercise. Imagine you wanted to sell a PC or a car. Your colleague should play an interested buyer – someone who definitely wants what you've got for sale, but nonetheless intends to get the best deal they can. Undertake an e-mail negotiation. You might like then to try reversing the exercise, with your colleague trying to sell you something different.

Feedback In doing the exercise, aim to make the best of the medium, using its strengths to get your message across. Don't just type and send off an e-mail. Re-read it a couple of times, polishing it up as you go. I must reiterate that face-to-face is always best for significant negotiations, but e-mail has generated a very effective niche in these smaller concerns.

Outcome With e-mail added to your negotiating armoury you can take on a broader scope of negotiations – or use e-mail to encourage between-sessions movement in a major negotiation.

Variations As always, a simulation is no substitute for the real thing. If any opportunity arises for a real online negotiation, try it out.

Time management	✪✪
Stress Management	✪
Negotiation skills	✪✪✪
General development	✪✪
Fun	✪✪

23.5 Technique: Appearing naïve

Preparation None.
Running time Two minutes.
Resources None.
Frequency As required.

This is an apparently simple technique that can be remarkably powerful. In a negotiation you may find some points the other stakeholders bring up to be unacceptable. Rather than challenging them outright, use what politely could be described as a naïve response. (The less polite description is dumb.) Say that you don't understand them. Admit to your stupidity and ask them to explain the point in more detail. Be prepared to do this several times. Try this out next time you are in a meeting when something is said that seems strange or incomprehensible.

Feedback To be successful with this technique you have to be without pride, because you have to admit to not understanding. In practice, this is something people should do a lot more – if they did, there would be less disasters due to poor communication. But that isn't the reason for doing it.

As the other stakeholder has to expand on their point a number of things can happen. It can be exposed as unsubstantiated. As he or she tries to justify it, it may be that a pit is dug that can't be escaped from. Alternatively, the stakeholder could open up new variables. You might still not be able to do anything about this point, but the justification of the point might loosen up another point for movement. Or the repeated analysis of the point may encourage the stakeholder to give way. Even if there is no movement, you will have found out valuable information. But often an attack of naïvety can loosen up the arguments. And the great thing is, though you are effectively questioning the point, you are doing it in a non-aggressive way. You are admitting that you are being stupid about this, after all.

Outcome By seeming naïve you can achieve considerable movement without being threatening.

Variations This technique shouldn't be used too often or it will begin to seem to be a scheming tactic. It is a scheming tactic, but you don't want it to look like one!

Time management	✪
Stress management	✪✪✪
Negotiation skills	✪✪✪✪
General development	✪✪✪
Fun	✪✪✪

Unit 24: Finding the levers – making negotiation work for you

We've seen that negotiation is an essential skill. Negotiation normally involves change. The levers are the elements in the topic being negotiated that can be changed – the variables. Almost always there are more levers than are immediately apparent. A typical negotiating stance may be to state many variables as if they were fixed and constant. You have an opportunity by pulling on these levers to move the negotiation in your direction.

The techniques here are mostly group oriented, but you can try out the first as an exercise, and still make sure to read through the techniques. Make notes about how and when you can use them. And make sure you give them a try in the next appropriate forum.

Unit book

I'm recommending a straightforward negotiating title for this unit – *Everything is Negotiable* by Gavin Kennedy. It makes an excellent accompaniment to this unit as it stresses that everything you can think of is a lever, can be modified, can be negotiated.

You can find more information on our unit books, or buy them, from our support site: www.cul.co.uk/crashcourse.

Web links

Web links on the art of negotiation can be found at www.cul.co.uk/crashcourse.

24.1 Technique: It's yours right now

Preparation None.
Running time Two minutes.
Resources None.
Frequency As required.

In some negotiations theory and reality are widely separated. The other stakeholders know in their minds what the value of your offering is, but it's quite another thing to see it in the flesh. Whether you are buying or selling, trading or establishing facts, you can sometimes make a breakthrough in the negotiation by bringing reality to the table.

If you were selling something you could bring it to the table, or take the stakeholders to it and say 'Here it is. It's yours right now. Just...' If you are buying you can put cash or a cheque in front of them. Because it minimizes risk, the human urge to get something NOW if we can without waiting is very strong (just check out the subtitle of this book). If you can make that come true, especially with an actual physical presence on the spot, your chances of getting the negotiation to conclude successfully will be enhanced. Just spend a couple of minutes thinking through the practicalities of this approach for the sort of things you negotiate.

Feedback This harks back to one of the oldest techniques in the book – you see it in the movies all the time – slapping down the hard cash in front of someone's nose until they give way and accept it. It is, realistically, a very crude technique. But bearing in mind how much negotiation operates at the gut level, this isn't necessarily a bad thing. There are times when a figurative punch between the eyes can make all the difference.

Outcome By giving the stakeholders a view of the reality – and possibly the chance to walk away with it right now – you can maximize the chance of closing a deal.

Variations Even with an intangible like a job you can employ a variant of this technique. If you are headhunting, for instance, don't talk in a distant agency office. Walk them through the job, expose them to the place and the people. Tell them 'This is all yours.'

Time management	✪
Stress management	✪✪
Negotiation skills	✪✪✪✪
General development	✪✪
Fun	✪✪✪

24.2 Exercise: Starting prices

Preparation None.
Running time 10 minutes.
Resources None.
Frequency Once.

Price is inevitably important in buying and selling negotiations. When you are selling you must come up with a starting price. It's something most inexperienced negotiators can get very uncomfortable about. Try making a decision on each of these right now. You might not ever have to make such a decision, but think yourself into the position:

- You are a selling a house that has an unusual construction. The agent recommends starting it at 20 per cent under the typical market price for such a house. What would you do?
- You have written an excellent business book, but it's quite short. Books of this length are typically £9.99, but the publisher wants to sell it at £16.99 to focus on the senior management market. How would you react?
- Your company is bidding to provide a regular service for another company. Your first stab at an initial price is £150,000, but your accountant finds out that most of the competition are coming in at around £100,000. What do you do?

Note down what you would do, including a couple of reasons in each case.

Feedback In the first case, I would argue that by marking the house down we are saying there is something wrong with it. I'd suggest starting 20 per cent over market price, arguing that this is a unique opportunity.

In the second case, I'd suggest to the publisher that such a strategy needs to be more extreme. At £16.99 it seems like an overvalued thin book. It might be worth making it £79.99 with an expensive binding. It would be sold with a lot of very specific messages about the value of the book to a company, and its executive nature.

In the third case I would go in with an initial price of £110,000, but tell the buyer that I couldn't move on price like that. I would emphasize how much I had come down in price because I really valued the opportunity to work with them, as £150,000 really reflected the quality of my company's service, but I could make that big drop just to work with them.

You might not agree with all my arguments, but the important thing is that you are prepared to go in with a shocking price where appropriate, have the arguments to back it up, and don't cave in straight away. Similarly, you should know when to start reasonably and not move. It may seem strange that I've marked an exercise that's often painful for beginners highly on fun – the more you get into thinking boldly, the more fun it becomes.

Outcome Being able to set a bold but appropriate starting price is a great asset. Note that appropriate doesn't mean acceptable – just one that isn't going to cause the buyer to go elsewhere without discussing the matter with you.

Variations Take any opportunities you have to experiment with starting prices in real but safe negotiations.

Time management	✪
Stress management	✪✪
Negotiation skills	✪✪✪✪
General development	✪✪✪
Fun	✪✪

24.3 *Exercise/Technique: Throwing in the condiment*

Preparation None.
Running time 10 minutes.
Resources None.
Frequency Once.

Once upon a time, when you stayed in a bed and breakfast in the UK you were charged extra for 'use of cruet' – the salt, pepper, vinegar and sauces. This use of a small charge on the side for something everyone wants is still widely used to bump up income, if not in the hotel trade any more. A related approach can be used in negotiation to move things in your direction.

What the condiment can do for your negotiation is not so much add a little income as generate a new set of levers. If you can split off small elements of the cost as separate packages, you can then throw those back into the deal as a bargaining chip. 'If you can give us a guaranteed order for two years, we'll cover the packaging cost', or 'If you can see your way to doubling the order, we won't need to charge for either the pre-installation checks or the first year's servicing.'

Spend 10 minutes thinking about your products and services and identifying the condiments – the small items that are essential to the overall requirement but can be separated off as an individual charge.

Feedback The great thing about this approach is that you can generate movement from nothing, because you never intended to charge for the condiment elements in the first place. Make sure that there aren't too many and they are all known up front. There is nothing worse than a whole page full of add-on costs, or costs that are only revealed late in the day.

Outcome By dropping various near-fictional condiment costs you can achieve a considerable amount in return.

Variations None.

Time management	✪
Stress management	✪✪
Negotiation skills	✪✪✪✪
General development	✪✪
Fun	✪✪

24.4 Technique: There's always an 'if'

Preparation None.
Running time Five minutes.
Resources None.
Frequency Once.

When negotiating it's easy to feel positive about the other people involved. That's good – you want them to like you, and that is often best achieved by liking them back. But don't let this liking, or some obscure sense of chivalry, push you into the biggest mistake known to any negotiator. Don't forget the 'if'. Never give the other stakeholders anything for free – make them pay for it.

Say, for instance, they want you to cut your price, you can say 'I can see that would be advantageous, and it would be practical for me if we could up the order by 25 per cent.' Or you may be buying and the sellers say 'You'll have to wait four weeks for delivery.' Don't meekly take it between the eyes. Still be positive, but positively say, 'That's fine, if it's possible to throw in the maintenance for free, otherwise my cash flow is shot to pieces.' Or whatever.

Feedback I don't really understand why, but there's often a lemming-like urge to give things away, sometimes when they're not even asked for. Guard against this. Make sure the 'if' or 'providing' is always there. That way, any negative movement is to some extent countered. Otherwise, you are simply indulging in charity.

Outcome 'If' is as powerful a two-letter word for negotiation as 'No' is to time management. Each can be surprisingly hard to use, but once you do, you are well on the way to success.

Variations None.

Time management	✪
Stress management	✪✪
Negotiation skills	✪✪✪✪
General development	✪✪✪
Fun	✪✪

24.5 Exercise/Technique: Doing a special

Preparation None.
Running time Five minutes.
Resources None.
Frequency As required.

Every now and then there's a need for a little push to get a negotiation over the final hurdle. In particular, if you are selling, you might have use for this technique.

You have announced your 'final' price. The buyer says that she can't go that far, for apparently legitimate reasons. You feel that a small price reduction (well within your room for manoeuvre) should clinch the deal, but don't want to offer it as you feel that the buyer will want to go further. All the other variables have been explored. Where do you go? Think about it for a moment before proceeding.

Feedback A handy technique is to say 'I can't go any further – as I've said, this is my limit. But if I ring my boss, he might be able to give me another five per cent, provided you don't mind giving him an endorsement for the company. Would that be a problem?' You then ring the boss and leave them waiting a minute or two. Finally the boss rings back and okays the deal.

This technique not only puts a clear bottom on your pricing, it has the sneaky advantage of putting you on the other stakeholders' side. It's no longer them versus you, but both of you versus the boss. They will have a sense of relief when they get the go ahead, even if it's for something they hadn't intended to accept. Manipulative? A trifle. I wouldn't overuse this technique. But it will help out when you need to go a little further without losing control of the process, as has been proved in many used car and replacement windows sales.

Outcome Bringing in a special from the boss can often tip a teetering negotiation over the edge.

Variations Technically you don't have to bring in the boss on the phone, you could take note of a special offer or deal that hadn't been available up front, but the power of this approach is in the psychological effect of anticipation during the delay.

Time management	✪
Stress management	✪✪
Negotiation skills	✪✪✪✪
General development	✪✪✪
Fun	✪✪

Unit 25: Selling yourself – don't shoot yourself in the foot

Modesty and embarrassment are powerful enemies of effective negotiation. We don't like to push ourselves too much, and we often start crumbling, giving way on variables without even a negotiation taking place, because our stance seems too aggressive. It's important to be able to sell yourself effectively, without ruining your case, if you are to make a move towards getting what you really want out of life.

Do try out the exercises as you go. Put them off until later and you probably won't ever do them. Read through the techniques. Make notes about how and when you can use them. And make sure you give them a try in the next appropriate forum.

Unit book

This unit's book is an unashamed selling book. Called *Getting Everything You Can Out of All You've Got*, Jay Abraham's book is subtitled *21 ways you can out-think, out-perform and out-earn the competition*. This makes it sound about being the sort of aggressive sales-person who fleeces his or her customers – but it's not. This is about assertive selling, and is equally applicable to selling yourself as to selling consumer goods.

You can find more information on our unit books, or buy them, from our support site: www.cul.co.uk/crashcourse.

25.1 Technique: Talking yourself down

Preparation None.
Running time Two minutes.
Resources None.
Frequency As required.

You can be one of your own worst enemies in a selling negotiation. Unless you are hard as nails and don't give a damn about anyone else, the chances are you don't like to upset people – in fact, you quite like to please them. So before they've even got a chance to speak you can end up talking yourself down.

For example, you are asked 'What's your hourly rate?' (or unit price, or whatever), and you say '£100'. All of a sudden that sounds a trifle excessive. After all, you are dealing with a small company, or you've heard they are in financial difficulties, or the negotiator has a nice face. So you quickly add, 'But of course, it's negotiable.' Why not just stab yourself in the back straight away?

In fact, you can do attack yourself without even adding the rider. If you answer 'Around the £100-mark', or something similar, you are actively inviting the other stakeholders to lower your price for you. Even the number 100 sounds like a negotiating stance. It might be better to quote £99 or £101.

Feedback The other stakeholders are going to make it their goal to chip away at your price anyway without you helping them out. Now that you are aware of this danger, make sure that you are very clear about your price up front – and very happy that it is a sensible price to ask. Now get it fixed in your mind that this is the price that you are asking, however pathetic the other negotiators look. And tell them as if you were doing them a favour, not apologetically. Why should you apologize about your price if it's fair?

Outcome This is a painless technique that will increase your chances of getting a reasonable price in an instant. Don't give way to temptation.

Variations None.

Time management	✪
Stress management	✪
Negotiation skills	✪✪✪✪
General development	✪✪✪
Fun	✪✪

25.2 Technique: Getting endorsements

Preparation Target endorsers.
Running time 30 minutes.
Resources Mail and e-mail.
Frequency As required.

All negotiation requires an element of trust. The more the other stakeholders trust you, the easier it is to get some movement. In most cases, the other parties to the negotiation don't know you very well. This is where endorsement can come in. If you can get a respected third party to endorse your input to the negotiation, it is liable to give more weight to your case.

Endorsements can be both about you as a person and about parts or all of your case in the negotiation. Who you get to provide the endorsement depends on a combination of willingness to take part and suitability. The important thing is that someone respected by one or more of the other stakeholders has come in on your side.

As an exercise, put together a list of people you have dealt with in the last six months who might be prepared to give you an endorsement. Why not go the extra mile, and actually ask for it too?

Feedback Getting endorsements is something that feels harder than it actually is. It is easy to assume that you won't get endorsements, so you don't bother to try. And yet it often takes very little effort (beyond embarrassment) to get in touch with someone and ask for an endorsement. It's rare to get them if you don't ask.

While the obvious endorsers are other customers if you are trying to sell something, you can consider a much wider range of people. Provided the subject of the negotiation is interesting, or your case is strong it's surprising how often you can get perfect strangers to endorse your side. If those strangers happen to be famous, or influential in the eyes of the other stakeholders you have got a real advantage.

Outcome Endorsements increase the value of your argument and make it more likely that the other stakeholders will move in your direction.

Variations Don't give way to embarrassment about contacting strangers if necessary – it will be worth it.

Time management ✪
Stress management ✪
Negotiation skills ✪✪✪✪
General development ✪✪✪
Fun ✪

25.3 Technique: Delightful deals

Preparation None.
Running time Two minutes.
Resources None.
Frequency As required.

It is easy to underestimate the emotional content of negotiation. Because numbers and facts are being bandied around we can forget that this is, in the end, a human interaction driven by very human responses. How stakeholders feel will influence the negotiation, whether you like it or not.

For this reason, there is a big benefit to encouraging a positive atmosphere during negotiation. Your best weapon is delight. Delight in your products or services. Delight in the pleasure of dealing with the other stakeholders. Delight in the win–win outcome.

Regularly during the negotiation, remind yourself of all the good aspects that could come out of it. Smile at the other people. Force any negative thoughts away and think positively. You will be surprised at the results. As an exercise now, think through the last negotiation you were involved in. What could you have delighted in with a bit of effort? Don't let yourself say 'Nothing' – come up with at least five things.

Feedback Like most positive emotions, delight is a lot harder to fake than a negative. In fact, unless you've had lots of practice, the chances are that any attempt to fake delight will come across as false and smarmy. Instead, you will need to work on actually feeling delight. If you are selling, look for reasons to love your products or services. Whatever the negotiation, look for the good points in it. If you can get a good outcome, you and your company will benefit. That's something to look forward to, something to be positive about. Really try to enjoy the negotiation and the company of the other stakeholders. It might seem difficult to begin with, but it will come with practice.

Outcome Delight is a wonderful negotiating tool as it is very delicate and yet powerful. Done right, it is almost irresistible. And you'll enjoy the process more yourself – a good side advantage.

Variations None.

Time management	✪
Stress management	✪✪✪✪
Negotiation skills	✪✪✪✪
General development	✪✪✪
Fun	✪✪✪✪

25.4 Exercise: Selling your wider strengths

Preparation None.
Running time 10 minutes.
Resources Pen and paper.
Frequency Once.

Imagine that you are applying for a job. Thanks to excellent intelligence, you find out about all the other applicants. There are three others, each with exactly the same qualifications, experience and skills as you. There is nothing to choose between you on the area of the job itself.

Spend five minutes establishing what your wider strengths are. What sells you as an individual other than the specific experience and skills associated with your job? Spend a further five minutes looking at how you would use those wider strengths to sell yourself. How would you link them to the needs of the job and the company? How would you emphasize just how important these wider strengths are? What lessons for your work area can be drawn from the areas where your wider strengths apply?

Feedback At first sight this hasn't a lot to do with negotiation, but bear in mind that a lot of negotiation is about selling your side of the deal (even if the negotiation is actually about buying). Part of the preparation for a negotiation ought to be an exploration of wider strengths, and tying them back to the main requirement, just as you did in the exercises above. It needn't take much longer than 10 minutes, but it can have immense value. Don't overlook strengths that don't seem to have a lot to do with the deal – as (I hope) you saw in your own case, the impact of diversity is the whole point.

Outcome Giving thought to wider strengths and using them to influence a negotiation can tip the balance where the other stakeholders have little reason for making a choice. The more you can look out for wider strengths and their application, the better chance you have.

Variations If you have recently undertaken a negotiation, or are soon about to, take a few minutes to check out wider strengths.

Time management	✪
Stress management	✪✪
Negotiation skills	✪✪✪
General development	✪✪✪
Fun	✪✪

25.5 Exercise: Being you

Preparation None.
Running time Five minutes.
Resources Pen and paper.
Frequency Once.

Split a sheet of paper into two. In the left hand column, write down a series of keywords or short sentences that describe how you appear to the other stakeholders when you are negotiating. Think about how you speak to them, how you act, what you talk about and so on.

In the right hand column perform the same exercise, but describing when you have gone out for a meal with some old friends. Look at the differences between the two. Are there ways you could move the experience for the stakeholders towards that of your friends?

Feedback I am not suggesting that the stakeholders become your friends, nor am I suggesting that you go out for a meal with them – though that wouldn't be a bad idea. What would be very valuable in negotiation is if the stakeholders caught a glimpse of the real you, the one you show to your friends, not the artificial front most of us put on for formal events like a negotiation.

Anything you can do that helps the other stakeholders get to know and like you as a person will help with the trust that makes it so much easier to achieve win–win. The more you can become a real person to them, the less likely they are to stab you in the back and the more likely they are to extend human courtesy and warmth. This is why face-to-face is so important in negotiation – although people have fallen in love via e-mail or online chat, you are much more likely to get on in a reasonable timescale if you are in the physical presence of another person.

Outcome Make it hard for the other stakeholders to be impersonally nasty to you. If they know and like you as a person, they are much more likely to help you to a win–win outcome.

Variations None.

Time management	✪✪
Stress management	✪✪✪
Negotiation skills	✪✪✪
General development	✪✪✪
Fun	✪✪

Unit 26: Making the choice – supporting your decisions

All through our life, dealing with our time, dealing with others, dealing with events, we are making decisions. Often those decisions are made with little conscious input – we may not even realize a decision has been made. Sometimes, however, we need to bring the decision process into the open and consciously select the criteria on which the decision is to be made.

Do try out the exercises as you go. Put them off until later and you probably won't ever do them. Read through the techniques. Make notes about how and when you can use them. And make sure you give them a try in the next appropriate forum.

Unit book

David Freemantle's book *How to Choose* is interesting because it looks at how the very small choices we make – whether or not to smile, how we are going to behave, which route we take to work – can have a major influence on our success or failure. It's a very unconventional book about the nature of choice.

You can find more information on our unit books, or buy them, from our support site: www.cul.co.uk/crashcourse.

Web links

Web links for decision support and an Excel spreadsheet demonstrating simple option evaluation can be found at www.cul.co.uk/crashcourse.

26.1 Exercise/Technique: Taking notes

Preparation None.
Running time 20 minutes.
Resources Pen and paper.
Frequency As required.

Note-taking is an essential skill in managing a negotiation. You need to be able to take notes while keeping most of your attention focused on the discussion. Even more importantly, you need to be able to find a note without losing concentration. Graphical notes are ideal for this requirement. In this exercise, take about 20 minutes to make graphical notes of the main points you know about negotiating.

Start at the centre of a page or whiteboard and draw an image that represents the core of the issue. From this, radiate out branches that represent the major themes of the issue. From each of these draw progressively lower and lower level themes.

On each of the branches write one or two keywords above the line to say what that issue is. For instance one branch might be profit, splitting into costs and revenues, with revenues splitting into direct sales and indirect and costs splitting into the major cost drivers.

In general try to make the image organic. Start with larger and fatter branches at the centre moving to smaller and smaller ones and eventually twigs at the extremities. You might also use different colours for each major branch (and make all subsidiaries the same colour as the major branch).

Feedback Note-taking while keeping focus improves with practice. This exercise is one-off in terms of learning the basics of visual note-taking, but should be repeated by putting the technique into use. Every time you go to a meeting, try taking notes this way (whether or not you need any) as practice.

Outcome Better note-taking will result in staying on top of the negotiation and being able to respond instantly to any opportunity. It's a must.

Variations There are various alternative note-taking strategies but none can compare with this approach for negotiations.

Time management	✪✪
Stress management	✪✪
Negotiation skills	✪✪✪
General development	✪✪✪✪
Fun	✪✪

26.2 Technique: The timescales game

Preparation None.
Running time Two minutes.
Resources None.
Frequency Regularly.

Often stress is generated unnecessarily because we get a problem or a task out of all proportion. A handy way to put a problem in its place is to think about time. You'll find a number of exercises in this book that are about time management. This one is more about understanding time and its impact.

Next time you've got a problem or task that is nagging at you or causing stress, take a couple of minutes to think about two aspects of time. Is this really a problem now, or are you anticipating something well into the future? When does the task actually *need* to be completed by? Secondly, think yourself well into the future. Looking back from 10 years away, how significant would this problem or task be? How much difference is it going to make to the rest of your life?

Feedback Sometimes the answer will be 'It needs doing today' or 'It's going to change the rest of my life'. Fine – this may well be a circumstance where a little stress is desirable. If, however, it's one of the many, many problems and tasks that aren't urgent, or that you wouldn't even be able to remember existed in 10 years' time, however it turned out, it's time to loosen up.

Outcome Giving a time context to a problem or task, and looking back on it from an imaginary future is a valuable approach to remove plenty of unnecessary stress.

Variations This is an exercise that you can do whenever a problem or task gets on top of you.

Time management	✪✪✪
Stress management	✪✪✪
Negotiation skills	✪✪✪
General development	✪✪
Fun	✪✪

26.3 Exercise/Technique: Basic option evaluation

Preparation None.
Running time 15 minutes.
Resources Notepad, pen.
Frequency Once.

Where you have a number of options to choose between, a simple option evaluation can make it much more practical to go for the right choice. Try out this exercise on a real life evaluation, like choosing a new car.

List the options on a piece of paper. If there are more than three or four, try to eliminate some immediately as totally unacceptable.

Now list the criteria by which you will decide between options. What will you use to distinguish them? Again, keep to a handful of the most important criteria.

Finally score each option against each criterion. Either use a 1 to 10 scale or a High/Medium/Low scale. Combine the results.

This should give you a ranking of the options according to these logical criteria. However, it shouldn't be used as a fixed decision, but rather a guide to put alongside your intuition. If your gut feel differs from the logical assessment, try to see why. Are there criteria you are ignoring? Are some much more important than others?

Feedback Options can arise at several stages in a negotiation. You could be choosing between different bids, between different suppliers and products, between different combinations of variables. The only requirement is that you have a known set of options to choose between. This process helps you understand your decision better and come to a more effective choice.

Outcome By taking a systematic approach you can ensure that you have considered all the options, and that you are picking one with a conscious awareness of the criteria by which you will make the choice – the outcome is a more rational, thought-through decision.

Variations If you are finding wide variation between criteria, try *Sophisticated option evaluation* (below).

Time management	✪✪
Stress management	✪
Negotiation skills	✪✪✪✪
General development	✪✪✪
Fun	✪✪

26.4 Exercise/Technique: Sophisticated option evaluation

Preparation None.
Running time 20 minutes.
Resources Notepad, pen.
Frequency Once.

Sometimes criteria aren't enough to decide between options. You need to be able to give different weightings to say that, for example, price is twice as important as delivery times. The process used is much the same as in *Basic option evaluation*, but will take a little longer. As before, use the selection of a new car, or something similar, for the exercise.

List the options on a piece of paper. Even more so than with a simple evaluation it is important you restrict the list to perhaps three or four. Then list the criteria by which you will decide between options. What will you use to distinguish them? Again, keep to a handful of the most important criteria. Before going any further weight the criteria. Give one criterion the value 1 and give each other a value that reflects its relative importance compared with that key criterion – for example, if it's half as important, give it a value 0.5. If it's twice as important, make it 2.

Finally score each option against each criterion using a 1 to 10 scale. Then multiply each score by the criterion weightings before adding up the results.

This should give you a ranking of the options according to these logical criteria. However, it should only be a guide to put alongside intuition. If your gut feel differs from the logical assessment, try to see why. Are there criteria you are ignoring?

Feedback Options arise at several stages in a negotiation. You could be choosing between bids, between different suppliers and products, between different combinations of variables. Adding weighting to the process makes the evaluation more finely tuned.

Outcome By taking a systematic approach you can ensure that you have considered all the options, and that you are picking one with a conscious awareness of the criteria by which you will make the choice – the outcome is a more rational, thought-through decision.

Variations If the numbers are getting a bit of a strain, you may find it helpful to use a spreadsheet instead of paper. See the support Web site www.cul.co.uk/crashcourse for an Excel spreadsheet that demonstrates the basics of using a spreadsheet for option evaluation. One advantage of using a spreadsheet is that it makes it much easier to play with the effect of changing weights and scores which is essential if you are properly to understand the decision.

Time management	✪✪
Stress management	✪
Negotiation skills	✪✪✪✪
General development	✪✪✪
Fun	✪✪

26.5 Exercise/Technique: Options with guts

Preparation *Sophisticated option evaluation.*
Running time 15 minutes.
Resources Notepad, pen.
Frequency Once.

Logic can only take you so far – but many successful business decisions are based on gut feel. Does that mean you can ignore the concept of option evaluation? Not at all – but you need to flex the result. As a starting point you will need the output of the sophisticated option evaluation exercise. Look at the outcomes. Re-rank the options according to your feeling. Don't worry about the detail and the criteria, how would you rank them yourself?

If there is a difference between your gut-feel ranking and the mechanical one, get an idea of what it would take to move from the 'official' evaluation to yours. Play around with some of the criteria to see if you could make your gut-feel ranking come true by altering the scores or weights. For instance, you might be able to increase an option's ranking by decreasing the importance of price and increasing the importance of appearance (or whatever criteria you used).

If there isn't a difference, you are a very logical person. Don't give up on the exercise though. Play around with the scores and weights to see how sensitive the outcome is to changes.

Feedback Getting a feel for the ease with which you can change a decision is extremely valuable in coming to the right outcome. Performing this sort of sensitivity analysis can really help get a handle on what you are doing in preferring a particular option. Unfortunately the numbers quickly get messy, especially when there are several variables. There are a number of computer software packages on the market to assist with decision analysis (a spreadsheet alone can help a lot).

It is interesting to look at some historical decisions, whether taken by your organization, another organization or government. Look for the 'obvious' criteria and how those 'should have' influenced the decision. Often you will find that it is gut feel or hidden criteria that were given more weight, consciously or unconsciously.

Outcome As we've seen, options arise when choosing between different bids, between different suppliers and products, between different combinations of variables and so on. If you can understand the logical choice, and how much you have to contort it to match your gut feel outcome, you are in the best position possible.

Variations None.

Time management	✪✪
Stress management	✪
Negotiation skills	✪✪✪✪
General development	✪✪✪
Fun	✪✪

Unit 27: Going beyond the obvious – dealing with others differently

There are conventions on how we are going to behave when we deal with other people. Some are designed to help the process, but all too often they are based on greed – as in the typical business convention 'persuade the customers you are acting in their best interest, while screwing every penny out of them'. Others are there because this is the way things have always been done – for example, the assumption that the only transactions between a company and another company or individual should be based on cash. By going beyond the obvious, breaking these conventions, you can achieve a whole lot more.

Do try out the exercises as you go. Put them off until later and you probably won't ever do them. Read through the techniques. Make notes about how and when you can use them. And make sure you give them a try in the next appropriate forum.

Unit books

The success of fantasy books is often in going beyond the obvious. As well as providing good, stress-relieving distraction, an effective fantasy book is always challenging convention and the expected. This can be seen in the superb way that J. K. Rowling surprises the reader in the Harry Potter stories (if you are the one person left who hasn't read them yet, start with *Harry Potter and the Philosopher's Stone* (*Sorcerer's Stone* in the United States), with sudden twists that disrupt the apparently cosy, surprisingly conventional world she paints. The master, however, of challenging fantasy is Gene Wolfe. Try *There are Doors* for a delightful trip through twisted convention, or *Pandora, by Holly Hollander*, as much a murder mystery as a fantasy, but superbly effective on multiple levels.

You can find more information on our unit books, or buy them, from our support site: www.cul.co.uk/crashcourse.

Web links

Taking a different approach often implies being more creative – Web links on business creativity, plus some key areas of fantasy fiction can be found at www.cul.co.uk/crashcourse.

27.1 Technique: I agree... ish

Preparation None.
Running time Five minutes.
Resources None.
Frequency Occasionally.

There's no doubt that other people can be particularly stressful. Sometimes a desert island sounds attractive. A particular cause of stress is when someone has something to moan about. It's even worse if the person is aggressive too. You can just feel the stress meter shooting up as a finger is poked towards your nose.

This technique is particularly useful when dealing with such a person. Assuming that you don't want to agree with everything he or she says and give in entirely (this may be appropriate – if so, go with the flow), find some part of the argument you can agree with and stress your agreement. Don't answer the person's complaint directly, just confirm how much you agree with him or her.

For example, say you were dealing with someone who says she has been a customer for 20 years and is really upset by something that has happened, and wants compensation. You have no intention of paying compensation, so help to remove stress from the situation by saying: 'Yes, I can see that this is very upsetting for you, especially when you've been a customer so long'.

Feedback The technique doesn't just apply to a customer/retailer situation, but anywhere you might have a Mr(s) Angry who wants to complain.

The customer's response to the comments suggested above may be, 'That's all very well, but what are you going to do about it?', and at that stage to continue saying 'I understand how upsetting this is' will just irritate them. However, in many cases the de-stressing nature of agreement will be such that you can reach a compromise before the opportunity arises to fight back.

Outcome Reducing the level of anger in a confrontation will increase the chances of reaching an agreement – and will reduce the stress you are being subjected to.

Variations If you don't have someone angry with you right now, congratulations. Try getting a friend to play the part.

Time management	✪
Stress management	✪✪✪✪
Negotiation skills	✪✪✪✪
General development	✪✪
Fun	✪✪

27.2 Exercise: Exploring trust

Preparation None.
Running time 15 minutes.
Resources Paper and pen.
Frequency Once.

If you can establish a state of trust with the other stakeholders you are much more likely to achieve a win–win outcome. This exercise helps you explore the mechanics of trust.

Spend five minutes thinking about the trusting relationships you have had. With family, friends, colleagues – and in negotiation. What made you trust the other people? How was the trust built up? Note some key factors.

Now take another five minutes to consider how those factors can be built into the negotiation process. For instance, one might be 'delivering on a promise'. What can you do during a negotiation to be seen to deliver on a promise? The delivery would have to take place before the negotiation was over to ensure that the stakeholder got the message.

In a final five minutes, pull out the longer-term implications of trust. If you aren't just having a one-off negotiation, how can you use your key factors of trust to develop a trusting relationship over time? What should you avoid if you don't want to demolish trust?

Feedback Trust is probably the single most important success factor that is regularly absent from business. Parties in negotiations don't trust each other. Bosses don't trust workers. Workers don't trust bosses. Vendors don't trust customers (and vice versa). The need to establish trust is not out of a sense of moral values (though that isn't a bad thing) – it is demonstrably the only way to sustain a win–win relationship.

If it seems strange that the archetype of trust I'm recommending for you to use is the trust within your existing relationships, it shouldn't be. Negotiation is a personal human interaction. Effective negotiation has to be based as much on your own characteristics as on any theory.

Outcome The exercise delivers a better understanding of how you can build trust. It's then up to you to put it into practice in your negotiations. If it's a big turn around it may take a while before the other stakeholders believe you. Give it time.

Variations None; this is one you can't do without.

Time management	✪
Stress management	✪✪✪✪
Negotiation skills	✪✪✪✪
General development	✪✪✪✪
Fun	✪✪

27.3 Exercise/Technique: Beautiful barter

Preparation Prepare barter items.
Running time 10 minutes.
Resources Barter items.
Frequency Once.

When selling we often miss out on a real opportunity – barter. With barter, the goods or services you offer are worth cost price to you, but retail price to the other stakeholders: instant leverage. This means you can afford to be generous and still do well. Trade on retail price and each of you gets goods or services at cost. A wonderful win–win.

It may well be that you want to buy something from someone who doesn't need your goods or services. So what do you do? Find an intermediary. Someone who wants your output and has something desirable to the other party in your negotiation. Let's say that you were a holiday company and wanted to buy a fleet of vans. A garage is unlikely to want holidays. But your local radio station would love them as prizes. So barter your holidays for radio advertising, which can be offered to the garage, undercutting the radio station's rates. Again everyone benefits. The garage gets cheap advertising. The radio station gets a superb prize for 'free' slots, and you get your vans cheaply.

You won't undertake barter in 10 minutes. The purpose of this exercise is to examine your products and services and determine what and how you can barter. Then next time you enter into a negotiation you will have a secret weapon.

Feedback A while ago, a major pharmaceutical company was negotiating with an airline to provide all its air travel. The pharmaceutical's purchasing director had recently flown with the airline and noticed that it used a competitor's products in its first-class soap bags. At a crucial point in the negotiation, he pointed this out. The airline changed its soap bag supplier, and got the contract. No money changed hands to tip the balance – the movement was powered by barter.

Outcome Barter can change the face of a negotiation, bringing big percentages to play that weren't in the equation before. It's hard to understand why barter isn't used more.

Variations As an alternative, start from a look at your suppliers and customers. Are there ways that instead of using money you can use products and services in any of your transactions? Draw a quick map of how cash flows in and out of your organization. Each of those interfaces is an opportunity for barter.

Time management	✪
Stress management	✪
Negotiation skills	✪✪✪✪
General development	✪✪✪✪
Fun	✪✪✪✪

27.4 Technique: You won't win them all

Preparation None.
Running time Evening.
Resources Expenses.
Frequency After failed negotiation.

This is a special technique, as it should only be undertaken after a negotiation has failed. You will be feeling down. You could have won, but you didn't. We're not talking here about giving way on a few variables, but total collapse of the negotiation. No deal. Perhaps a competitor has walked all over you.

You could go into a corner and sulk, but it won't do you any good. Instead, consider having a wake. Celebrate the collapse of the negotiation and what you've learnt from it (make sure you do learn something from it).

If it's a big negotiation, go out for a meal or go to a show. Otherwise, you might celebrate by getting yourself a small treat. Whatever you do, though, do it with the intent of burying the failure and moving on. Celebrate in the knowledge that next morning you are going to start something even better – and make sure that you do make a start.

Feedback This isn't hiding your head in the sand. You have failed, and it is bound to be disappointing. After all, unless you go into a negotiation knowing that you are going to win, you are handicapping yourself with your own inability. But there is no benefit to be had from wallowing in the misery that can accompany failure. There are three key elements here – learning from the failure, giving the negotiation a send-off celebration and moving quickly on, ideally to something bigger and better.

Outcome There will be failures. Everyone has them. But coping effectively with failures is an essential if you are going to be successful as a negotiator.

Variations None.

Time management	✪
Stress management	✪✪✪
Negotiation skills	✪✪✪
General development	✪✪✪✪
Fun	✪✪✪✪

27.5 *Exercise/Technique: Aim high to get more*

Preparation None.
Running time 10 minutes.
Resources Pen and paper.
Frequency Once.

Look at the prices of a couple of your products and services (or equivalent). For each, jot down at least three good reasons for doubling the price. Now consider any recent contracts. Now jot down at least three good reasons for doubling the quantities involved.

Feedback Of course in every instance there will be a hundred reasons why you shouldn't double the prices. All the competition are operating at about the same price. That's how things have always been priced. And so on. But maybe you have been looking at the wrong competition. Maybe what you have to offer is so much better than the opposition that it's worth twice the price. There are always arguments for aiming high – bear in mind also that you will have to sell less to make the same amount of money. Of course, you still have to sell some. There is a balance. But you don't get anywhere by underselling yourself.

You will have seen some of this happening in *Starting prices* in Unit 24, but I wanted to pull it out as an exercise in its own right because it's a fundamental issue that goes across the whole of negotiating, not just starting prices. You will fail more if you aim high, and you need to support that high aim with great follow-through – it's no use bidding for a contract that's way out of your league and not fulfilling it – but aiming high is the only way you can rise above the rest. It is worth the risk.

Outcome Aiming high is necessary to exceed expectations. And if you don't exceed expectations, you will be never more than moderately regarded or successful. No more to say.

Variations Try the same exercise, quadrupling the prices.

Time management	✪
Stress management	✪✪
Negotiation skills	✪✪✪✪
General development	✪✪✪
Fun	✪✪

Unit 28: Be prepared – planning for success

It's easy to picture negotiation, dealing with others, as depending purely on your ability to wing it – to make it up as you go along. And there's no doubting that it can be very helpful being able to pull verbal rabbits out of the hat. However, it's equally true that you can't beat preparation. If you know what's at the heart of your sell, you can improvise – if you don't, you will flounder. If you know what you are aiming for you can be flexible. If you don't, you are simply blundering about. Being great at spur-of-the-moment dealings is helped vastly by preparation.

Do try out the exercises as you go. Put them off until later and you probably won't ever do them. Read through the techniques. Make notes about how and when you can use them. And make sure you give them a try in the next appropriate forum.

Unit book

Being prepared implies to some extent looking into the future, inevitably a flawed exercise at best. A fascinating insight into what's possible, and the limitations of any such attempt, is Alvin Toffler's *Future Shock*, a book from the last century looking forward at the way society might change, particularly under the influence of technology.

You can find more information on our unit books, or buy them, from our support site: www.cul.co.uk/crashcourse.

Web links

Links on planning can be found at www.cul.co.uk/crashcourse.

28.1 Technique: Stage fright

Preparation Requirement to give presentation.
Running time 15 minutes.
Resources None.
Frequency Occasionally.

Most of us have to speak to a large audience occasionally. For some it comes naturally, but for many it is a frightening experience. Next time you have a large presentation to give, use this planning exercise to counter that stress. As soon as you know you are presenting, put together a rough set of milestones. Something like: presentation ready, script ready, rehearsed, packed. Some of the stress with presentations comes long before the event – the more you are prepared, the less it will hover in your mind.

Several days before you are due to present, run through the presentation in full. You may feel stupid standing in front of your PC talking to the air, but a run-through helps with timings and enables you to spot sections that need rewriting or don't work. If necessary do this two or three times, until your notes are just an occasional reference. It's fine to write a detailed prose script, by the way, but don't read it. Condense it down to keywords to use on the day.

When it comes to the event, explore the venue first if possible – it's less stressful to present in a familiar environment. Make sure the technology works (and you've got a backup in case it doesn't). Just before the presentation do a breathing exercise. Get yourself into a positive frame of mind. Smile a lot. Know it's going to succeed. Then go out and enjoy it. While presenting, scan the audience, but stick longer with the faces that give positive feedback.

Feedback Everyone who goes on stage gets butterflies in the stomach. Some professional actors suffer terribly from stage fright. Don't let this perfectly natural reaction turn to excessive stress. When you give a presentation you are acting. Act yourself into a positive role. Enjoy it – everyone can.

Outcome Presentations always involve stress, but by being appropriately prepared you can limit this to positive stress.

Variations None.

Time management	✪✪
Stress management	✪✪✪✪
Negotiation skills	✪
General development	✪✪✪
Fun	✪✪

28.2 Exercise/Technique: Your USP

Preparation None.
Running time 10 minutes.
Resources None.
Frequency Once.

Whether or not you are literally selling in a negotiation, the act of negotiating will have an element of selling in it – selling your proposition, selling your side of the argument. In marketing, an important contributory factor is the USP – the unique selling proposition. Spend a few minutes thinking what your USP should be for a particular deal coming up. If you don't have one lined up, develop the USP for you as a person that you might use in getting a job.

A USP should be short, sharp and memorable, getting through to the key essence of the selling proposition in a single sentence. It might be as broad as 'Never knowingly undersold' or 'We try harder' or as specific as '20 per cent cheaper than any competitor' or 'The only all-night chemist that delivers'.

Feedback You may not necessarily come out with your USP in a negotiation (though if it's a good one, you ought to – and to hammer it home however you can). Even if you don't, though, it's valuable to have it in mind as a focus for your argument of why things should go your way.

If your negotiation is primarily about finding an acceptable outcome – for instance union negotiations with a company – don't make the assumption that this isn't for you. Like it or not, you are still selling your position, your point of view. Even if the whole concept of selling is one that sits uncomfortably, you can benefit from a USP for a negotiation.

Outcome As a condensation of the unique value of the proposition, the USP has proved a fundamental marketing tool – it can also benefit anyone involved in a negotiation.

Variations None.

Time management	✪
Stress management	✪✪✪✪
Negotiation skills	✪✪✪✪
General development	✪✪✪✪
Fun	✪✪

28.3 Exercise/Technique: Setting targets

Preparation None.
Running time 30 minutes.
Resources None.
Frequency Once.

When you are sitting in a negotiation and pressure is coming from all directions, it is no time to be indulging in higher mathematics. It's then that any preparation you can put in pays off. This exercise focuses on two prime targets – trade-offs and final positions.

As an exercise, put together a list of variables for an imaginary negotiation. For each draw up a table showing the best, worst and fair outcome. The best outcome is the value that you could reach if everything went your way, being realistic. The worst is the value beyond which you simply can't go because it makes the whole negotiation non-viable. The fair value is one that you would be comfortable with, being neither outstanding nor disastrous.

On the same sheet of paper, if possible, draw up some potential trade-offs. Consider the variables in combination. If the other stakeholders gave way on one variable, what would you give in return?

Feedback If you have information on a real historical negotiation, use that in the exercise instead. Remember *Another lever* from Unit 1 when undertaking this exercise. Once you have got your targets together, take a few minutes to look for other variables that you could bring into the equation.

Outcome A positions and trade-offs document is one of the most important you can take into a negotiation. If you have a superb memory, you would be best memorizing it. If you can't manage this, make sure it is in a form that you can read easily – but the other stakeholders can't.

Variations It is worth practising using your targets. Come up with (or even better get someone else to come up with) a series of random movements of variables. See how you would react, given your targets.

Time management	✪
Stress management	✪✪✪
Negotiation skills	✪✪✪✪
General development	✪✪✪
Fun	✪✪

28.4 Exercise: Future visions

Preparation Read up on a negotiation.
Running time Five minutes.
Resources Pen and paper.
Frequency Once.

Find a negotiation that is just about to start or is underway. It could involve your company, or just be a negotiation that is in the news. Read up as much you can on the negotiation (this isn't part of the five minutes).

Now take a pen and paper and try to put down a word picture of the ideal outcome from your viewpoint. If you are any good at drawing, you might like to include actual pictures too. Capture as much as you can in this vision of the way things could be as a result of the negotiation.

Feedback All negotiations are about the future, something that we can't see. Because the future is inevitably a fuzzy commodity we all benefit from being handed concrete examples of what it is going to be like. This could be anything from a description, through an artist's impression to a full scale mock-up, depending on the resources you have and the type of negotiation that is under way.

It can be a huge benefit to your side of the discussion if you can realize a vision in this way, making the fuzzy possibilities of what might be into a clear future. The crudest version of this involves money. Actually putting cash money or a cheque into someone's hands, the technique described in *It's yours right now* (Unit 24). 'Here you are, a cheque right now, if you accept the deal.' The physical presence of the cheque can seem much more real than the concept of payment. Similarly, anything that can be done to help the other stakeholders to visualize the outcome as you want it to be, and to make it seem more concrete, will help your chances of making it come true.

Outcome Human nature will ensure that the other stakeholders will prefer an outcome they can clearly visualize, or even touch. Help them to make it happen.

Variations None.

Time management	✪
Stress management	✪✪
Negotiation skills	✪✪✪
General development	✪✪✪
Fun	✪✪✪

28.5 Exercise/Technique: Don't leave the next step in others' hands

Preparation None.
Running time 10 minutes.
Resources None.
Frequency As required.

You've reached a stage in the negotiation when the other stakeholders need to withdraw. Perhaps they have to go back to base and talk. Maybe they're just embarrassed about counting on their fingers in front of you. Whatever reason, the negotiation is temporarily suspended. There's danger lurking here. When the others get back to their normal environment they may be distracted. Keep them on track. The same day as the negotiation ends, drop them a note, stating positively what has been agreed so far.

Very often letters like this end with something like 'Thanks for taking the time to discuss the matter with us – if you'd like to take it further, please get in touch.' Sounds harmless? It's not, because you have just relinquished control. Instead say something like 'I'll be back to you in a week's time to fix up the next session,' or whatever is appropriate. Keep the initiative and move the process forwards. It only takes a few minutes to send a letter like this and follow it up – but it can be a very valuable few minutes.

Spend 10 minutes thinking through the tasks and activities you are currently involved in. How many of them are out of your control? What could you do to get them moving?

Feedback I don't know quite why, but it's difficult to keep the reins in this way. Perhaps it feels as if you are being pushy. But without it, you have lost control of the process. Be sensitive to the other stakeholders' reactions. If, for instance, when you ring up they are evasive about fixing a date to get together, say something like 'You are obviously very busy now. Can I call you again in a week and see how things are going?' Again, you've kept the initiative. Don't let go.

As an additional exercise, come up with a response to each of these threats of losing the next step:

- A customer says 'someone else is taking over my job. I'll get her to contact you'.
- You finish a contract and receive a letter thanking you for your work.
- You can't reach someone on the phone and are told 'I'll get him to contact you,' by his PA.

Outcome The chances of reaching a successful conclusion to your negotiations are crucially dependent on keeping in control.

Variations None.

Time management	✪
Stress management	✪✪
Negotiation skills	✪✪✪✪
General development	✪✪✪
Fun	✪✪

Unit 29: Putting it across – communicating your message

We have already looked at the importance of listening properly, but communication is a two-way process and this penultimate unit looks at ways of getting your message across to your benefit.

Do try out the exercises as you go. Put them off until later and you probably won't ever do them. Read through the techniques. Make notes about how and when you can use them. And make sure you give them a try in the next appropriate forum.

Unit book

Take time off in this unit to catch up on the reading you haven't quite finished from the previous units. You could pick up a book on communication skills, but ironically I've yet to find one that's good enough to recommend.

29.1 Exercise: Using emotion

Preparation None.
Running time Five minutes.
Resources Pen and paper.
Frequency Once.

Emotions are an inevitable part of a negotiation. It might seem logical to try to remove emotion and make a negotiation clinical, but in fact emotions can work to your benefit. Spend five minutes considering how you might employ the following emotions in a negotiation. Don't go on to the feedback section until you have done this.

- anger;
- warmth;
- excitement;
- gut feel.

Feedback Anger needs careful use. You should always be in control of it, rather than the other way around. Use anger as a short sharp shock if you are being misused, to express your distress. It should be switched off quickly as soon as there is a response, whether it's apology or more anger. Positive emotions like warmth and excitement can be used a great deal more than they are. Warmth will help others be comfortable with the deal. Excitement will stress your commitment and energy. When things are going well, put that excitement across, not in terms of 'I'm really stomping on you', but 'We're getting along excellently.'

Gut feel is a special case. It's very important – your reaction to what is happening is just as important as the numbers, but make sure that your gut feel is applied correctly. Gut feel is great on concepts and directions, but often lousy on numbers. Almost everyone's gut feel can be misled by statistics, and even as simple a concept as percentages can confuse – be wary of small percentages of large numbers, as they seem insignificant, but can, of course be just as significant as large percentages of small numbers. Go with your gut feel, but do so after conscious and cool assessment.

Outcome Using emotion correctly can tip the balance your way in a negotiation which is logically straightforward. We are emotional beings, so any attempt to ignore emotion will play into the hands of those who use it.

Variations None.

Time management	✪
Stress management	✪✪
Negotiation skills	✪✪✪
General development	✪✪✪✪
Fun	✪✪

29.2 Exercise: I'll be honest...

Preparation None.
Running time Five minutes.
Resources None.
Frequency Once.

You are in the midst of a negotiation to sell a single item. You have the following pieces of information. Which should you let the other stakeholder know?

- You have been approached by two other potential buyers.
- You have dealt with the stakeholder's competitors in the past.
- You can't afford to drop the price much because of development costs.
- Another potential buyer is ringing this afternoon.

Spend a couple of minutes jotting down what you would let them know in each case.

Feedback While we like to keep cards hidden, being more open will often get better results. In this example I'd consider letting the other stakeholder know all four pieces of information. You may feel you need to protect your other potential buyers, but the knowledge of their existence may hurry things along. Just saying 'I have to be honest with you, I have two other companies interested,' won't do a lot, because it sounds like a bluff, but with appropriate backup it can build towards openness and trust.

The second item can be very powerful. Everyone is interested in competitors. While you won't give away trade secrets, the stakeholder will be interested to hear just how you got on with his or her competitor. For instance, when selling a book to a publisher, I usually take books I've written for other publishers. The publishers are genuinely interested in the way their competitors produce books and how they do business.

Honesty as your reason for holding price can also reap dividends. If practical, show them a costing breakdown and why you have cut prices to the bone (of course with appropriate mark-up – you have to survive). The more you can open up, the better the chances of winning the other stakeholder's confidence.

Outcome Opening up is a great way to encourage win–win, because you are both working on the same information base. It may encourage the other stakeholder to give more information too, and will certainly encourage trust.

Variations As a variation, imagine that you are on the other side of the deal. In each case, imagine first that the whole process goes through with the other side not telling you about each of the four points above. Then think how you would feel in each case if they had been up-front about it. Let the feelings you would get on the receiving end help guide your approach when making the choice yourself.

Time management	✪
Stress management	✪✪
Negotiation skills	✪✪✪✪
General development	✪✪✪
Fun	✪✪

29.3 Technique: Yes... eventually

Preparation None.
Running time Two minutes.
Resources None.
Frequency As required.

It is in the nature of negotiating that there are no fixed rules, but a principle that comes close to being a rule is that you should never say 'Yes' first time. It's the inverse of the concept that everything is negotiable – so to say 'Yes' to whatever is first on offer is simply missing the opportunities to negotiate.

The chances that the starting conditions are exactly how you want things to be are negligible – and you will normally be able to lose something you don't want in order to gain something you do. There's not much of an exercise here, except to bear this in mind each time you negotiate. It's not a matter of being nasty or negative – just don't rush in and agree without getting some benefit. As an exercise, monitor the next few discussions you have and watch out for the over-eager 'Yes'.

Feedback You may not have major negotiations every day, but this is an exercise you can practise in many dealings with other people. It may not be a good idea for your day-to-day social interactions with family and friends, but bear in mind next time you buy something for the house, or a member of staff wants to talk about a pay rise.

One way to avoid sounding negative as a result of this policy is make sure that you are very open and positive about agreeing with anything that isn't setting a variable. Plenty of 'Yes, you're right' and nodding when the stakeholder is discussing how great his or her company is (or whatever) will stand you in good stead when you don't say 'Yes' to his or her first offer.

Outcome This is a balancing exercise. A number of other exercises encourage you to take a positive and likeable attitude to the other stakeholders. With this balance, you can stay positive but not give too much away.

Variations None.

Time management	✪✪
Stress management	✪✪
Negotiation skills	✪✪✪✪
General development	✪✪✪
Fun	✪✪

29.4 Exercise/Technique: Using silence

Preparation None.
Running time 15 minutes.
Resources Stooge (for exercise).
Frequency As required.

For this exercise you need a stooge who is unaware of your intentions. The aim is to get some practice at using silence. Get into conversation with a friend or colleague, in a situation where you would expect to chat for 20 minutes or so. This exercise won't work if either of you is in a hurry.

Once the conversation has got going, start to use silence consciously. When the other person has said something, don't jump in. Instead, look fascinated. You might nod or smile or make a 'hmm' noise for encouragement, but try to force the stooge to continue, using only silence. You may find this difficult at first – work at it. You will have to be unusually careful about your expression to ensure that you don't come across as bored (or vacant), without appearing to suffer from painful facial contortions.

Feedback Silence is one of the negotiator's best weapons, yet it is rarely used to full effect. Most of us find it embarrassing to remain silent for long. We feel the urge to jump in and fill the gap. When we do so, we let the other stakeholders off the hook. They too feel the need to say something – so give them a chance.

Just occasionally you will hit a Mexican standoff, where everyone involved is good at handling silence, and the lack of input becomes silly. If nothing has been said at all for five minutes, it might be worth speaking. But not to give anything away. Say something like 'I think we're getting bogged down here. We could all do with some fresh air. I suggest we have a five-minute stretch break.' Or words to that effect.

Often the response to your silence might be to ask you a question. Don't be silent then – that could be interpreted as rudeness. But as much as possible use silence in response to statements ('we could offer a 10 per cent discount,' 'we want to do this…'). Let the other person, and the silence, open up the options.

Outcome Getting some practice at overcoming the embarrassment of silence is important if you are going to use it effectively. Otherwise, no matter what your intention, you will cave in and speak.

Variations It would be best if you could undertake this exercise in a natural social meeting, rather than an engineered one, which may make you feel even more uncomfortable. The exercise has to be a one-to-one – if there are other people in the conversation, they will do the leaping in, and silence will no longer be in use.

Time management	✪
Stress management	✪
Negotiation skills	✪✪✪✪
General development	✪✪✪
Fun	✪✪

29.5 Exercise: Body language

Preparation Find a stooge.
Running time 10 minutes.
Resources Video camera.
Frequency Once.

Your body language will always contribute to the quality of your negotiation. Try this little exercise. Get someone else to act as a participant in a tough negotiation. Video a few minutes' discussion as you argue the fact that you can't go any cheaper while the stooge tries to beat down your price. Lie blatantly.

Now check out the video. Look for any signs of closing up – crossing your arms, curling up on the chair, avoiding eye contact and so forth. Similarly look for occasions when you are open and warm.

The point of this exercise is to be aware of what your body language is like, so that you can do something about it in a real negotiation. Some of your body language will result from the artificial nature of the situation, but it should still be an effective guide.

Feedback I am not suggesting that you lie blatantly in real negotiations, but by forcing yourself to lie you are more likely to indulge in the sort of negative body language that could come out in the pressures of a normal negotiation.

Be conscious of your body language when negotiating. Make sure that you use open positions more – sitting back, arms apart, open handed, smiling, looking the other stakeholders in the eye. Before long it will seem quite natural, even if it feels very uncomfortable at first.

Outcome By employing more open body language, even under stress, you will come across as honest and positive. Don't let your body give the game away, or even worse misrepresent your stress as dishonesty.

Variations None.

Time management	✪
Stress management	✪✪✪
Negotiation skills	✪✪✪✪
General development	✪✪✪✪
Fun	✪✪

Unit 30: A sense of calm – further relaxation

As the course comes to an end there's a chance to put in a little more work on your relaxation skills. Don't be tempted to skip this last unit – it's an important completion section for the course.

Unit book

There's something strangely relaxing about fear combined with comfort – it's why theme parks are so effective, and this is also part of the reason for the success of the superb TV series *Buffy the Vampire Slayer*. What should be a feeble teen show has been instead a revelation thanks to a combination of razor-sharp scripts, a constant dose of humour and a strong, comfortable central unit, all surrounded by horror. The novelizations of the *Buffy* series fail miserably to achieve this same effectiveness (they really are just teen shlock), but one book that manages that same combination of nightmare and warmth is Ray Bradbury's classic *Something Wicked This Way Comes*. It's an ideal final recommendation.

You can find more information on our unit books, or buy them, from our support site: www.cul.co.uk/crashcourse.

Web links

Links on *Buffy* (including links to buy the series on DVD or video) and Ray Bradbury can be found at www.cul.co.uk/crashcourse.

30.1 *Exercise/Technique: Relaxing by numbers*

Preparation None.
Running time Five minutes.
Resources A quiet place.
Frequency Occasionally.

If life is getting on top of you, try a little systematic relaxation. It needn't take long, but you do need somewhere quiet to be able either to lie down or sit in a very comfortable chair. Close your eyes, lie back and relax. Try to clear your mind of all thoughts.

Now focus your attention on the parts of your body, working from your head down to your toes. As you consider each section, tense and relax the muscles a few times, holding them tense for a couple of seconds, then relaxing to a long, slow breath. Try to keep your concentration on the area you are exercising – don't let your thoughts drift off to problems or concerns.

When you have worked down the body, lie still, breathing slowly, keeping as much as possible to a mind blank of thought for another minute or so. While doing so, keep your muscles as relaxed as possible. When you have finished the exercise, don't jump up, but gently open your eyes and stand slowly.

Feedback Interestingly, a very similar technique is used in the companion book to this, *Instant Brainpower*, as a way of improving your visualization skills, an important part of knowledge management. In that case, as you work through your body you are visualizing, but the important component is the parallel feeling of relaxation.

Outcome Although this technique requires a haven from the stressful world, it can be carried out quite quickly, and is a good emergency defence when things are getting on top of you.

Variations You can combine this exercise with a breathing exercise.

Time management	✪
Stress management	✪✪✪✪
Negotiation skills	✪
General development	✪✪✪
Fun	✪✪

30.2 *Technique: Music soothes the savage breast*

Preparation Get appropriate CDs or tapes.
Running time Five minutes.
Resources Tape or CD player.
Frequency Regularly.

Often stress strikes at a time when we can't do anything about it. One of the reasons road rage is so common and extreme is that you are highly restrained by the physical and mental requirements of driving a car. You can't start exercising or have a massage – but you can use music. The right sort of music will lower your heart rate, get you thinking in a more relaxed way and generally put your stress into perspective.

Note 'the right sort of music'. Not all music is de-stressing. Anything with a fast beat and a heavy, pulsing bass will act more as an adrenaline booster than a relaxant. And don't think just because it's classical it's calming – there's plenty of classical music that will push up your heart rate.

Look for slow, calm music, reminiscent of flowing water and happy, untroubled times. It can be anything from classical to folk as long as it has the right effect. I find Tudor and Elizabethan church music, which combines a steady, flowing quality with spiritual depth, particularly effective. The best idea is to try a few different styles and see which suits you best.

Feedback Make sure that the music that is relieving your stress isn't stressing others. The tinny rattle of overheard Walkman headphones or the booming bass of a car passing with its stereo up too loud causes plenty of irritation for others. Try to keep your music to yourself.

Outcome With appropriate music you can distance yourself from stress and put it into perspective. It slows down your heart rate and even helps regular breathing. There's nothing better if you are stuck in a traffic jam.

Variations Music isn't just valuable in the car. The right kind of music can be an aid to relaxation and stress relief wherever you are. See www.cul.co.uk/music for recommendations on appropriate music.

Time management	✪
Stress management	✪✪✪✪
Negotiation skills	✪
General development	✪✪✪
Fun	✪✪✪✪

30.3 Exercise: Cornered rats

Preparation None.
Running time Five minutes.
Resources None.
Frequency Once.

Spend a few minutes thinking about negotiations you have been involved with. They could be the formal negotiations of business, or the (more frequent) social negotiations from 'What shall we have for dinner?' to 'Where shall we go on holiday?' List a handful of negotiations where both sides have backed themselves into a corner and been unable to move. What happened? How did you feel? How did you get out of the deadlock?

Feedback All too often you can reach a point where none of the stakeholders have any room for manoeuvre. Immediately, what could have been a very amicable negotiation passes into something closer to warfare. In fact, actual warfare is generally generated by just such conditions. The best cure is to avoid it happening in the first place. If you see the possibility looming, take a step to try to stay on the same side. Bring the potential deadlock explicitly into the conversation and look for ways to avoid it.

Failing that, a brief cooling-off period is usually valuable. Once you have dug yourselves into your respective positions you won't be in any mood for compromise. Step back from the negotiation for a while. When you return, don't keep on the same line, only look at places where there is a chance for movement. Make sure you are working together in partnership, rather than against each other (at least until you are out of the hole). Phrase your language inclusively and positively – make it all about 'we' not 'you' and solutions, not problems.

Outcome Your own practical experience of deadlocks will come in very useful; don't waste it – build on it.

Variations None.

Time management	✪
Stress management	✪✪✪
Negotiation skills	✪✪✪
General development	✪✪✪
Fun	✪✪

30.4 Technique: Meditation

Preparation None
Running time 10 minutes.
Resources Quiet space.
Frequency Regularly.

For some, meditation is a natural part of life, for others a symptom of the lunatic fringe. In fact, there is nothing extreme about meditation, nor does it require acceptance of a particular philosophy. Find somewhere you can sit quietly and comfortably – unless you are very supple, cross-legged positions should be avoided. Reduce sensory distractions to a minimum. Breathe slowly and evenly. Imagine that everything is slowing down.

Then, find a focus. This can be a meaningless set of syllables, a simple phrase, or a very calm image like a great, unruffled lake, or a single leaf. To begin with, you may find it helps to have a physical object to provide the focus, but before long you will be able to do without it. If you use an object, don't think about any associations or properties it has. Keep your focus on the entire object. For a few minutes (with your eyes closed unless you are using something physical), let your focus fill your mind. The stress will drain away – but don't think about it, or its causes.

Feedback Initially you will find it hard to keep focused. Your mind will wander. When you notice this, bring yourself back. Don't go too long to start with. Begin with a few minutes and build up to maybe 15 minutes.

Most of the world's religions from Christianity to Zen Buddhism, and plenty of non-religious groups, practise meditation. You can see it as an opportunity to explore inner spirituality or as simple mental/physical exercise. One effect is to change the brainwave pattern to a less reactive one (see the Introduction). Whatever your view, it works.

Outcome Meditation is hard to do without a quiet space and a few undisturbed minutes, but its powerful impact on stress levels makes it well worth trying.

Variations Try using a kitchen timer to avoid worrying about how long you have been meditating, particularly if you have another activity to undertake later.

Time management	✪
Stress management	✪✪✪
Negotiation skills	✪
General development	✪✪✪
Fun	✪✪✪

30.5 Exercise: Low power dressing

Preparation None.
Running time Five minutes.
Resources None.
Frequency Once.

The way we dress contributes to our state of relaxation and stress. Tight, formal clothes increase stress levels. Loose, informal clothes help us to relax. Be particularly wary about restrictions about the throat, chest and waist, which can all be significant contributors to stressing.

Spend a few minutes mapping out your week. Which clothes do you wear when? How do the different types of clothing make you feel? How can you get the positive feeling of power that formal dressing gives without adding to your stress levels with tight, stiff clothing? Look for opportunities to overthrow any dress code, at least part of the time.

Feedback When I worked in a corporate office daily I never questioned the need to wear a suit to work. Yet once you have managed to work for a while, still doing a high-pressure job but without the need to dress up for it, you can never go back. Yes, you will wear a suit, but only where absolutely necessary. Look at what people wear when they come into work for a special effort at the weekend. If the clothes are suitable then, why aren't they at other times?

If you have to stay with tight clothing, accept the facts of life. It is natural as you grow older that your neck and waist will increase in size. If you're a mature man, you don't fool anyone by holding onto the 14 inch collars that fitted at college. All these shirts do now is choke you through the day. If you feel the need to undo your collar button when you're under pressure, then your collar is too tight. Either buy a new shirt or keep the top button undone.

Outlook Almost everyone who has changed to wearing more casual work clothes finds it a positive move. There are good physical reasons for avoiding tight, constricting clothes. Finding a way to work in casual wear more often will help your underlying stress levels.

Variations None.

Time management	✪
Stress management	✪✪✪
Negotiation skills	✪
General development	✪✪✪
Fun	✪✪✪

4 Review

PULLING IT TOGETHER

In the 30 units of the course you will have tried out a wide range of exercises and added a whole collection of techniques to your toolbag. Where now?

Begin by re-reading Chapter 1. Get the basics well established. Make sure you are familiar with the essential nature of time management, stress management and negotiating. Get familiar with the underlying principles of establishing what your personal goals are, then setting in place a direction. In the appendices at the back of the book you will find listings that will enable you to pick out techniques particularly appropriate for one of the aspects, but bear in mind that the divisions are arbitrary – it really is all about personal development.

Next, achieve some visibility of what you are trying to do. If you are using a top ten list of the week, get it somewhere anyone can read it. You might not want to make your record of personal principles and focus quite so visible, but make sure it's somewhere that *you* at least can see it on a regular basis. Check what you are doing against it when you make plans.

From a time-management viewpoint, use the tools on a regular basis. Don't let them run your life, but let them help you to run your life the way you want it to be. For stress management, look to your anchors and aspects of control. And remember that every encounter with someone else is a chance to brush up your negotiation skills.

What might be useful is to use the checklist in Chapter 2 not just as a marker that you have finished a unit of the course, but as a reminder. Revisit the elements of the course several times over the next year to ensure that they are well embedded in your way of doing things.

One final thought – read. Reading is one of the easiest and most pleasurable ways to develop yourself. Read voraciously and as widely as possible. If you didn't have time to read all the unit books as you went along, continue picking them off. But make sure you read.

COLLECTED READING LIST

An overview of the unit books from the course

Abraham, J (2000) *Getting Everything You Can Out of All You've Got*, Piatkus, London

Aird, A (ed) (2002) *The Good Pub Guide*, Ebury

Albery, N (ed) (1997) *The Time Out Book of Country Walks*, Penguin, London

Allingham, M (1950) *Sweet Dangers*, Penguin, Harmondsworth

Ashcroft, F (2001) *Life at the Extremes*, Flamingo, London

Austen, J (1994) *Northanger Abbey*, Penguin, London

Bates, H E (1961) *The Darling Buds of May*, Penguin, Harmondsworth

Bradbury, R (1998) *Something Wicked This Way Comes*, Pocket Books, London

Bryson, B (1998) *Notes from a Big Country*, Doubleday, London

Buzan, T and Buzan, B (2000) *The Mind Map Book*, BBC, London

Clegg, B (2001) *The Professional's Guide to Mining the Internet*, Kogan Page, London

Clegg, B (2002) *The Complete Flier's Handbook*, Pan, London

Clegg, B (2001) *Light Years*, Piatkus, London

Cooper, C L and Palmer, S (2000) *Conquer Your Stress*, CIPD, London

Covey, S (1999) *The Seven Habits of Highly Effective People*, Simon & Schuster, London

Edstrom, J and Eller, M (2000) *Barbarians Led by Bill Gates*, Henry Holt, New York, NY

Emmett, R (2001) *The Procrastinator's Handbook: Mastering the art of doing it now*, Fusion, London

Fiennes, R (1999) *Fit for Life*, Little Brown, London

Firth, D (1995) *How to Make Work Fun*, Gower, Aldershot

Forster, M (2000) *Get Everything Done and Still Have Time to Play*, Hodder and Stoughton, London

Freemantle, D (2002) *How to Choose*, FT/Prentice Hall, London

Handy, C (1998) *The Hungry Spirit*, Arrow, London
Handy, C and Handy, E (1999) *The New Alchemists*, Hutchinson, London
Hemsath, D and Yerkes, L (1997) *301 Ways to Have Fun at Work*, Berrett-Koehler, San Francisco, CA
Jay, A and Lynn, J (1989) *The Complete Yes Minister/The Complete Yes Prime Minister*, BBC, London
Kennedy, G (1997) *Everything is Negotiable*, Random House, London
Larson, G (1996) *Last Chapter and Worse*, Time Warner, London
Law, A (1999) *Open Minds*, Orion, London
Mortimer, J (1983) *The First Rumpole Omnibus*, Penguin, Harmondsworth
Peters, T (1994) *The Tom Peters Seminar: Crazy times call for crazy organizations*, Macmillan, London
Pratchett, T (1989) *Wyrd Sisters*, Corgi, London
Rowling, J K (1997) *Harry Potter and the Philosopher's Stone*, Bloomsbury, London
Semler, R (2001) *Maverick!*, Random House, London
Singh, S (1998) *Fermat's Last Theorem*, Fourth Estate, London
Toffler, A (1985) *Future Shock*, Pan, London
Vidal, J (1997) McLibel, Pan, London
Wodehouse, P G (2002) *Summer Lightning*, Penguin, London
Wolfe, G (2001) *There Are Doors*, Orb
Wolfe, G (1993) *Pandora, By Holly Hollander*, Tor

Appendix

TECHNIQUES WITH HIGH TIME MANAGEMENT RATINGS

Ref.	*Title*
1.1	Where did it go?
1.2	The top ten list
1.3	A personal project
2.1	Talent spotting
2.2	If I were rich
2.3	Dream day
2.4	Obstacle map
2.5	What's it worth?
4.1	Principles
4.2	Focus
4.3	Priorities
4.4	Pareto
4.5	Drawn and quartered
5.1	Scrap the briefcase
5.2	How long?
5.4	Banning homework
5.5	Because I'm worth it
6.1	The red hat
6.2	Deflecting distraction

6.4	Waiting room
6.5	Caught in the Web
7.1	Chunking
7.2	Tasks, tasks
7.3	Task list stragglers
7.4	We don't deliver
7.5	Against the buffers
8.1	Why not 'No'?
8.2	No, I can
8.3	Meet yourself half way
8.4	No action, no report
9.1	Agenda bender
9.2	Garbage in, garbage out
9.3	Crowd control
9.4	Go casual
10.1	Cherry-picking
10.2	Little treats
10.3	Doggie chocs
10.4	Pat on the back
11.1	Quiet corners
11.2	How wide is your door?
11.3	Home, sweet home
12.1	Letting go
12.2	Be prepared
12.3	Delegation difficulties
12.4	It's mine
13.1	The e-mail of the species
13.3	Calling by numbers
13.4	Fluffy phones
13.5	Paper mountains
14.1	TV turn-off
19.1	Don't bury yourself
20.1	Penalizing pen-pushing
20.2	A file in a cake
21.1	Hot spots

TECHNIQUES WITH HIGH STRESS MANAGEMENT RATINGS

Ref.	*Title*
1.4	Little successes
3.1	Control freaks
3.2	The big stuff
3.3	How do you react?
3.4	Physical checks
3.5	Emotional and spiritual checks
4.1	Principles
4.2	Focus
4.4	Pareto
5.1	Scrap the briefcase
5.2	How long?
5.3	Reading up
5.4	Banning homework
5.5	Because I'm worth it
6.3	Jump-start
8.5	No news is good news
10.2	Little treats
10.3	Doggie chocs
10.4	Pat on the back
10.5	I did that
11.4	Environmental stuff
11.5	Coping with change
12.4	It's mine
13.2	E-mail it away
14.3	Play!
14.4	The spiritual path
14.5	Different values
15.1	Handling confrontation
15.2	Laugh!
15.3	Rage
15.4	Don't do that
16.1	Touchy-smelly
16.2	Ritual relaxation
16.3	Breathing is good for you
16.4	Pushing waves
16.5	Medicinal reading

17.1	Sulkers
17.2	Nemesis
17.3	Bully off
17.4	Cut the aggro
18.2	Broken record
18.3	Broken CD
18.4	Setbacks
19.2	Café life
19.3	Get away
19.4	Walkies!
20.4	Bureaucratic bounce-back
21.2	Stress workout
21.3	Sleep!
21.4	Stimulants stink
21.5	Integral exercise
22.1	Capture ideas
25.3	Delightful deals
27.1	I agree… ish
27.2	Exploring trust
28.1	Stage fright
28.2	Your USP
30.1	Relaxing by numbers
30.2	Music soothes the savage breast

TECHNIQUES WITH HIGH NEGOTIATION SKILLS DEVELOPMENT RATINGS

Ref.	*Title*
1.5	Another lever
15.1	Handling confrontation
17.5	Slowing the pace
18.1	Are you assertive?
18.2	Broken record
18.3	Broken CD
18.5	Personality types
22.2	Lifetime value
22.4	Knowing the opposition
22.5	Knowing your products and services

23.1	Listen well
23.2	Are they telling the truth?
23.5	Appearing naïve
24.1	It's yours right now
24.2	Starting prices
24.3	Throwing in the condiment
24.4	There's always an 'if'
24.5	Doing a special
25.1	Talking yourself down
25.2	Getting endorsements
25.3	Delightful deals
26.3	Basic option evaluation
26.4	Sophisticated option evaluation
26.5	Options with guts
27.1	I agree… ish
27.2	Exploring trust
27.3	Beautiful barter
27.5	Aim high to get more
28.2	Your USP
28.3	Setting targets
28.5	Don't leave the next step in others' hands
29.2	I'll be honest…
29.3	Yes… eventually
29.4	Using silence
29.5	Body language

TECHNIQUES WITH HIGH GENERAL DEVELOPMENT RATINGS

Ref.	*Title*
1.1	Where did it go?
1.3	A personal project
2.1	Talent spotting
4.2	Focus
4.3	Priorities
4.4	Pareto
5.1	Scrap the briefcase
5.2	How long?

5.3	Reading up
5.4	Banning homework
5.5	Because I'm worth it
6.3	Jump start
6.5	Caught in the Web
11.5	Coping with change
12.5	Mentor mine
14.2	You are what you eat
14.3	Play!
14.4	The spiritual path
14.5	Different values
15.1	Handling confrontation
15.3	Rage
16.5	Medicinal reading
18.1	Are you assertive?
18.4	Setbacks
19.3	Get away
23.1	Listen well
26.1	Taking notes
27.2	Exploring trust
27.3	Beautiful barter
27.4	You won't win them all
28.2	Your USP
29.1	Using emotion
29.5	Body language

TECHNIQUES WITH HIGH FUN RATINGS

Ref.	*Title*
1.3	A personal project
2.2	If I were rich
10.2	Little treats
10.3	Doggie chocs
10.4	Pat on the back
14.3	Play!
15.2	Laugh!
16.5	Medicinal reading
19.3	Get away
25.3	Delightful deals

Also available from Kogan Page...

Other titles in the Crash Course series:

Crash Course in Creativity, Brian Clegg and Paul Birch
Crash Course in Managing People, Brian Clegg and Paul Birch

...and by the same authors, in the Instant series:

Instant Brainpower, Brian Clegg
Instant Coaching, Paul Birch
Instant Creativity, Brian Clegg and Paul Birch
Instant Interviewing, Brian Clegg
Instant Leadership, Paul Birch
Instant Motivation, Brian Clegg
Instant Negotiation, Brian Clegg
Instant Stress Management, Brian Clegg
Instant Teamwork, Brian Clegg and Paul Birch
Instant Time Management, Brian Clegg

The above titles are available from all good bookshops. For further information, please contact the publisher at the following address:

Kogan Page Limited
120 Pentonville Road
London N1 9JN
Tel: 020 7278 0433
Fax: 020 7837 6348
www.kogan-page.co.uk